Seeing Female

Recent Titles in
Contributions in Women's Studies

Seeing Female

SOCIAL ROLES AND PERSONAL LIVES

EDITED BY

Sharon S. Brehm

CONTRIBUTIONS IN WOMEN'S STUDIES,
NUMBER 88

GREENWOOD PRESS

NEW YORK • WESTPORT, CONNECTICUT • LONDON

Library of Congress Cataloging-in-Publication Data

Seeing female.

(Contributions in women's studies, ISSN 0147-104X ; no. 88)
Includes index.
1. Women—United States—Social conditions.
2. Feminism—United States. 3. Women—United States—Psychology. 4. Social role—United States. I. Brehm, Sharon S. II. Series.
HQ1420.S35   1988   305.4'2'0973   87-15039
ISBN 0-313-25589-X (lib. bdg. : alk. paper)

Library of Congress Catalog Card Number: 87-15039
ISBN: 0-313-25589-X
ISSN: 0147-104X

First published in 1988

Greenwood Press, Inc.
88 Post Road West, Westport, Connecticut 06881

Printed in the United States of America

The paper used in this book complies with the Permanent Paper Standard issued by the National Information Standards Organization (Z39.48-1984).

10 9 8 7 6 5 4 3 2 1

Copyright Acknowledgments

Grateful acknowledgment is hereby given for permission to reprint the following:

Reprinted by permission of the publisher and the Trustees of Amherst College from *The Poems of Emily Dickinson*, edited by Thomas H. Johnson, Cambridge, Mass.: The Belknap Press of Harvard University Press, Copyright 1951, © 1955, 1979, 1983 by The President and Fellows of Harvard College.

I stepped from Plank to Plank
A slow and cautious way
The Stars about my Head I felt
About my Feet the Sea.

I knew not but the next
Would be my final inch—
This gave me that precarious Gait
Some call Experience.

—Emily Dickinson

CONTENTS

Acknowledgments

By definition, an edited book is a collective effort, and this particular collaborative endeavor has been a pleasure from conception through publication. I am grateful beyond adequate words to all of the contributors for their fine work delivered up in timely fashion. I deeply appreciate the encouragement given to this project by Mary R. Sive, Social and Behavioral Sciences Editor at Greenwood Press, and the efficient work of Arlene Belzer during the production process. My greatest debt, of course, is to all those women—among the living and the dead—whose dignity and courage in their social roles and personal lives continue to sustain the hopes of their sisters.

Seeing Female

Introduction: Sightedness, Near and Far

SHARON S. BREHM

The essays in this volume share a common preoccupation with obtaining the gift of sight for and about women. Since a woman's view of her own and other women's lives is necessarily a multifaceted phenomenon, the authors who have contributed to this collection have selected widely differing angles of perspective. Some have looked through the eyes of children: observing the differences in socialization provided for girls and boys (Huston), and recounting those events of childhood that shape our identity (Horowitz) and cast our imagination (Schultz). Other contributors examine women's lives through the medium of literature. From the works of women writers, we can learn about their own development as women (McNall) and about their response to the social forces confronting them (Marx). Other authors have chosen the lens of a sociocultural perspective, describing the dilemma faced by Afro-American women as they resist racist propaganda (Pennington) and the difficulties faced by all women as they engage in the political process (Campbell and Jerry; Sprague).

The chapters included here also consider a variety of women's roles. Indeed, the breadth of inquiry runs all the way from an examination of apparitions of the Virgin Mary (Zimdars-Swartz) to an analysis of the rhetorical devices employed by Senator Nancy Kassebaum and other women politicians (Campbell and Jerry). In addition, there are chapters on the professional and personal conflicts encountered by women in counseling psychology (McDermott), the effects on women of historical changes in the ethos of medical practice (Morantz-Sanchez), and the excitement as well as disillusionment found by women who dare to tread into male-dominated professional domains such as journalism (Bowles) and administration (Springer).

Throughout this book, the concerns of modern feminism are apparent, although again the angle of perspective varies. Some authors, for example, focus on the possibilities for discovering a way of seeing the world that is more compatible with women's experiences and values (Schultz; Sprague; Weick), and on the complexities inherent in transmitting such a viewpoint across generations of women (Albrecht). Societally induced and sustained conditions of female dependency are considered in terms of their impact on depression among women (Ford and Berkman), while various psychological motives that serve to maintain patriarchal structures are discussed in the context of intimate relationships between women and men (Brehm).

In light of this degree of diversity, it may seem a drastic step to try to ferret out a small number of "major themes" reflected in all the contributions to this volume. Fortunately, however, setting forth a few general dimensions, touched on in one way or another by every chapter, need not become an exercise in reductionism. These dimensions provide continuity in a context of variety; they do not substitute for the particular vision conveyed in each chapter. To gain the particulars, one must read, and see, for oneself.

Among the thematic dimensions found throughout this book, the most visible is the dimension of time. Past (women's history), present (contemporary issues), and future (yet unrealized possibilities) are all represented here. Moreover, every chapter—no matter what its specific chronological focus—has a sense of time about it. To be female in the United States of the late twentieth century is to be sensitive to the reality of history. Women's present cannot be understood without knowledge of women's past; knowledge of women's past would be unendurable without hope for women's future. It is this sense of time, running on and being lived in, that informs all of the essays here.

These essays are also concerned with the relationship between an individual woman (with her dreams, fears, conflicts, and convictions) and the social context in which she resides (with its prohibitions, admonitions, and normative definitions). Whether they emphasize the interior life or external social arrangements, the chapters in this collection manage to encompass both the sharp edge of a woman's inner struggle and the blunt mass of convention poised against her. Such an inclusive perspective could not have occurred if the social roles described in this book had been restricted to those of which we, the contributors, approve. Rather, these chapters point to a steadfast determination on the part of their authors to understand women's social roles and women's personal lives as they have been and as they are, regardless of how these roles and lives might ultimately be judged. This determination derives directly from that sense of history I mentioned before. If a more generous future is to be created for women, we are obliged to study the defeats as well as the triumphs of those who went before us.

The third theme winding its way throughout the chapters in this book is that of personalism. One of the most extraordinary (and, to some, most outrageous) aspects of women's scholarship in our time has been its admission of the personal into the academy. The radical nature of such a step should never be underestimated. In one sweep, this new broom has brought in "facts" that never existed in male-defined scholarship and brought down the inflated pretensions of that contradiction in terms, "objective knowledge." As a marginalized group, women are acutely aware that all knowledge is subjective, that it cannot escape the influence and limitations of our experience.

This awareness, however, does not translate into a prescription for the form that the convergence of scholarly reflection and personal insight should take. The goal of feminist scholarship is not to make sure that every scholar includes some sort of personal note at the beginning, middle, or end of her or his article, chapter, or book! Instead, this goal is the far more difficult one of encouraging free play between scholarship and experience so that all of us, female and male, see more than we did before. The chapters of the present book offer, I believe, compelling evidence of the benefits to be derived from free play. There was no editorial rule; there is no homogeneity. Each author speaks as much about herself as she decided was appropriate for her subject matter, and every chapter comes straight from that new feminist organ: the mind-and-heart.

Free play might also characterize the spirit in which this book would be best read. I doubt that this book lends itself very well to being consumed, much less digested, in a single sustained march from beginning to end; it seems to me to work better as a collection of glimpses than as one long, hard stare. I'd like to think this book might be kept around for awhile, ready at hand for browsing, or for searching. However it is read, the book's organization into several sections of several chapters each should be considered merely an optional path to follow. Since I often strayed from this path in my summary of chapter topics at the beginning of this introduction, I can only applaud such straying by others. Indeed, there are so many connections among various chapters that one can change perspective at will simply by grouping together one rather than another set of chapters.

These interconnections—these echoes, amplifications, reverberations—suggest that this book may not be a book at all; in some ways it is more like a discussion among friends and colleagues. The formal structure, of course, is that of a series of monologues, with each contributor (singly or in pairs) speaking in turn. But this overt structure rests on a deeper foundation of dialogue and community. The authors of the essays you are about to read know one another. Many of us work at the same place; many of us live in the same town. Those who now live at a distance once dwelled among us and still keep in touch. There are years of shared thoughts, feelings, concerns, and interests woven into the fabric of this text. We produced this book together so that we might see better close at home, and so that we might extend the reach of our vision by enlarging the circle of conversation.

PART ONE

WOMEN'S DEVELOPMENT AND IDENTITY

Gender, Socialization, and the Transmission of Culture 1

ALETHA C. HUSTON

Gender differences in personality, cognition, and behavior have been disputed by social scientists for most of the twentieth century. Despite the fact that unexamined assumptions and loaded political agendas on both sides have often guided empirical investigations, some consistent patterns emerge that deserve careful scrutiny. Some gender differences appear in very early childhood, suggesting that they are influenced by constitutional factors and/or early experience. Others follow similar patterns across cultures and across species, suggesting that they are determined by biological attributes of the human species or by common characteristics of many human societies.

This essay has two purposes. In the first section, socialization practices by adults that might contribute to different personality attributes and behavioral skills are examined. The focus on socialization is not intended to deny the role of biological contributors to gender differences, but is based on the premise that from the earliest days of life social experience has an impact on organisms whose biological make-up leaves them highly malleable. In the second section, some of the implications of gender-related socialization for individuals and for the society in which they live are discussed.

Any discussion of gender differences must begin with a few caveats. The most important of these is that females and males are more similar than different. On any of the attributes described, male and female distributions overlap much more than they diverge. The average levels may differ, but there are many individuals of both genders who depart from those group averages by a wide margin. Jessie Bernard (1976) cautions scholars against describing these findings with phrases such as "Men are more aggressive than women" because of the implication of an absolute difference. Alternatives are "Men are more often aggressive than women," or "More men than women are highly aggressive."

The second caveat is political. Feminists have resisted admitting any differences between the genders, particularly in early childhood, because of the real danger that such differences will be interpreted as genetic and immutable, and as evidence of the inherent inferiority of women. Some scholars, on the other hand, confirm the feminists' fears. Sociobiology is the latest manifestation of the tendency to argue that human behavior and social systems are the products of evolution and other biological processes that are "natural" and inevitable (Wilson, 1975). Unfortunately, some individuals advocating these views jump to a tautological conclusion that what exists presently defines what must and ought to be.

Sensible scholars can tread the path between these views. We can examine human behavior in our own and other societies, attempting to observe as accurately and carefully as possible. We can admit that gender has some biological components without falling into the simplistic trap of biological determinism (e.g., cf. Hall, 1985). Perhaps most important, we can escape from the assumption of male superiority; when the genders are different, qualities possessed more often by women than by men can be valued and examined for their contribution to society.

Gender Differences in Socialization Patterns

Socialization can be broadly defined as "the process by which individuals acquire the knowledge, skills, and dispositions that enable them to participate as more or less effective members of groups and the society" (Brim, quoted in Goslin, 1969, p. 2). It is a process of transmitting and receiving values, social norms, and specific skills that are valued in a culture, usually across generations. The term "socialization" is sometimes used as a noun describing the product—a person who has incorporated culturally important knowledge and norms. In the present essay, I use "socialization" as the process and "being socialized" as the product.

Socialization by Adults

In virtually every human society and in most other mammal species as well, females assume primary responsibility for socializing the young (D'Andrade, 1966; Draper, 1985). The biological asymmetry of reproductive roles has been interpreted by many scholars as one major basis for the universal division of social roles (e.g., de Beauvoir, 1949). Because females bear the young and are biologically equipped to feed them, it follows "naturally" that females are assigned most other responsibilities for childrearing. Some have gone further to argue that processes of natural selection have favored the evolution of a biologically based disposition in females to be oriented to long-term social relationships (Draper, 1985). Such arguments are difficult to evaluate because most women's adult lives until quite recently were occupied by relatively uncontrolled and uncontrollable childbearing. The changes in life span and reproductive control that characterize highly developed societies today are at best only a few generations old, so human societies have had little time to learn whether behavior patterns of women will change without the imperative of lifetime responsibility for young children.

Whatever the reasons, women are the ones who care for young children at home, teach them in school, and carry out most other adult activities with children. When mothers are employed outside their homes, their children are usually cared for by other women. For the first several years of most children's lives, their principal guides, disciplinarians, teachers, and nurturers are female adults.

Female children also participate as recipients in the socialization process more readily than male children do. Observational studies have consistently found that girls more often than boys spend time in settings and activities where adult guidance is readily available. Observations in the homes of young children indicate that girls are in the presence of a parent, usually the mother, more often than boys (Fagot, 1978). In preschool and elementary school years, girls gravitate to activities that are supervised and directed by adults; boys more often choose activities with little adult involvement (Carpenter and Huston-Stein, 1980; Serbin, 1980; Serbin, O'Leary, Kent, and Tonick, 1973). For example, during observations of eight to ten year olds in a summer day camp, girls spent 60 percent of their time in adult-supervised activities; the comparable figure for boys was 36 percent (Huston, Carpenter, Atwater, and Johnson, 1986).

The same pattern appears in investigations of cultures outside the United States. Girls spend more time than boys in and near the home, often doing household chores and caring for younger children (Whiting, 1980). Girls in later childhood and adolescence are subject to "chaperonage," adult supervision that is not based on their immaturity or inability to behave responsibly, but on their sexual vulnerability and the societal concern with protecting their virginity. During these same years males are encouraged to become independent and self-reliant (Block, 1984; D'Andrade, 1966; Newson and Newson, 1976). As a result, females remain close to the adult world, especially to the world of female adults. Males move away not only from the female adult world, but from adults in general. Male adults take over some socialization roles for boys as children get older, but they do not occupy the same central role in children's daily lives as adult women do.

My colleague, Jan Carpenter, and I began several years ago developing a theoretical model designed to describe some of the consequences of gender differences in socialization (Carpenter, 1983; Huston and Carpenter, 1985).

We proposed that one major function performed by adults is to provide "structure"; that is to provide rules, guidelines, and suggestions about appropriate ways to behave. In settings where adults supervise children's activities or tasks, adults provide structure by direct instructions, suggestions, and corrections and indirectly by modeling. For example, when an adult and child play with a bat and ball, the adult is apt to demonstrate throwing, batting, and running from base to base, and the child is likely to learn the rules associated with the adult game.

If adults are not present or involved, the children themselves must create a structure—they must invent ways to use materials or make up rules for a game. A group of children presented for the first time with a bat and ball might decide to lay the bat on the ground and jump over it while juggling the ball. They might also hit each other over the head with the bat.

We proposed that experience in adult-directed activities leads children to be compliant, to accept the structure given, and to depend on adults for guidance, and that experience in unstructured activities encourages leadership, independence, creativity, and aggression. On the whole, these hypotheses have been supported by our own research and that of others (Huston and Carpenter, 1985; Smith and Connolly, 1980). Children in highly structured settings exhibit relatively high levels of rule obedience, compliance to adult requests, responsibility, and attentiveness to curriculum activities. Children in low structure settings exhibit relatively high levels of imaginative fantasy, leadership, and aggression. Perhaps more interesting, when girls and boys were observed in the same activity, sex differences in behavior did not occur (Carpenter, 1983; Huston and Carpenter, 1985). It appears that some differences in behavior attributed to gender may be a function of the different types of activities in which girls and boys are usually observed.

Because girls spend more time in adult-structured activities than boys do, the theory leads to the prediction that girls will be more compliant, responsible, rule obedient, and attentive to a teacher, while boys will be more imaginative, assertive, and aggressive. For the most part, a large body of research supports this prediction. One of the most consistently observed behavioral gender differences occurs on a dimension of compliance-conformity vs. disobedience-aggression. Throughout childhood and adolescence, girls more often conform to adult demands, requests, and norms, obey rules, and enforce rules on others. When adults ask children to do something, girls more often comply at the first request; boys more often have to be asked again. Boys more often disobey adults and are more frequently punished. Males at all ages (and in most other species) are more often aggressive than females. The data on conformity to peers are mixed, but it is fairly clear that females are more apt than males to conform to the demands and standards set by adults (Block, 1984; Huston, 1983; Maccoby and Jacklin, 1974).

Quiet, obedient, attentive behavior serves children well in school, and girls succeed in school more often than boys do. Girls have higher grades than boys throughout the school years and in college. Women now get the majority of all bachelor's and master's degrees in the United States (Carnegie Foundation, 1986). Boys more often have learning problems (e.g., poor reading, learning disabilities) and behavior problems (Huston, 1983; Wittig and Petersen, 1979). In many cases, higher grades are not accompanied by higher achievement test scores. In fact, by the college years, males have higher average scores than females on tests such as the SAT. Behavior patterns are probably partially responsible for the discrepancy between test performance and school achievement. Girls more often sit quietly, listen to instruction, complete assignments on time, and less often present behavior problems to teachers. Some of the advantages of willing compliance to teacher demands decline, however, as individuals reach advanced educational levels. Success increasingly requires initiative and independent creativity, as well as responsibility and ability to follow others' direction.

Peer Group Experiences

Girls' and boys' peer group experiences differ because children's groups are segregated by gender and because groups of girls more often incorporate adult direction and leadership than do those composed of boys. Gender segregation characterizes peer interactions from at least age three onward. When children play in large groups, where potential companions of both genders are available, they generally spend more time with children of their own gender than with those of the other gender. The prevalence of gender segregation increases into the elementary school years so that for most children in middle childhood (roughly seven to eleven), the great majority of their play with other children occurs with members of their own gender.

One basis for gender segregation may be adult expectations and reinforcement. For example, the amount of gender-segregated play varies considerably depending on the philosophy of education in a school (Huston, 1983).

Preferences for activities that are sex-typed by society (which are probably taught very early) also contribute to choosing same-gender playmates. Many children show pronounced preferences for toys that are socially stereotyped as appropriate for their gender before their second birthdays. For instance, in several observational studies of children from fifteen to thirty-six months, boys played more often with trucks, trains, and toy tools while girls played more often with baby dolls (O'Brien and Huston, 1985). These children were sufficiently young that they played individually, rarely interacting with other children in conjunction with toy use; they were probably not highly influenced by other children. By age three and older, when children are in preschool classrooms, the children who congregate in play areas that are feminine sex-typed (e.g., housekeeping toys, dolls) are apt to be girls; those who congregate around masculine sex-typed toys (e.g., trucks, blocks) are likely to be boys (Eisenberg, Tryon and Cameron, 1984). Therefore, gender segregation may result from acquired sex-typed toy preferences.

Still another basis for gender segregation is the child's own cognitive organization of the social world. Between age two and three, children learn to classify themselves and others as female and male; they frequently use gender as a social category. By definition, a category provides a structure for grouping some individuals together and differentiating them from others. The human mind relies on categorical thinking to reduce the vast complexity of individual events to a level that can be comprehended. Because gender is a dichotomous and socially salient means of categorizing people, it is not surprising that it is one of the earliest social categories that children use.

Once the basic differentiation exists, children search actively for information to "fill in" each category; they are primed to notice and incorporate their society's norms about what females and males should and should not do. As a result, most preschool children have acquired social stereotypes about "sex-appropriate" and "inappropriate" play to which they adhere rather rigidly. They enforce those norms on one another. A boy who joins a group of girls in doll play is likely to be ostracized not only by other boys, but by his female playmates. Females sometimes have a little more latitude in joining predominantly male activities, but they also receive a considerable amount of negative feedback from their peers (Fagot and Leinbach, 1983).

Another hypothesis to account for both gender segregation and for females' greater closeness to adults rests on the observation that boys more often are aggressive and dominant. It is argued that, because girls resist or dislike boys' aggression, they play with other girls and/or stay close to adults on the assumption that adults will prevent the more egregious forms of male dominance (e.g., grabbing toys, pushing others out of one's way). There have been few efforts to test this hypothesis thus far, but it is supported by the observation that selective play with same sex peers occurs at a slightly younger age for girls than for boys (Maccoby and Jacklin, 1985).

Even though both genders form same-sex peer groups, male groups move away from adults much more distinctly than female groups. When males choose activities outside the range of adult supervision in preschools or daycamps, they are often in groups (Huston and Carpenter, 1985). As a result, the male peer group becomes an autonomous unit, supporting its members without much influence from adults. In leisure time activities at home, boys spend more time than girls with peers in unsupervised activities outside their homes (Carpenter and Huston, 1983). Girls' peer groups more often include adult-directed activities and other forms of adult involvement.

Hence, at both the individual and peer group levels, females are exposed to and seek adult influence more than males do. Their peer groups are more apt to incorporate adult values and norms and are often less autonomous than those of their male counterparts.

In summary, gender differences in the socialization process appear to result in a closer socialization bond and a more intensive process of adult-child socialization for females than for males. Female adults are almost universally responsible for the socialization of children. Female children more often than males are exposed and choose to expose themselves to socialization influences from adults. As a result, female children frequently accept adult norms and values; they comply with requests and rules; and they are relatively unlikely to step outside the boundaries of behaviors that are socially prescribed for both genders. Peer groups become sex-segregated at an early age, and female peer groups more often incorporate adults and adult standards. Male peer groups are apt to become more autonomous from adults and to reinforce somewhat different norms than those given by adult socializing agents.

Models for Understanding Gender Based Socialization Patterns

The basic theme emerging from this analysis is that adult women act as socializing agents and that female children are especially willing recipients of the knowledge, values, and beliefs taught by adults. From a societal perspective, it can be argued that the intergenerational connections among females are important links for maintaining cultural norms and aassuring continuity of beliefs and values. Although I speak of female and male socialization patterns, these are of course not linked to gender in any immutable or absolute way. Undoubtedly, one can find many females who do not follow the pattern of acceptance and conformity to societal norms just as there are many males who do not rebel and reject those norms. Nevertheless, the former pattern does more often characterize females and the latter more often males. The purpose of this analysis is to understand better some of the implications of these patterns for individuals and the society in which they live.

This analysis is a product of my own intellectual history which, in many ways, parallels the evolution of feminist scholarship in the social sciences. Alice Rossi's (1976) three models of equality represent some steps in that revolution. In the *pluralist* model, differences among groups are accepted as given; efforts to produce equality focus on valuing each group equally. Rossi argues persuasively that equality in a pluralist model is virtually impossible to obtain because one group is inevitably defined as superior and the other(s) inferior.

In the *assimilationist* model, members of the minority group attempt to change their behavior to be more like the majority group (i.e., to be able to succeed in the society as it currently exists). The attributes of the majority group are explicitly or implicitly valued more than those of the minority. Abundant examples appear in the literature on women: advice to women about how to be more assertive, competitive, and achievement-oriented and devaluation of traditional female activities such as homemaking and childrearing. In psychology, theories have been conceived to explain male personality or behavior; then they are applied more or less successfully to women. The assimilationist model has dominated much of the social science research on women; even strongly feminist scholars are often influenced by it despite their best efforts.

In the *hybrid* model, changes in both majority and minority groups as well as some changes in social institutions are anticipated. Characteristics previously associated with both groups may come to be socially valued, and social institutions will reward new combinations of individual attributes and skills. In the case of gender issues, this model implies that both "feminine" and "masculine" attributes and interests may be socially valued as their association with gender gradually withers away (Bem, 1984). Theories are developed from observations of both genders rather than being grafted from one to the other. New patterns emerge, representing integration of earlier ones.

Gilligan's (1982) theory proposing two "voices" of morality and self-concept represents one effort to develop a hybrid model in that some of the theoretical constructs were derived from direct observations of women rather than being adapted from psychological theories based on males.

Jeanne Block (1973) proposed a less widely known, but comprehensive theory fitting the hybrid model. Developmental changes in sex role identity across the life span were posited; androgyny, the highest developmental level, was defined as an integration of masculine and feminine personality patterns. She used Bakan's (1966) concepts of agency and communion to describe the masculine and feminine aspects of personality. Agency is the concern with self as an individual and is manifested in self-assertion, independence from others, and self-expansion. Communion is the sense of self as part of a larger whole and is manifested in behaviors that support the social group such as cooperation and concern about others. Neither tendency is adaptive or positive by itself; the ideal personality is balanced with an integration of the two.

My own evolution from assimilationist to hybrid thinking has been repeated numerous times in different contexts. One of my first research interests was the relation between gender and achievement motivation. Most extant theories of achievement motivation were explicitly based on males; females were excluded because the available measures were not validated for them (McClelland, Atkinson, Clark, and Lowell, 1953).[1] The major theory explaining development of achievement orientation contained the proposal that males' achievement motivation was based on internalized standards of excellence that were applied independently of parents and other reinforcing agents. Females' achievement efforts were thought to be motivated "merely" by a need for social approval; they worked to please others rather than themselves (Crandall, Katkovsky, and Preston, 1960).

In a theoretical examination and reinterpretation of the literature concerning female achievement orientation (Stein and Bailey, 1973), we gradually shifted from an initial orientation that assumed the value of masculine patterns to an attempt to describe equally valid and valuable feminine patterns. We argued that males and females are equally responsive to social approval and disapproval, but are socialized to value achievement in different domains. Social skills are one domain of achievement for females. There is an important difference between social achievement and social dependency.

Jan Carpenter and I began our research on structured and unstructured environments because we were concerned that the qualities cultivated by structured environments (i.e., the female attributes) were socially maladaptive; we thought the qualities cultivated by unstructured environments (i.e., the male attributes) were more functional. We, like many other feminist scholars interpreting data on gender differences, proposed that female socialization patterns resulted in dependency, conformity, and passivity. Male socialization was expected to encourage qualities that lead to success in the occupational world such as the ability to create, to take unconventional views, or to assert leadership. After all, we argued, people who have been trained to be compliant and obedient are likely to remain in subordinate, relatively powerless positions. The qualities that serve well to please teachers are not so functional in the world of work.

As the data accumulated, it became apparent that those assumptions were wrong on two levels. First, children who had extensive experience in high adult-structured activities were not passive and dependent. They were indeed compliant, but they were also skilled in leadership and social interactions with adults. Their performance on tests of reading, math, and visual spatial skills was also better than the performance of children who spent relatively little time in adult-structured activities.[2] Second, those who spent a lot of time in low structure activities did, as expected, show leadership skills with peers, but they were often aggressive and uncontrolled, and they were not especially creative. We came to realize that both high and low adult structure might provide valuable experiences for children and that an optimal pattern was probably some balance between the two.

At a more functional level, we revised our model in the direction of a hybrid. Writers who stress the maladaptive character of female socialization take for granted the primacy of occupational success as a goal, and they implicitly accept the value of agentic qualities of competition, individualism, and disconnectedness that predominate in that world. If one expands

the valued contributions to the world to include traditionally feminine domains, then a different definition of "adaptive" emerges that includes communal qualities promoting group cohesion and caring about others.

Implications for Transmission of Culture

With this background, we can return to the implications of gender differences in socialization. One consequence (and perhaps cause) of females'
greater involvement in socialization experiences is that many females form
and retain close interpersonal bonds between parent and child more readily
than males do. Females throughout the lifespan are more apt than males to
maintain close ties with parents, children, and other family members. I am
arguing here, however, something more than close emotional ties. I am
proposing that the close relations between adult women and female children
form a link for teaching and learning, for modeling and imitating, for
conveying and accepting ideas, that is important to maintaining the continuity of society and culture. This "feminine" mode of socialization can
balance the "masculine" mode that promotes change and rejection of parental teaching.

The notion of balance is critical to this conception as it is to Block's
description of individual personality integration. Every society exists in
some tension between retaining its values and traditions on the one hand
and moving toward change and innovation on the other. The United States
has typically prided itself on its readiness to change and to innovate. One
could argue that our society currently falls near one extreme defined by
instability and flux. We value change almost for its own sake. We turn to
youth to find creative new ideas rather than age to find wisdom. Our popular
heroes are rebels who resist social convention and authority.

At the same time, we recognize that transmission of cultural values across
generations is a glue by which society retains organization and continuity.
The recent resurgence of fundamentalist religion and social conservatism
probably reflects a sense on the part of some that there is an imbalance
between change and continuity. Without endorsing the values of these
groups, we can recognize that the young need to be grounded in some sense
of values beyond the thrill of the moment and in awareness of connectedness
with the human groups to which they belong.

For individual children, a combination of socialization practices might
promote internalization of social norms while also teaching readiness to
challenge those norms. Because present practices emphasize the former for
females and the latter for males, socialization for equality may require us
to treat girls and boys differently. Young girls may need encouragement
to venture away form adult guidance, and young boys may need encouragement to accept it. If we succeed, both individuals and society may evolve
new integrations of continuity and change.

Notes

1. In retrospect, McClelland and his colleagues deserve considerable credit for testing their measures and theory on males and females separately and for restricting their conclusions to males rather than assuming that the theory applied to women as well.

2. The fact that males have better average performance than females on college entrance examinations measuring these same skills could indicate that the value of adult structuring declines as children reach higher educational levels that demand increasing independence. An alternative explanation is differential selection—poorly achieving males have dropped out of the educational process and do not take college entrance examinations, while females from a wide range of backgrounds do take them.

References

Bakan, D. (1966). *The duality of human existence*. Chicago: Rand-McNally.

Bem, S. L. (1984). Androgyny and gender schema theory: A conceptual and empirical integration. In T. B. Sonderegger (Ed.), *Nebraska symposium on motivation: Psychology and gender* (Vol. 32: pp. 179–226). Lincoln: University of Nebraska Press.

Bernard, J. (1976). Sex differences: An overview. In A. G. Kaplan and J. P. Bean (Eds.), *Beyond sex role stereotypes: Readings toward a psychology of androgyny* (pp. 10–26). Boston: Little, Brown.

Block, J. H. (1973). Conception of sex role: Some cross–cultural and longitudinal perspectives. *American Psychologist, 28*, 512–526.

———. (1984). *Sex role identity and ego development*. San Francisco: Jossey Bass.

Carnegie Foundation Report on Education at U.S. Colleges, Excerpts from (1986, November 2). *New York Times*, p. 15.

Carpenter, C. J. (1983). Activity structure and play: Implications for socialization. In M. B. Liss (Ed.), *Social and cognitive skills: Sex roles and children's play* (pp. 117–146). New York: Academic Press.

Carpenter, C. J. and Huston-Stein, A. (1980). Activity Structure and sex typed behavior in preschool children. *Child Development, 51*, 816–817.

Carpenter, C. J. and Huston, A. C. (1983, April). *Structuring of children's time in middle childhood*. Paper presented at the Biennial Meeting of the Society for Research in Child Development, Detroit.

Crandall, V. J., Katkovsky, W., and Preston, A. (1960). A conceptual formatulation for some research on children's achievement development. *Child Development, 31*, 787–797.

D'Andrade, R. G. (1966). Sex differences and cultural institutions. In E. E. Maccoby (Ed.), *The development of sex differences* (pp. 173–203). Stanford, Calif.: Stanford University Press.

de Beauvoir, S. (1949). *The second sex*. New York: Bantam.

Draper, P. (1985). Two views of sex differences in socialization. In R. L. Hall (Ed.), *Male-female differences: A biocultural perspective* (pp. 5–26). New York: Praeger.

Eisenberg, N., Tryon, K., and Cameron, E. (1984). The relation of preschoolers' peer interaction to their sex-typed toy choices. *Child Development, 55,* 1044–1050.

Fagot, B. I. (1978). The influence of sex of child on parental reactions to toddler children. *Child Development, 49,* 459–465.

Fagot, B. I. and Leinbach, M. D. (1983). Play styles in early childhood: Social consequences for boys and girls. In M. B. Liss (Ed.), *Social and cognitive skills: Sex roles and children's play* (pp. 93–116). New York: Academic Press.

Gilligan, C. (1982). *In a different voice: Psychological theory and women's development.* Cambridge, Mass.: Harvard University Press.

Goslin, D. A. (1969). *Handbook of socialization theory and research.* Chicago: Rand-McNally.

Hall, R. L. (Ed.) (1985). *Male-female differences: A bio-cultural perspective.* New York: Praeger.

Huston, A. C. (1983). Sex typing. In E. M. Hetherington (Ed.), P. H. Mussen (Series Ed.), *Handbook of child psychology: Vol. 4. Socialization, personality, and social development* (4th ed., pp. 387–467). New York: Wiley.

Huston, A. C. and Carpenter, C. J. (1985). Gender differences in preschool classrooms. In C. C. Wilkinson and C. B. Barett (Eds.), *Gender-related differences in the classroom* (pp. 143–168). New York: Academic Press.

Huston, A. C., Carpenter, C. J., Atwater, J. B., and Johnson, L. M. (1986). Gender, adult structuring of activities, and social behavior in middle childhood. *Child Development, 57,* 1200–1209.

Maccoby, E. E. and Jacklin, C. N. (1974). *The psychology of sex differences.* Stanford, Calif.: Stanford University Press.

————. (1985, April). *Gender segregation in nursery school: Predictors and outcomes.* Paper presented at the Biennial Meeting of the Society for Research in Child Development, Toronto.

McClelland, D. C., Atkinson, J. W., Clark, R. A., and Lowell, E. L. (1953). *The achievement motive.* New York: Appleton-Century-Crofts.

Newson, J. and Newson, E. (1976). *Seven years old in the home environment.* London: Allen and Unwin.

O'Brien, M. and Huston, A. C. (1985). Development of sex-typed play behavior in toddlers. *Developmental Psychology, 21,* 866–871.

Rossi, A. S. (1976). Sex equality: The beginnings of ideology. In A. G. Kaplan and J. P. Bean (Eds.), *Beyond sex-role stereotypes: Readings toward a psychology of androgyny* (pp. 79–88). Boston: Little, Brown.

Serbin, L. A. (1980). Sex role socialization: A field in transition. In B. Lahey and A. Kazdin (Eds.), *Advances in clinical child psychology* (Vol. 3: pp. 246–270). New York: Plenum.

Serbin, L. A., O'Leary, K. D., Kent, R. N., and Tonick, I. J. (1973). A comparison of teacher response to the preacademic and problem behaviour of boys and girls. *Child Development, 44,* 796–804.

Smith, P. K. and Connolly, K. J. (1980). *The ecology of preschool behaviour.* Cambridge: Cambridge University Press.

Stein, A. H. and Bailey, M. M. (1973). The socialization of achievement orientation in females. *Psychological Bulletin, 80,* 345–366.

Whiting, B. B. (1980). Culture and social behavior. *Ethos, 2,* 95–116.

Wilson, E. O. (1975). *Sociobiology: The new synthesis.* Cambridge, Mass.: Harvard University Press.

Wittig, M. A. and Petersen, A. C. (Eds.) (1979). *Sex-related differences in cognitive functioning.* New York: Academic Press.

In the Family Circle

2

LEONIE A. MARX

When Georg Brandes, the internationally renowned Danish critic and literary historian (1842–1927), included a portrait of Gabriele Reuter (1859–1941) in his collection of critical essays *Gestalten und Gedanken* (1903; Personalities and Reflections), he assigned to her 1895 novel *Aus guter Familie* (Of Good Family) considerable value as documentation of the state of family and society in the German Empire, founded in 1871 under Prussian aegis. Brandes, whose close ties with German culture were established well before this new empire, was nevertheless no stranger to it. He had resided in its capital of Berlin from 1877 to 1883 and had no difficulties accepting the depiction of the female tragedy in Reuter's novel as a reflection of actual conditions in German bourgeois families. In his opinion, the book constituted, for the time, a major "document" with respect to the mental coercion of young girls and the forcible treatment to which they were subjected in conservative families of certain social strata.

Reuter herself later expressed in a 1908 letter to Brandes that in this novel, subtitled "Leidensgeschichte eines Mädchens" ("A Girl's Story of Suffering"), she had presented a segment of German women's cultural history that would not lose its value with time. Not only did Reuter (1921) view the dynamics of her conservative upper-middle-class family life as a complex, detrimental force in her personal development, she also saw the restrictive, prescribed values of that environment create a typical pattern for daughters growing up in her social stratum. It was this pattern that she considered important to chronicle because the stamina and endurance re-

All quotations are my own translations and are based on the 1917 edition of Gabriele Reuter's 1895 novel *Aus guter Familie*. Research for this article was partially supported by a Hall Center Travel Grant.

quired by the daughter to live through and survive the mental battles, as well as the physical and emotional stress of her life in the family circle, amounted to a kind of dubious heroism. It begged to be brought to public awareness.

Reuter's commitment as an author reflects her proximity to the modern literary current of Naturalism whose major French, German, and Scandinavian works she had read. It is particularly the theory of milieu espoused by Naturalism, portraying people as the products of their environments, which corroborated Reuter's own experiences. Having chosen to focus primarily on the milieu she knew best, she felt that in the interest of "truth" she could contribute a knowledgeable account and transmit informed judgment of a critical situation (1921, p. 431).

This essay proposes that the enduring representational value that Reuter attributed to the novel in her letter to Brandes stems only in part from a truthful account of an overall factual situation with obvious autobiographical traits. Apart from its documentation of conditioning and subordination to female gender roles in the patriarchal family, which amounts "to an indictment of the patriarchal power relations in Wihelmine society" (Johnson, 1980, p. 240), a significant compositional aspect of Reuter's novel must be addressed. As will be demonstrated, the presentation of the actual conditions which the daughter of good family had to face receives its cultural and specific historical significance from Reuter's treatment of historical events, women's place in history, and their consciousness of it. Precisely here, in the critical depiction of what constitutes history for women vis-à-vis national history, can be found Reuter's particular contribution to a diagnosis of woman's cultural position in imperial Germany.

In this novel of 1895, the one responsible for her literary breakthrough, Reuter concentrates on the social sphere of the government official, the high level civil servant in Prussia during the latter half of the nineteenth century. Through historical events, which she chooses to combine with her protagonist's fate, Reuter's criticism, while directed at the ways and means of enforcing power in the family, points well beyond that social institution to the larger society and to the state. As evident in this novel, membership in the family circle is synonymous with the requirement that a woman must define her personal history within this sphere; at the same time membership in the family entails that she thereby also contributes to history in general. Reuter delineates the network of strictures this involves as she depicts the personal history from youth to early middle age of her protagonist Agathe Heidling; through Agathe, Reuter "popularized the character of the anti-heroine" (Alimadad-Mensch, 1984, p. 122). She accounts for Agathe's progressive isolation up to its tragic climax in mental illness and treatment at an institution by showing how ideologically generated myths—ranging from sexual taboos, idealized love, and marriage to the illusion of automatic self-fulfillment in gender roles—are responsible for Agathe's growing estrangement from her initially positive self-image whenever she experiences another clash between the facts of her life and these myths she was raised with. Ultimately, this estrangement, compounded by continuously frustrated attempts to free herself emotionally and intellectually, is responsible for her inability to break away from the family circle and seek an historical role different from the one assigned to her.

From the very beginning of the novel Reuter leaves no doubt that, within the territory of the immediate family and social circle, history and its significance as reserved for women equal myth. It is this myth which serves to distort Agathe's historical sense by teaching her a one-dimensional purpose in life, relegating her to reproductive tasks in the household and society, and belittling her intellectual capacity. Myth is passed off as history, when it actually is substituted for it and amounts to a predetermined, second-rate kind of history sustained by a patriarchal state and society that veil the harsh reality of strict conformity, double standards, and subordination under an authoritarian rule with a facade of sentiment about familial love and harmony.

As the novel opens, Reuter develops this thematic complex based on Agathe's confirmation, her symbolic initiation into the circle of adults. All the elements destined to shape her life are present here, gradually to be rendered into a composite picture of women's lives under a self-righteous patriarchal system for which the family circle of the upper bourgeoisie provides an important nucleus. Agathe's father, councillor to the government in the administration of a provincial capital, states his demands and expectations of her accordingly in his dinner speech after her confirmation. Agathe's duty and conditional significance as a citizen are laid out to be those of the female citizen: " . . . woman, the mother of future generations, the founder of the family, is an important member of society if she remains quite conscious of her position as an insignificant, concealed root" (p. 22). By conforming to the qualities attributed to the root, the woman Agathe can look forward to an allegedly noble destiny; if she behaves like the "silent, patient, immobile root, which seems to have no life of its own and yet is carrying the tree of mankind . . . " (p. 22), she can be certain of acceptance and respect as an adult member of society.

What Herr Heidling emphasizes metaphorically is not only woman's duty to subordinate herself to the point of negating her faculties except for those which cultivate submissiveness and center on motherhood; his remarks also reveal the underlying strategy employed in educating young women for that role. While, on one hand, it can hardly be denied that woman must be considered essential for human history, and for the maintenance of the state and its institutions, her role is nevertheless belittled. By assigning it such low significance as a mere service function, it receives the quality of a necessary but ancillary role that anchors woman's dependency on the structure of the family. This construct of a role is furthermore given the appearance of a fixed natural law to be followed as a self-evident matter, thus concealing the fact that it could possibly be changed and affect society, as well as the course of history.

Heidling's preposterous directives complement those of the pastor whose religious guidance had instructed Agathe in her duties as a prospective citizen in the kingdom of heaven. Although the pastor alludes to her rights as well as obligations, he uses the same ambiguous procedure as her father, but in so abstract a fashion that, in its vagueness, it amounts to strenuous double-talk. Having thoroughly confused and frustrated Agathe, the pastor also manages to lay a solid foundation for a good many future guilt feelings should she stray from the prescribed path of duty leading to the heavenly kingdom. This path consists of regulations for her daily life as they concern "the modern young lady of good society" (p. 20). She certainly has the right to enjoy nature, artistic creativity, and reading—all in the circle of family and with girlfriends her own age; yet she is required to adhere to only these sources of joy and entertainment, and even these in one particular way. For it is pure, meaning religious, art she must seek pleasure in, while socially necessary events such as dances must be enjoyed only in an honorable way. Especially targeted is the material with which she might educate herself further. Here Agathe is given the stern warning to beware of modern science "which would only lead her to doubts and loss of faith"; her whole life is to be love, completely selfless, a love "that does not request what it is entitled to" (p. 20). For the nearly seventeen-year-old Agathe, who has finished her schooling and religious education, who is about to have her social debut at her first dance in order to be looked over as a potential wife and mother, for this young woman the pastor sums up his restrictions in the cryptic advice for her adult life: be happy and "enjoy as if you did not enjoy" (p. 20).

The obvious common denominator both speeches share is the requirement that Agathe give up her individual personality, above all her intellectual curiosity, in order to comply with the legally anchored conditions of domination administered by state and church down to the family level (Gerhard, 1978). It is a pattern of patriarchal domination that has been aptly termed the "triumvirate" made up of authoritarian father figures: "the father of the church, the father of the people, and the father of the family" (Hermand, 1975, p. 60). The rights granted to Agathe by these figureheads and their representatives are as second-rate as the historical role she is allowed to play. These rights are integral elements in a system that fosters idealism but simultaneously exploits it by pruning it to suit the narrow interests of those in power. This is poignantly underscored by the two confirmation gifts Agathe is most elated over. One of them is the deluxe edition of the book "Woman's Life and Activity as a Maiden, Spouse, and Mother." Its title and elaborate binding promise the longed-for explanations of Agathe's important duty and destiny, when, in fact, such an exterior belies the unglamorous reality of the mythicized roles. The underlying restrictive formula, 'children, church, and kitchen,' was firmly established for the German nuclear family during the nineteenth century (Weber-Kellermann, 1974).

The other book gift, a volume of poetry by Georg Herwegh (1817–1877), sent to Agathe by her cousin Martin, immediately causes reproach and condemnation, because its fighting spirit in the interest of radical ideals such as liberty, equality, and democracy represents an ideological threat to supporters of the existing authoritarian monarchy. A reminder of the 1848 revolution, this kind of poetry is deemed unsuitable for girls. The immediate confiscation of the book, whose liberal ideas horrify Agathe's father and the pastor alike, demonstrates the censorship that contributes to the effectiveness of this patriarchal system. Ideals Agathe was taught and refers to in defending her wish to read Herwegh's revolutionary poems, such as the ethic to stand up and fight for one's convictions, are termed applicable only when they support "a good conviction" (p. 24), meaning the one espoused by Heidling and the pastor; rebellion, on the other hand, is treated like an illness that threatens society. Censorship and tutelage exercised over women by representatives of church and state prepare Agathe, similarly to innumerable other girls since Luther's time, "to follow in the footsteps of a mother who also was kept as a minor" (Lorenz, 1980, p. 28).

By having interrupted Heidling's effusions about woman's due and rightful place in society with ideas that run counter to his reactionary ideology, Reuter has sketched some basic characteristics of the pattern ruling women's lives in the late 1860s. Through the conflict between Heidling's authoritarian stance and the liberal ideas of 1848 expressed in Herwegh's poetry, Reuter succeeds in contrasting the spirit of the two historical epochs—before and after the 1848 revolution—as well as two generations in one, essentially nuclear, family. This constellation provides the novel with a dialectical potential by means of Heidling's nephew Martin, who advocates the egalitarian ideals of the bourgeois revolution, which had failed in 1848, and introduces Agathe to them. Thus the historically prevailing conflict between the egalitarian revolutionary movement and the authoritarian conservative system is not only alluded to but runs parallel to the development of Agathe's personal history. Through flashbacks to her childhood the reader becomes a witness to the tight parental control over her life that is comparable to the increasingly rigid rule and censorship employed in Prussia during the 1860s, particularly affecting the state's civil servants. Prevention of rebellion at the state level is matched at the family level by the effort to prevent or crush disobedience.

Yet, in the figure of Martin, Reuter points to a possible liberating change in these conditions, for it is through Martin, who emancipates himself from his conservative family background and eventually offers to help Agathe free herself, that a decisive change in her life becomes a possibility. Through Martin's example Reuter illustrates that a change in the system is needed by both women and men; she also shows how important and difficult mutual assistance is in achieving this goal. Martin, the orphan under the guardianship of Agathe's father, his uncle, is financially independent due to a small inheritance. He can become a student and a social democrat (albeit much resented for it), can study working-class conditions in England as Marx and Engels did before him, and can engage in political opposition and journalistic activity; even when forced to escape from Germany into Swiss exile, he is able to continue his studies in Zürich and become a respected author abroad.

In Agathe's case her father has the leverage to enforce the subordination to his censorious rules of any political, intellectual, or social awareness. Since those who instruct Agathe include the most respected adults in her family—the pastor is her uncle—and in her immediate social circle, which primarily consists of acquaintances from her father's professional sphere, these adults automatically have maximum credibility; to be obedient to them is necessary for Agathe in order to prove her good moral standing, win their approval, and remain a beloved member of the family circle. What she is allowed in terms of an appropriate political and historical consciousness is evident in the reception of the Franco-Prussian war events of 1870–1871 and centers on the emotional level, around the heroic victor and around patriotism for the new-founded empire; grenade fragments are made into inkwells and cute little flower vases to decorate the boudoirs of the young ladies, for "the German girl's right and duty it was to honor the military" (p. 96).

The fact that Agathe tries to join conventional society despite her perception and dislike of the ruling double standards indicates the predicament her upbringing toward the exclusive goal of marriage has created for her. It forces her personal history into a mental and social straitjacket of numerous restrictions. Only through the discrepancies between myth and reality, between theory and practice, such as the increasing number of betrayals that shape Agathe's life, does she develop an acute sense for women's position in the socio-political system she lives in.

For the period spanning Agathe's twentieth birthday until she is a defeated individual in her thirties at the novel's end, Reuter juxtaposes her protagonist's learning experiences and growing awareness with two main traits of the epoch after 1871: the consolidation of the empire's internal authority and the mounting tension between conservatives and opposing socialists. These traits are part of a period of expansion and modernization of the state; Agathe's "modernity," however, develops along the lines of Thomas Mann's 1904 definition of that term, that is, through her steps toward consciousness and the truth about her existential conditions as a woman (1974, p. 394).

During the period after 1871 Agathe's parents also consolidate their control over her, continuously imposing yet another restriction on a life with already very limited options. For Agathe, in contrast to Martin, the German universities are closed, only permitting women to enroll as of 1900, in Prussia not until 1908 (von Soden and Zipfel, 1979); she must seek parental permission, frequently even in order to go out, has no financial means at her disposal except for whatever she can eke out of her allowance for clothing. Barely past twenty, she is judged too old for marriage by her childhood friend (now her sister-in-law), has been appraised at the marriage market of society balls, and is finally rejected at twenty-four by a middle-aged bachelor in her father's profession who subsequently warns other prospective suitors that she has no dowry. Her father, legally the sole administrator of the family's finances, had used Agathe's dowry to secretly pay off the debts that her brother, a young and rising lieutenant in the imperial army, had accumulated at cards. This betrayal of Agathe's options thus is perfectly legal, even though the funds had been set aside for Agathe from her mother's dowry, and it underscores further the priority granted to male interests (Gerhard, 1978).

From the beginning of the novel, Reuter has provided links between Agathe's personal history, especially her growing awareness, and the situation of women outside her class; but she lends her depiction a political dimension through Martin, the active social democrat whose journalistic criticism of the system is not only rejected by Agathe's family but eventually also forbidden by Bismarck's legislation which banned the Social Democratic Party in 1878. Through Martin's endeavors to create awareness of the conditions of the suffering lower classes, Reuter adds another dimension of women's plight to her novel, thereby pointing to the political nature of the daughter's situation without having to leave the social milieu of the upper-class daughter. After all, the daily lives of upper- and lower-class women, though worlds apart, were nevertheless closely linked in the bourgeois family, since they lived in the same house or large apartment and to some extent shared the work load as well. Reuter elucidates a vicious circle of domination in which the bourgeois household corresponds to the pattern of social Darwinism in state and society on the whole, subjecting the servants to sexual exploitation, a low quality of food, and long workdays. Reuter's depiction is by no means exaggerated when one considers the rigid discipline to which the Prussian labor laws for servants—effective from 1810 until the end of the German Empire in 1918—subjected the servants. The underlying feudal spirit of these laws is best reflected in clause #77 entitling the employer to exercise corporal punishment; this clause remained in effect until 1900, by which time 98 percent of household servants were women (Gerhard, 1978).

Martin, in his appeal to Agathe's conscience before his departure into exile, entrusts a bundle of his publications to her and urges her to recognize that she and women of her class are the worst enemies of the servants. Reuter has prepared the reader for the urgency of this statement by having depicted two contrasting figures in the household of Agathe's parents. "Kitchen-Dorte," who never loses sight of the fact that she can rely only on herself, survives in the system, not however without an occasional half sarcastic, half cynical remark about its conditions. She succeeds in obtaining the reward "for twenty-five years of loyal service with one family and faultless moral conduct" (p. 273). The tokens of recognition, a Bible and a silver medal with an official document—all traditionally awarded by the queen of Prussia, now empress of Germany—again underscore the intimate connection among church, state, and bourgeois family. Through this award, celebrated with gifts and, ironically, with a cake Dorte baked herself, the system bestows as great an honor on her employer. It enhances the Heidlings' image in society by casting a veil of harmony and high moral standards over Agathe's family.

The actual conditions behind this facade are more accurately illustrated by the fate of Wiesing, the unspoiled naive country girl who had gone to confirmation with Agathe and whom the pastor had entrusted to the moral guidance of an equally naive Agathe when Wiesing became a servant in the Heidlings' city-household. The tragic irony of this mentorship becomes apparent when Wiesing turns to Agathe for protection, after having been exploited sexually by Agathe's brother; while Agathe has been warning her of the dangerous dance halls, she is actually not safe in her room. Even though Agathe secretly installs a bolt on Wiesing's door and confronts her brother with reproaches, she also punishes Wiesing with cold distance, thereby turning against her protégée whose untidy room, as the scene of her elegant brother's erotic pursuit, has filled Agathe with disgust. It is on the aesthetic level that Agathe resents Wiesing, and on this level she can find an emotional outlet for her abhorrance over her brother's "dishonorable," in fact, criminal, behavior. Aesthetic sensitivity, a privilege of her class, also proves to be an ideological tool for obscuring the truth, a tool instrumental in her own education, veiling facts and gender roles with a mythical aura. How miserably Agathe has failed as a mentor is evident in her relief when her mother angrily dismisses Wiesing, because the girl is pregnant. By leaving Wiesing to her fate, Agathe not only becomes an accomplice to her brother by covering up his violation; she also shares in the responsibility for the child's and Wiesing's death in a slum quarter of town a few years later. At that point, all Agathe can do to help is to pay for a coffin and a funeral in order to save the child's body from automatically being sent to the dissecting rooms of the medical school.

Frau Heidling's callous reaction to Wiesing's fate, her statement that servants "are good for nothing and only created for our torment" (p. 292), proves, at this point in the novel, that prejudice, discrimination, authoritarian orders, and aesthetic taboos serve to prevent solidarity among women due to class interests; they serve also as a refuge for the likes of Frau Heidling, who otherwise would not be able to cope with their roles as wives, mothers, and housekeepers in the only sphere of power they have been assigned to. The strict subordination to the state required of her husband is passed on to his family circle, where it is imposed on those who have minimal rights. By exemplifying the slave mentality that Frau Heidling has accepted for herself and for her daughter and enforces upon the servants, Reuter stresses the feudal aspect of the system that governs women's lives and how it is perpetuated in the conservative bourgeois family. With Agathe's expanding consciousness, the political nature of these conditions is gradually given a central focus. As the state fortifies its ideological system, creating role models for servants with awards such as Dorte's, Agathe senses that twenty-five years of officially rewarded self-denial have, in fact, deprived Dorte "of the best part of her existence" (p. 277).

Betrayal through myths and deprivation characterizes a system that utilizes the claim of protecting women in order to protect itself, that is to say, male interests, from women's competition, above all by depriving them of the necessary intellectual basis for any competition: knowledge. Aimed at reserving jobs for men, particularly in the Civil Service sector which had to absorb yearly "a large number of mustered-out officers and under-officers" from the military (Bebel, 1904, p. 213), official denial of educational opportunities for women is paralleled by censorship in the family. When Agathe chances upon Ernst Haeckel's *Natürliche Schöpfungsgeschichte* (1868; History of Natural Creation) and experiences a thorough intellectual revelation through this first acquaintance with Darwin's theories, she begins to sense how extensive her intellectual deprivation is. She envies men, because, in contrast to them, she is not allowed to learn, much less to engage in research, but must accept that "silly love" will be her main concern in life (p. 303). Of course history only repeats itself for Agathe, for again she does not receive the books she needs to study further and, moreover, her father locks his bookcase to save a crumbled myth. He refuses to admit that she could have understood Haeckel's work correctly, fearing perhaps that she did comprehend it. The gifts she receives instead, a book about "The Flora of Central Germany—for the Use of Our Daughters" accompanied by a flower press, symbolize how she herself is classified and conserved eternally to be the young girl and good daughter for whom life is barred just as certain doors are.

Agathe is unable to accommodate herself in this system, because, unlike her girlfriends, she has not learned early on how to utilize it to her advantage; instead, she has believed in its facade only increasingly to find her expectations, her ideals, and ultimately herself betrayed. If despite this realization, which she finally communicates to Martin, she fails to leave the circle of selfish parental love, it is not paternal authority alone that keeps her in it. It is also Agathe's disposition to approach life predominantly on an emotional level that confines her. Whether it was the reception of such ideals as liberty and democracy or Martin's challenge to help the lower classes,

Agathe was enthusiastic about the high motivation and grand gestures, about the powerful language and the noble image of such a cause. This explains why, in growing up, she could apply the same strong enthusiasm to religious, romantic, or historical myth. With her intellectual growth stunted, Agathe developed an intensified emotional perception, exactly as was considered proper for girls.

Although she comes close to accepting Martin's help, the offer to copy manuscripts for him in Zürich, she cannot, at this point, emancipate herself from the emotional, strictly romantic bond she had developed toward him. A definite alternative for Agathe is present in Martin's suggestion that she change the course of her life and play an active, socially and historically important role for other women outside the restricting circle of her family by writing a book about her experiences as she related them to him. She fails to seize this opportunity, because she cannot conceive of her life outside the family circle in terms other than those of romantic devotion to another person; yet Martin, who openly shows his erotic attraction to other women, is not the proper candidate to fulfill Agathe's visions. Above all, Agathe cannot think of working for her own benefit now, when her entire life has consisted of training to be selflessly devoted to others, in her case a training in absolute filial duty, which now leaves her deprived of even the essential survival instincts. However, Martin's project to assist Agathe in creating a self-defined historical role for her life must also be considered a failure on his part, since he, angry and critical of Agathe's jealous and highly emotional reaction to his flirting with others, fails to comprehend the depth of her dilemma and leaves Agathe under the rigid control of her father and her sister-in-law.

In keeping with the thesis of this essay it must be considered symptomatic for the essence of this novel and for its contribution to the clarification of German women's cultural position in the latter half of the nineteenth century that Reuter concludes her novel at a spa, where mostly young upper-class women from all over Germany are treated for iron deficiency. Under the direction of a cynical doctor, who is as contemptuous of his patients as he is sought after by them at social gatherings, the microsociety of this spa is presented as a stark reminder of the conditions in Wilhelminian society at large. It is here that Agathe lucidly perceives "the great deception they all had committed against her—Papa and Mama and the relatives and girlfriends and the teachers and preachers" (pp. 373–374). The sociopolitical gesture of this protest against the abuse of women's options and potential is openly directed at the state when Reuter changes the well-known phrase Bismarck had used to credit the "blood and iron" of war for the unification of German states. Instead, Reuter observes that it seemed "as if the wealth of blood and iron with which the German Empire was forged into powerful great-ness, had been sucked from the veins and bones of its daughters and they could not recover from the loss" (p. 369). Against the background of this statement Reuter demonstrates who the actual losers are, as Agathe, neither the first nor the last of many, loses her ability to cope rationally with her anger over an existential situation she finds unacceptable and lapses into insanity, the daughter's illness or "female malady" (Showalter, 1985) which was not restricted to Wilhelminian society alone.

Had rebellion been viewed as an illness before, it now coalesces with it, only to be remedied by the institutional straitjacket which accomplishes what its intellectual and social variants failed to achieve. Defeated in her quest for love and truth after she has seen her ideals violated and has suffered through the distorting myths imposed on her life, Agathe—heretic because of her insubordination—finally is subjected to one more form of torture: various methods of psychiatric treatment. Reuter's analogy between an ascending national and a descending personal history is completed after Agathe too is granted peace following her battles. Hers is the peace dictated to losers; it is rooted in a partial loss of memory following two years of treatment in a mental hospital. In exchange for this loss she can now be a tolerated and compliant member of society.

References

Alimadad-Mensch, F. (1984). *Gabriele Reuter: Portrait einer Schriftstellerin.* Bern, Frankfurt/M., Nancy, New York: Lang.

Bebel, A. (1904). *Woman under socialism.* D. De Leon (Tr.). Reprinted from the New York Labor News Press. New York: Schocken Books, Inc., 1971.

Brandes, G. (1903). *Gestalten und Gedanken.* München: Langen.

Gerhard, U. (1978). *Verhältnisse und Verhinderungen.* Frankfurt/M.: Suhrkamp.

Hermand, J. (1975). Biedermeier-Kids: Eine Mini-Polemik. *Monatshefte, 67, 1,* 59–66.

Johnson, R. L. (1980). Men's power over women in Gabriele Reuter's *Aus guter Familie.* In M. Burkhard (Ed.), *Gestaltet und gestaltend* (pp. 235–253). Amsterdam: Rodopi.

———. (1982). Gabriele Reuter: Romantic and realist. In S. L. Cocalis and K. Goodman (Eds.), *Beyond the eternal feminine* (pp. 225–244). Stuttgart: Akademischer Verlag Hans-Dieter Heinz.

Lorenz, D. (1980). Vom Kloster zur Küche: Die Frau vor und nach der Reformation Dr. Martin Luthers. In B. Becker-Cantarino (Ed.), *Die Frau von der Reformation zur Romantik* (pp. 7–35). Bonn: Bouvier.

Mann, T. (1904). Gabriele Reuter. *Gesammelte Werke, 13* (pp. 388–398). Frankfurt/M.: Fischer, 1974.

Reuter, G. (1895). *Aus guter Familie: Leidensgeschichte eines Mädchens.* Berlin: Fischer, 21st–22nd ed., 1917.

———. (1908). Unpublished letter to Georg Brandes. Brandes-Archive, Royal Library, Copenhagen, Denmark.

———. (1921). *Vom Kinde zum Menschen.* Berlin: Fischer.

Showalter, E. (1985). *The Female malady: Women, madness, and English culture, 1830–1980.* New York: Pantheon Books.
Soden, K. v. and Zipfel, G. (1979). *70 Jahre Frauenstudium.* Köln: Pahl-Rugenstein.
Weber-Kellermann, I. (1974). *Die deutsche Familie.* Frankfurt/M.: Suhrkamp.

Afro-American Women: Achievement through the Reconciliation of Messages and Images

3

DORTHY L. PENNINGTON

I learned about Black feminism from the women in my family—not just from their strengths, but from their failings, from witnessing daily how they were humiliated and crushed because they had made the "mistake" of being born Black and female in a white man's country. I inherited fear and shame from them as well as hope. These conflicting feelings about being a Black woman still do battle inside of me. It is this conflict, my constantly ... "seeing and touching/Both sides of things" that makes my commitment real (Smith, 1983, p. xxii).

Afro-American women have received conflicting messages and images about themselves throughout their history in America. The messages and images have been both positive and negative, and in order to resolve the ambivalence that these multiple messages and images created, Afro-American women have used specific strategies of reconciliation. Most of the negative messages and images resulted from Afro-American women's status as slaves and that legacy, their being compared to Caucasian women and their being the antithesis of what it meant to be a Caucasian male. Afro-American women were a "contrast conception." During the Antebellum period, the images that outsiders had of Afro-American women were of their being breeders, concubines, mammies, mules, contrasted with the ideals of womanhood—delicacy, shrinking mannerisms, sexual innocence, and social grace (Burgher, 1979). While these images and messages emanated from Caucasians, they were entrenched in the thinking of Afro-Americans. As shown in the quote from Smith, Afro-American women inherited both fear and shame, as well as hope, from older women in their families. Many of the images and messages came to Afro-American women vicariously, often through unspoken means.

This essay explores some of the messages and images that Afro-American women received and some of the strategies that they employed to reconcile the conflicts involved. It argues that Afro-American women reconciled the messages and images, rather than treating them as either/or propositions. It further argues that religion and an African worldview of compassion and tenacity, along with the exigencies they faced, served as the motivation and principles guiding Afro-American women toward specific strategies of achievement, in spite of their ascribed status of being Afro-American, female, and often, poor.

Religious Values as Guiding Principles

Religion permeated all aspects of life in traditional Africa (Mbiti, 1970), and Africans who were brought to America brought with them their religious values (Woodson, 1936; Bourguinon, 1970). African women, often having served as religious leaders in their families, were in a unique position to embody and transmit these values. The African worldview emphasized reverence and respect for the Supreme Being, believed to have the ability to intervene into the affairs of humans; compassion for fellow humans; and the belief that humans were in an unpredictable world over which they exercised little control, thus requiring a tenacious faith, humility, and ongoing communication with supernatural beings. This worldview, coupled with the African understanding that motherhood was a cosmic necessity for women, placed upon African women the responsibility of being nurturant and loving; women were often the healers in their tribe. While some African women were, undoubtedly, dissatisfied with this responsibility, it was an expectation nevertheless. And while African women had leadership and social roles in their tribes and communities—such as being traders, political leaders, ritual leaders, drummers, craftswomen, and warriors (Sertima, 1984)—it was their role as mother and life-giver that was considered by the society as being the most important.

When brought to America and placed in the roles of breeder, concubine, mammy, and beast of burden, Afro-American women integrated these roles with the African emphasis on compassion and faith and thereby reconciled them into a positive self-image. "Obviously unable to ignore the role forced on them by their masters, they blended the external shields of strength and tenacity required of them with an inner core of tenderness and compassion" (Burgher, 1979, p. 108). The resulting image was a transcendent one that went beyond its separate parts. This, undoubtedly, led to the image of Afro-American women as being "strong."

While religion taught Afro-American women compassion and tolerance, it also gave them a sense of motivation. They wanted to improve their condition and that of Afro-American people. Religion provided hope. It translated into a sense of "mythication," that is the belief that God, the right, or some superrational force was on their side. It gave a sense of holiness, sanctification, and mission to their cause. The articulation of religion as a reconciling agent for Afro-American women became a part of their rhetoric, as shown in "On Being Brought from Africa to America" by Phillis Wheatley (1786):

> Some view our sable race with scornful eye,
> "Their colour is a diabolic die."
> Remember, Christians, Negroes black as Cain,
> May be refin'd, and join the angelic train.

The conflicting messages here were those of Afro-Americans' color as carrying an ascription of inferiority, on the one hand, and the belief that religion provided a basis for positive self-worth, on the other. Though sometimes expressed in more general terms, Afro-American women's view of Christian values as a means of reconciling their conflict showed that they often made analogies between their condition and that of Christ, as seen through the eyes of Harper (1871):

> How to solve life's saddest problems,
>   Its weariness, want, and woe,
> Was answered by one who suffered
>   In Palestine long ago.

Just as religion served as a basis of hope for Afro-Americans, it also served as a basis for the motivation needed to actively resist oppression. The religious values of Afro-American women caused them to employ strategies that combined compassion with forcefulness in order to reconcile conflicting messages and images, and to advance their cause. Before being able to argue for their rights as capable citizens, however, they had to argue for more basic rights: the right to be viewed first as humans and then as women; the right not to be viewed as beasts of burden, "the mule of the world" (Walker, 1984, p. 237).

Attempting to Forge an Identity as Women

Because early America had certain images of womanhood—delicacy, shrinking mannerisms, sexual innocence, social grace—the roles (often necessary ones) that Afro-American women were assigned were not conducive to their fitting into the American image of womanhood. Caucasian women, in many instances, were placed on "pedestals," in cosmetic, seemingly nonsubstantive positions. The more affluent among them were given a sheltered, genteel existence in which their womanhood could be taken as a given. Afro-American women, on the other hand, had to seek an identity as humans and as women. The external image of them as beasts of burden served to justify the brutalities imposed upon them:

> No chance was given her for delicate reserve or tender modesty. From her childhood she was the doomed victim of the grossest passions. All the virtues of her sex were utterly ignored. . . . So likewise was it her lot to wield the heavy hoe or to follow the plow or to gather in crops. She was a 'hewer of wood and a drawer of water.' She had to keep her place in the gang from morn till eve, under the burden of a heavy task, or under the stimulus or the fear of a cruel lash. . . . Her home life was of the most degrading nature. She lived in the rudest huts, and partook of the coarsest food, and dressed in the scantiest garb, and slept, in multitudinous cabins, upon the hardest boards (Crummell, 1883).

And likewise, Sojourner Truth, formerly called Isabella, speaking at a Woman's Rights convention in 1851, agitated for the need of Afro-American women to be treated humanely and with dignity:

> Dat man ober dar say womin needs to be helped into carriages and lifted ober ditches, and to hab de best place everywhar. Nobody eber helps me into carriages, or ober mud puddles, or gibs me any best place! And a'n't I a woman? Look at my arm. I have ploughed, and planted and gathered into barns, and no man could head me. And a'n't I a woman? I could work as much and eat as much as a man—when I could get it—and bear de lash as well. And a'n't I a woman? I have borne thirteen children and seen 'em mos' all sold off into slavery, and when I cried out with my mother's grief, none but Jesus heard me! And a'n't I a woman?

Sojourner here sought to reconcile the image of Afro-American women as being heavy laborers with that of their ability to be tender, compassionate mothers. The sense of "mythication" for her cause came through her allusion to her communication with Jesus and the hope that this instilled in her. "A'n't I a woman," strategically repeated, implied her need for humanity and womanhood, while she, at the same time, acknowledged her toughness in withstanding adversity.

Even in the middle of the twentieth century, Afro-American women did not share in the image given to white womanhood. One means of separation was that of titles. Traditionally, Afro-American women were referred to by their first name, while Caucasian women expected to be addressed as Mrs. or Miss, an obvious status difference. Thus, in the novel *The Street*, Lutie, an Afro-American female, is met at the station by her new Caucasian employer with "Hello, there, I'm Mrs. Chandler. You must be Lutie Johnson" (Petrie, 1946, p. 35). Although the negative images held of Afro-American women instilled in them a sense of humility, the values of moral integrity served as an impetus to them to go forward. Afro-American women viewed education as a means of going forward.

Becoming Trained and Educated

The sense of "mythication" was present as Afro-American women sought to reconcile the image of their being uncultured and unrefined with their belief in themselves as worthy vessels with a divine mission. Religion sanctioned them and gave them a sense of purpose. Thus, as they sought to improve themselves through the strategy of becoming trained and educated, religion was a motivating force. Maria Stewart, an Afro-American orator speaking in 1883, asked "Why cannot we become divines and scholars?" Going further to reconcile the unlearned state of most Afro-American women at that time with their innate abilities and spirituality, she continued "Although learning is somewhat requisite, yet recollect that those apostles, Peter and James, were ignorant and unlearned. They were taken from the fishing boat and made fishers of men" (in Foner, 1972, p. 66). For the mission of education, therefore, Stewart viewed religion as being central. To those who chided her for speaking so much about religion, she replied, "I have regardless of the frowns and scoffs of a guilty world, plead up religion and the pure principles of morality among you. Religion is the most glorious theme that mortals can converse upon" (Foner, p. 66).

In expressing a similar notion, Cynthia Hope, an Afro-American leader in Atlanta in 1908, used the religious phrase "love thy neighbor as thyself" to guide the founding of a neighborhood union related to education. Two major functions of the union were (1) "to provide playgrounds, clubs, good literature, and neighborhood centers for the moral, physical, and intellectual development of the young, and (2) to establish lecture courses, classes, and clubs for adults for the purpose of encouraging habits of cleanliness and industry, promoting child welfare, and of bringing about culture and efficiency in general homemaking" (Neverdon-Morton, 1978, pp. 44–45). "Love thy neighbor as thyself" was a motivating theme that Hope and other educated Afro-American women adopted to show their concern for the masses deprived of educational and training opportunities. This legacy inspired much of the effort of Afro-American women in the Club Movement. Their motto was "Lifting as We Climb." The most prominent organization of the Club Movement was the National Association of Colored Women, formed in 1896.

Afro-American women in the Club Movement were concerned not only with matters of race, but also with health care, childrearing, and training in caring for the home. This training was aimed at women because they played a central role in the home and in child care. Morality and Christian principles were constantly emphasized. At the same time that Christian principles, such as "love thy neighbor," were the motivating force behind women in the Club Movement, Christian principles were also the message of these women, passed on as a foundation on which to build; this became a part of their lore. They believed that a foundation of morality, established in the home, would be a way of helping Afro-American women to cope with and reconcile the conflicting messages and images they received. As Josephine Bruce (1905), a noted Afro-American woman, said, "The Negro home is distinctly becoming the center of social and intellectual life; it is building up strength and righteousness in its sons and daughters and equipping them for the inevitable battles of life which grow out of the struggle for existence" (in Giddings, 1984, p. 100). For these women, therefore, "the home was not so much a refuge from the outside world as a bulwark to secure one's passage through it" (Giddings, p. 100). These women did not try to repress or deny the negative forces that Afro-Americans encountered; they wanted, rather, to reconcile the various forces in carving out a life for themselves and their race.

Afro-American women in the Club Movement also paved the way for Afro-American women leaders, many of whom were educated, to reconcile political and community activism with traditional values of marriage and motherhood. Women leaders, such as Mary Church Terrell and Ida B. Wells-Barnett, saw this as a personal conflict. While the traditionalism of the society regarding women's roles, as well as the Afro-American emphasis on procreation, may have imposed on these women the need for maternity, they, themselves, recognized the merits of motherhood. Wells-Barnett felt that not having children deprived women "of one of the most glorious advantages in the development of their own womanhood" (recounted by Duster in Giddings, 1984, p. 111). Having families of their own allowed these activists to devise creative ways of reconciling the conflict, such as shared child care. Equally as important, it allowed them to become examples of the messages that they carried. This process of enactment enhanced their credibility as leaders. They became flexible in the roles that they played, for the need to be flexible was a conscious part of Afro-American women's experiences and awareness.

Exercising Role Flexibility and Functionality

In slavery, there was little division of labor between Afro-American women and men, as the women were put to work in the fields right alongside the men. This resulted from not only the planters' desire to produce a large labor force, but also from their conscious attempt to prevent Afro-American women from enjoying the privileges of womanhood accorded to Caucasian women. This sentiment was articulated shortly after the emancipation of the slaves as "all over the South, planters complained that freedwomen were 'putting on airs,' desiring to 'play the lady' and be supported by their husbands like the white folks" (Sterling, 1984, p. 321). These behaviors, which seemed to place Afro-Americans on an equal footing with Caucasians, angered the ruling class. The planters wanted to maintain their image of Afro-American women as beasts of burden.

In actual fact, emancipation did not release Afro-American women from their traditional role as heavy laborers. They worked alongside the men on farms that they acquired or on which they were sharecroppers. The women plowed and planted, as well as harvested the crops. Many of them took the harvest to market, thus acquiring skills in business. In some ways, women seemed to have worked harder than men: "Most of the field-work was done by the women and girls; their lords and masters were much interrupted by their political and religious duties. When the days of 'conwentions' came the men were rarely at home; but the women kept steadily at work in the fields" (Botume, cited in Sterling, 1984, p. 324).

While the planters viewed these women as beasts of burden, the women combined this image with their view of themselves as industrious and reconciled the two. The resulting image was that of Afro-American women as being self-reliant and sturdy. Just as women plowed in the fields, they also sewed and nursed babies. Many of them had large families. Afro-American men participated in more organized religious activities than the women, and many men took training to become ministers. During these times, the women supported their husbands and families. This practice resulted from religious teaching and respect for their marital responsibility, as well as from the affection between women and men. In Georgia, for example, the would-be preachers viewed their wives' working to support them as a "lawful tribute," and "generally [had] an extempore sermon on hand from some of Paul's dicta about women" (Sterling, 1984, p. 326). These women, therefore, had a clear sense of duty not only to their husbands and families, but also to the law of marriage. While the law provided the form for their behavior, their circumstances provided the content; they did whatever was necessary to make ends meet. There was no stigma attached to duties requiring heavy physical labor on the part of women.

Socially, Afro-American women were also flexible. They adjusted to life with or without a spouse. While marriage was the socially defined base for the Afro-American community, unmarried females functioned well. Single women often remained at home with their parents and carried on the work in which the family was engaged. Some, however, became schoolteachers and other types of professionals. Mary Jane Patterson was one such person. She was a prominent teacher and principal in Washington, D.C., and she, like her two sisters who were also teachers, never married (Sterling, 1984). These women were respected and participated in societal activities just as did Afro-American women who were married.

The Strategies in Perspective

This essay has described a number of strategies employed by Afro-American women in their efforts to reconcile the negative images and messages they received from Caucasians with the positive images of black womanhood they received from their African traditions. These negative images and messages functioned to try to prevent the integration of Afro-American women into the larger American society. For example, Afro-American women were not integrated into the industrialized work force not only because "white women had no intention of working alongside black women, but also because there were widely held racial stereotypes of Afro-American females as being immoral which prevented their becoming a part of the growing female factory labor supply" (Harley, 1978, p. 8). Yet, Afro-American women took such images, transcended them through love and endurance, and were able to survive the most ignominious circumstances as well as to pave the way for the more militant responses in modern times (Dance, 1979). Thus, negative images played two roles. They kept Afro-American women humble, but they also served as a source of motivation for Afro-American women to excel.

The ability of Afro-American women to reconcile conflicting messages and images has been influenced by the African worldview, which emphasizes integration and synthesis of phenomena rather than analysis and dispersion. Thus, "complementary opposites" work together to create balance. This ability to integrate and to reconcile is passed on through lore among Afro-American women. Margaret Walker referred to this phenomenon in "Lineage" (1942) where she described Afro-American grandmothers as being strong and sturdy, plowing and bending at toil, while at the same time, touching the earth and making grain grow, singing and being full of memories. The lore handed down from generation to generation has been both spoken and unspoken, as in the case of grandmothers who told their granddaughters how to reconcile sexual assaults by slave masters or in the case of the writer, Alice Walker, who noted how her mother had organically "handed down respect for the possibilities—and the will to grasp them" (Walker, 1984, p. 242). Afro-American women often reconciled conflicting messages and images by viewing life in the metaphorical terms of war or struggle. In war, a warrior absorbs the blows along with the victories. Thus, the dominant image of Afro-American women as being "strong" has validity. From negative appellations like "beast of burden," "crude," "immoral," Afro-American women have reclaimed earthiness, swarthiness, and sturdiness. They have walked between the highly negative images held of black women and the highly passive images held of white women to find a vision of women, strong *and* tender. Under the most difficult of circumstances, Afro-American women have struck a balance for all women.

References

Botume, E. (1893/1984). In D. Sterling (Ed.), *We are your sisters: black women in the nineteenth century* (p. 324). New York: W. W. Norton.

Bourguinon, E. (1970). Afro-American religion: traditions and transformations. In J. F. Szwed (Ed.), *In black America* (pp. 191–192). New York: Basic Books.

Bruce, J. (1905/1984). In P. Giddings (Ed.), *When and where I enter* (p. 100). New York: Bantam.

Burgher, M. (1979). Images of self and race in the autobiographies of black women. In R. P. Bell, B. J. Parker, and B. Guy-Sheftall (Eds.), *Sturdy black bridges: visions of black women in literature* (p. 108). Garden City, N.Y.: Anchor.

Crummell, A. (1883/1972). The black woman of the south: her neglects and her needs. In P. S. Foner (Ed.), *The voice of black America* (p. 511). New York: Capricorn.

Dance, D. (1979). Black eve or madonna? In R. P. Bell, B. J. Parker, and B. Guy-Sheftall (Eds.), *Sturdy black bridges: visions of black women in literature* (p. 130). Garden City, N.Y.: Anchor.

Duster, A. (1970/1984). In P. Giddings (Ed.), *When and where I enter* (p. 111). New York: Bantam.

Harley, S. (1978). Northern black female workers. In S. Harley and R. Terborg-Penn (Eds.), *The Afro-American woman: struggles and images* (pp. 7–9). Port Washington, N.Y.: Kennikat Press.

Harper, E. W. (1871/1981). The burden of all. In E. Stetson (Ed.), *Black sister* (p. 7). Bloomington: Indiana University Press.

Mbiti, J. (1970). *African religions and philosophy*. New York: Doubleday.

Neverdon-Morton, C. (1978). The black woman's struggle for equality in the South. In S. Harley and R. Terborg-Penn (Eds.), *The Afro-American woman: struggles and images* (pp. 44–45). Port Washington, N.Y.: Kennikat Press.

Petrie, A. (1946). *The street*. Boston: Houghton Mifflin.

Sertima, I. (1984). *Black women in antiquity*. New Brunswick, N.J.: Transaction.

Smith, B. (Ed.) (1983). *Home girls: a black feminist anthology*. New York: Kitchen Table.

Sterling, D. (Ed.) (1984). *We are your sisters: black women in the nineteenth century*. New York: W. W. Norton.

Stewart, M. (1883/1972). What if I am a woman? In P. S. Foner (Ed.), *The voice of black America* (pp. 66–68). New York: Capricorn.

Truth, S. (1851/1972). Woman's rights. In P. S. Foner (Ed.), *The voic of black America* (p. 123). New York: Capricorn.

Walker, A. (1984). *In search of our mothers' gardens*. New York: Harcourt Brace Jovanovich.

Walker, M. (1942/1981). Lineage. In E. Stetson (Ed.), *Black sister* (p. 94). Bloomington: Indiana University Press.

Wheatley, P. (1786/1981). On being brought from Africa to America. In E. Stetson (Ed.), *Black sister* (p. 5). Bloomington: Indiana University Press.

Woodson, C. G. (1936). *The African background outlined*. Washington, D.C.: The Association for the Study of Negro Life and History, Inc.

The American Woman Writer in Transition: Freeman, Austin, and Cather

4

SALLY ALLEN McNALL

When, as a very young woman, I began consciously to identify myself as a writer, the models I looked to were writers of the Modernist period. I did not notice for many years that the Modernist image of the artist—isolated, driven—would prove awkward to combine with the other image I had of myself, as wife and mother. I first read Cather's 1915 novel of an artist's development, *The Song of the Lark*, in 1955, when I was fifteen. Rereading Cather's novel in the 1980s, I can now see the ways in which she was not so uncompromising as she seemed in my first reading. Reading a similar work, *A Woman of Genius* (1912), by Cather's contemporary, Mary Austin, I see more compromises, greater difficulties. Reading Mary Wilkins Freeman's *The Butterfly House* (1912), I am made aware of an even wider context of practical problems, social stigmata, and psychological barriers to be overcome by the woman writer. Freeman, born in 1852, wrote until 1917, without coming to terms with the twentieth century. But Austin and Cather, born in 1868 and 1873, were in every sense contemporaries of American Modernist writers such as Hemingway and Fitzgerald, just as Virginia Woolf was the British contemporary of Joyce and Lawrence.

The three American women do not illustrate a steady progression in women's literary history. The similarities are as instructive as the differences, and so this essay will be one in what Showalter has termed "gynocritics," which concerns itself with the "history, themes, genres and structures of literature by women" (Showalter, 1985, p. 128). It will also be an essay in biography, as I turn from the Künstlerromane, or novels of the artist's development, to what I take to be their sources in these writers' lives. Cather wrote no autobiography, but much of *Song of the Lark* is autobiographical. Austin wrote both an autobiographical novel, *Woman of Genius*, and an autobiography, *Earth Horizon* (1932). Freeman's most autobiographical novel is *By the Light of the Soul* (1907), and I will be referring to it as well as to *Butterfly House*.

The New Woman

Freeman was one of the last of a group Mary Kelley (1984) has called the "literary domestics," and Freeman wrote in what Judith Fetterley defines as another woman's genre, regionalism.[1] The larger part of Freeman's work described up-country New England women's lives. However, *Butterfly House* is set in suburban New Jersey. In this novel, the figure of woman writer is split into four characters, a common literary (as well as psychological) maneuver among nineteenth-century writers (though usually a two-way split sufficed). Austin's and Cather's novels, on the other hand, portray psychic integration of a fairly high order, though it is not easily won. Available to both these women was the role of the "New Woman," who chose the public sphere over the domestic. As Smith-Rosenberg describes it, this cohort "inherited a consciousness of women's new role possibilities almost as their birthright" (1985, p. 176).

Freeman did not finish college, and married with enthusiasm at fifty; most critics say Freeman's writing deteriorated after her marriage. Austin finished college, meaning not to marry until she had made something of her education, and her teaching career lasted two years before her engagement to Stafford Austin. Her marriage turned out badly and yet, as her autobiography shows, she did not let it destroy her career as a writer. Cather did not marry. In the early 1890s she fell in love with Louise Pound, the exemplary New Woman of her generation at the University of Nebraska. Cather continued a career in journalism, already well begun while she was a student, after a move to Pittsburgh, Pennsylvania. There, in 1899, she met the love of her life, Isabella McClung. For Cather's New England mentor, Sarah Orne Jewett, loving another woman was socially acceptable; Jewett and Annie Fields, members of Freeman's generation, participated in the nineteenth-century female world of love and ritual (Smith-Rosenberg, 1985). However, young women who grew up in the nineties were subjected to the American male's reaction to the challenge of the New Woman, which saw her as an unnatural threat to the social order and regarded lesbianism with fascinated horror (Smith-Rosenberg, 1985; Sahli, 1979; Faderman, 1981; O'Brien, 1984). Concerning her loves, and her enduring relationship with Edith Lewis, Cather was silent.

Neither Austin nor Cather, then, broke free of the domestic sphere without paying a price. Yet while Freeman turns her autobiographical character into a sacrificial figure who never gets pen to paper, and splits the woman writer she does portray, Austin and Cather do something very different: each *enlarges* upon the riskiness of a woman being an artist by making her characters *performers*. Austin's character, Olivia, becomes an actress; Cather's character, Thea, becomes an opera singer. These projections are attempts to fuse idealization with its opposite, to portray the terrors as well as the power of public achievement in art.

The Modern Artist and the Other Self

For both Austin and Cather, Modernist ideas were of first importance, in particular the idea of art as "pure," or "objective," a value transcending all others. "The artist," Stephen tells his friend in Joyce's *A Portrait of the Artist as a Young Man* (1916) "like the God of the creation, remains . . . invisible, refined out of existence, indifferent, paring his fingernails." And at novel's end, Stephen goes gladly into exile with his art. Such an esthetic promises freedom not only *from* restrictive social institutions, but *to* create a work that is not (like creating more people?) merely another one of the products of time. Its appeal is obvious to women who need a way to value their own separateness. Writing of Katherine Mansfield in 1936, Cather said, "Every individual in [a] household . . . is clinging passionately to his individual soul. . . . Always in his mind each member . . . is . . . trying to break the net which circumstances and his own affections have woven about him." In Austin's autobiography (1932), she describes how she realized that her individuality would never be accepted, when her brother reproaches her for boiling her own egg her own way: "Somehow you never seem to have any feeling for what a HOME should be."

Both Austin and Cather were sturdy psychological adventurers, in their equally impressive access to unconscious materials. Here again, of course, the Modern climate encouraged them. Both of their heroines, Olivia in *A Woman of Genius* and Thea in *The Song of the Lark*, experience their genius as something beyond the everyday self. Olivia states that if she knows anything of genius, "it is wholly extraneous, derived, impersonal, flowing through and by." She calls it "That-Which-Walked-Beside-Me." In her autobiography (1932), Austin goes farther and tells of her very early sense of having two selves, the ordinary one, and the "I-Mary," who stood apart and observed, and with whom there was "always a sense of something assured and comforting." As an adolescent, Mary (throughout, she refers to herself in the third person) "was dimly aware of something within herself, competent, self-directive; she meant to trust it." Cather wrote no autobiography and seldom wrote or spoke candidly about writing, but her depiction of Thea indicates a trust in something very like the "I-Mary." "She [Thea] knew, of course, that there was something about her that was different. But it was more like a friendly spirit than like anything that was a part of herself . . . under her cheek, it usually seemed to be, or over her breast,—a kind of warm sureness." Austin's and Cather's impression of "genius" as comforting, warm, and assuring are quite different from the reports of the men of their generation. I will come back to this point.

Two themes, then, stand out in Austin's and Cather's Künstlerromane—a sense of separateness, and a sense of double identity that consoles. The first time Thea leaves home, it is easy because she "was all there, and something else was there, too... that warm sureness, that sturdy little companion with whom she shared a secret." In her first year in Chicago, emerging from the concert hall in an ecstatic daze, she is approached by two men, who rudely break the spell. She sees the world as "there to take something from her. Very well; they should never have it.... She would have it, have it—it!" When she leaves home again, she knows she is "going away to fight, and... going away forever." Unlike Thea, Olivia begins by believing what her culture believes about a woman's life: "And that was how I found myself farthest from Art and Life at the time when I found myself a young lady." But her marriage is a mistake; she becomes a mother too early; the child dies—she is driven "apart from the usual, and I still believe the happier, destiny of women." Humiliated by a man's advances, she finds that there is "nothing to whiten the burning of [the theatre's] shames but the high whiteness of its ultimate perfection. It is so with all art... one loses behind the yelping pack."

Identity: Fragmentation and Opposition to the Conventional

In Freeman's tradition, women characters did not get away with going off on their own, calling themselves geniuses. In *Butterfly House*, four women represent four different aspects, good and bad, of the woman writer. The best-selling writer Martha is young, egotistical, defensive, and Western (from Illinois!); she "has not mastered the art of dress and self poise." But she is an "almost brutal, clear-visioned young thing," who runs home in rage and confusion from the pretensions of Easterners. We hear no more of her. Meek, plain Annie, though she has also (anonymously, without even her grandmother knowing) written a best-seller, is so sheltered, so unworldly, that her very innocence is her inspiration: when she loses some of it, a friend claims that the person responsible has "stolen the light by which you wrote." The thief is Margaret, vain and lovely, with "the burning ambition of genius but... destitute of the divine fire." She claims authorship of Annie's book and is punished by having to maintain the lie. "If I do not tell I shall not have myself—It is a horrible thing not to have yourself," she says. But Annie and her friend, Alice, insist on this punishment. In Freeman's description, "Alice, large and fair in her white draperies, towered over Margaret... like an embodied conscience. She was almost unendurable, like the ideal of which the other woman had fallen short." Margaret, now unable to love herself, will learn to love her family and home—a very neat transformation from what Huf calls "The Monster in the Atelier" to "The Angel in the House." (Huf, 1983, p. 157). Of the reserved and marmoreal Alice the reader learns only that she has "had rather an eventful life," including college, and according to Margaret's husband, she has never "cared a snap about getting married. . . . Some women are built that way." Annie, in contrast, marries the town's leading clergyman, claiming her writing will never cause her to "neglect you or our own home."

For Freeman, then, having "it—it!" is not even a mixed blessing, but an occasion for shame and extravagant reparation. Not one of the four women in the novel is strengthened by her gift or aspiration. Even Martha, who has "whalebone" in her nature, is nearly as badly scorched by earned fame as Margaret is by the stolen sort. Only Alice, who *does not* write, who is *silent*, is strong. She has returned home to stay and to be good to "friends in distress," toward whom she is motherly. She is the provider of the warm, consolatory sense of personal promise that nourishes Olivia and Thea; Alice even loves Margaret. Did Freeman know how much a woman's self-reliance depends on whether or not she loves women? Thinking about the book's insistence on secrets (e.g., authorship, fraud, budding love), I wonder if Freeman, besides being led astray by the formulae of a popular genre, was not unconsciously expressing an awareness of the real sources of her own art, which was most successful when it dealt with independent, eccentric New England women. Here, they are absent, and repressions abound.

The question of self-reliance and identification is highlighted in Austin's and Cather's novels by the presence of the sort of character Huf refers to as a "sexually conventional foil" (p. 7). Olivia begins her story "It is strange that I can never think of writing any account of my life without thinking of Pauline Mills and wondering what she will say of it." Pauline—proper, complacent, rich—has led the life Olivia has not, and her smug misunderstanding of Olivia's life sharpens Olivia's self-image. Thea first has the iron enter into her soul at a recital. The little girl is performing on Christmas Eve, at the Opera House; she plays a piece that is over her audience's head. Then Lily Fisher springs her trick—a recitation and hymn tune in one, exactly right for the audience. Before bed, Thea looks at herself in the mirror. "Lily Fisher was pretty, and she was willing to be just as big a fool as people wanted her to be. Very well; Thea Kronborg wasn't. She would rather be hated than stupid any day."

If contempt for the sham in the lives of conventional women and mediocre artists spurred both Cather and Austin, it was also an irritant to Freeman. Freeman's *Butterfly House* begins, in fact, as a wicked satire of "fashionable" clubwomen, whose club program contains a stupid singer and a mechanical recitation. It also includes a guest lecture on "Where does a woman shine with more luster, at home or abroad?" and we may judge its quality by the fact that it is greeted with "bursts of shrill laughter." Unfortunately for her novel, Freeman is not able to make the excellence of Annie's work a sufficiently convincing contrast.

Mothers

Failures at what Austin calls "ordinary happiness," that is, fulfillment as wife and mother, are a familiar feature of biography, autobiography, and fiction by women. We would not be feminists if we had not noticed some deficiencies in that "happiness." Freeman, in common with most literary domestics, wrote novels portraying a "good" (and happy) mother and a "bad" (and punished) one. Her own mother was a sensible and strong-willed woman, whose early death was a shock to her daughter. In *Light of the Soul* (as is true of most domestic novels), the heroine is left motherless as a child; the mother seems to be an idealized portrait of Freeman's mother, and the stepmother (Freeman was spared this) is one of the nastier examples in the genre. None of the four women in *Butterfly House* has a mother. The issue is raised in another way, by focusing on the way Margaret neglects her small daughters. The opposition of good (Annie will be terrific; Alice, in her adopted role, is) and bad mothers is usual in the fiction of women who write in terms of their culture's prescribed roles, without confronting the internal contradictions produced in women's lives (McNall, 1981). But Freeman herself put off marriage until she was safely past childbearing. What might be made of that?

Both Austin and Cather make a better job of confronting their mothers. Austin's relationship with hers, as she details in her autobiography, was badly strained; though normally affectionate with her other children, her mother did not like Mary to touch her. Mary came at a bad time, and her precocity and oddness hardened attitudes present before her birth. Her father's death made matters worse. In *Woman of Genius*, Olivia speaks of her longing to be held close, and seeming to remember it. She is ill, and asks her mother to pick her up, and then to put her down again. "I have had drops and sinkings, but nothing to compare with this for there was nothing there . . . the release, the comforting . . . it wasn't there . . . *it was never there at all!*" In the novel, Austin effects a reconciliation. Eventually her mother takes the blame for not having wanted her, and Olivia comforts her. Mary Austin and her mother were not so lucky. Mary's only child was born hopelessly retarded, and the grandmother's response was "I don't know what you have done, daughter, to have such a judgment upon you!" (1932). This ended communication between them. Austin's inability to care for her own child may have resulted from the earlier failure of relationship.

Austin was a feminist, and Olivia's story includes a struggle with two central issues of a feminist cultural critique: birth control and economic independence. With Cather, we are in another distinct realm of discourse. Though not a feminist, she nevertheless had a horror of woman's traditional role, born in part, undoubtedly, from observing her mother's nineteen years of childbearing, "dragging the chain of life," as she puts it in the autobiographical short story, "Old Mrs. Harris" (in *Obscure Destinies*, 1932). Thea's eventual marriage is mentioned twice in the epilogue of *Song of the Lark* (only once, in Cather's 1932 revision). Perhaps because Cather had such profound reservations about including this sop to convention, she goes to great lengths earlier in the novel to establish Fred as a man who understands the claims of Thea's art; who, in fact, provides her with the opportunity to collect her strength and purpose. He sends her to Panther Cañon, where she discovers her artistic foremothers, in the broken pottery of the Indian women who once lived there, and resolves the dilemma of what was expected of her, and what she must expect of herself: "No more of that! . . . She had older and higher obligations."

Thea's mother, for whom Cather's was in many ways the prototype, is a very solidly realized character, and Cather does not offer any easy resolution to the tensions in the relationship. Like Virginia Cather, Thea's mother "did not chastise her children often, but she did it thoroughly." She "let her children's minds alone. She did not pry into their thoughts or nag them. She respected them as individuals and outside of the house they had a great deal of liberty. But their communal life was definitely ordered." Thea's mother takes Thea "more seriously" than the other children, and recognizes her special needs. She is dubious about letting her teach piano: "Even if Thea isn't apt to have children of her own, I don't know as that's a reason why she should wear herself out on other people's." Nevertheless, Thea knows her mother is "a part of the family, and she [is]not."

When her mother falls ill, Thea is in Dresden, on the eve of her first great opportunity as a singer. Mrs. Kronborg accepts Thea's decision as natural: "That's the way it goes, you see. . . . I guess I got about as much out of Thea's voice as anybody will ever get. . . . We gave her the dare . . . we ought not to complain, doctor; she's given us a good deal to think about." Her fierce pride in her daughter is clear to the doctor for the first time; he sees a similarity he had not imagined. Thea's playing of the operatic role of Elizabeth is illuminated by her grief, and later her Fricka is a memorial to her mother: she wears her hair as her mother did, and her interpretation of the role is a tribute to wisdom and domestic order. Each of the two women, in her own way, has given her best to the other. Yet Cather in no way minimizes the pain of the loss they sustain—they are like and unlike; they understand and do not understand each other; they can and cannot give what the other needs.

Mother Nature

For Freeman, Austin, and Cather, writing was, to a significant degree, bound up with a sense of place. This is different, in each case, from an attachment to a particular hearth. In Austin and Cather the attachment is specifically to the out-of-doors, to the land, to the earth itself. Freeman's stories of independent and eccentric women in Massachusetts or Vermont are filled with homely details of season and weather, of gardens and the produce of gardens; she illuminates the internal life of her characters with imagery of the natural world. Did Freeman's move, with her husband, to New Jersey cut her off from an important source? While her characters sometimes have moments, occurring in relation to the natural world, in which they feel a part of the scheme of things, these moments are described in the language of religious meditation and are among the least convincing passages in her work. For Freeman, it seems to me, the link to New England women may have been crucial; for her, in contrast to Cather and Austin, the natural world was not a reliable source of trust, warmth, or comfort, anymore than "genius" or mothers appear to have been.

Perhaps a sense of place must be an active choice, though surely some of its determinants are unconscious. For both Austin and Cather, the debt was incurred suddenly and dramatically, at a turning point in the life of each. Both were explicit about it. Cather moved with her family to Nebraska when she was nine, and after an initial response of terror and awful homesickness, she fell passionately in love with the prairie. This childhood passion was central to much of her work; the same was true of the passion she developed, as an adult, for the Southwest. Austin's discovery of the land she was to speak for was equally transformative. However, it was in her early adulthood that she arrived in the country that was to sustain her inspiration. On the way to the San Joaquin Valley, Austin saw in the land something "wistful, cruel, ardent, [which] when you turned from it, leaped suddenly and fastened on your vitals. . . . Beauty-in-the-wild, yearning to be made human. Even in the first impact, Mary gave back a kindred yearning" (1932). Her unconsummated passion for "the Spirit of the Arroyos" was fulfilled in the Tejon Range. On the family homestead Austin suffered an emotional breakdown and *could not eat*—until the "deadlock was broken by the discovery . . . of wild grapes in one of the Tejon canyons, and after a week or two of almost exclusive grape diet, Mary began to pick up amazingly" (1932). Intimate knowledge of the land saved Austin and became, as it did for Cather, the source of her best work, *The Land of Little Rain* (1903). A simultaneous release into a personal and active spiritual life was always associated for her with the natural world.

This intensity of feeling about the natural world brings us back to *Song of the Lark*, and Thea's experience in Panther Cañon, where she found nurturance. Cather herself visited Walnut Canyon in 1912, before her career as a novelist began, and had a similar experience of renewed confidence and purpose. Thea's ritual bathing, the deep rest and strength that she finds in Panther Cañon, are powerful images of rebirth. Moers (1976, p. 260) discusses this scene and other such fictional passages in terms of "oceanic feelings," associating them correctly with mystical experience, but not, explicitly, with the infant's inability to know her own boundaries. But the association must be made—and also made with the life-long consolatory companion of "genius," which is described in Austin's and Cather's novels as physical intimacy, tied to warmth, to odor, to childhood memories of immersion in the natural world. These sensual out-of-doors particularities are the occasion of Thea's spiritual growth, as Olivia is saved by Chicago's wind laying "bare the roots of my life . . . the undivided part that the earth had in me, . . . the unslumbering instinct that saves wild creatures."

Hoch-Smith and Spring (1978) remark that "if a woman is to devote her attention to spiritual concerns, she must not be hindered by physical fertility but come to develop instead the potential of symbolic motherhood" (p. 15). A new sort of home is made in these women's books, for eccentric spinsters, for immigrants, for social outcasts, for Indians, for troublesome daughters, for the endangered land. Austin's Olivia defines genius as "feeding others." Art as a substitute for religion or love was one of the great themes from the Romantic through the Modernist periods. Austin and Cather, I think, did not deal in substitutes, but in identities; their work clarifies for me the connections between love and self, love of women, and love of what remains of the natural world. Though we may not know how to take hold of these responsibilities, we are bound to feel them more strongly for the way in which these writers took hold of them in their art.

Note

1. Judith Fetterley, in a workshop given jointly with Marjorie Pryse, "American Women Regionalists," Eighth Annual Convention NWSA, June 13, 1986.

References

Austin, M. (1903). *The land of little rain.* New York: Houghton, Mifflin and Co.
———. (1912). *A woman of genius.* Garden City, N.Y.: Doubleday.
———. (1932). *Earth horizon.* New York: The Literary Guild.
Cather, W. (1915/1978). *The Song of the Lark.* Lincoln: University of Nebraska Press.
———. (1932). *Obscure destinies.* New York: Alfred A. Knopf.
———. (1936). *Not under forty.* New York: Alfred A. Knopf.
Faderman, L. (1981). *Surpassing the love of men.* New York: William Morrow.
Freeman, M. W. (1907). *By the light of the soul.* New York: Harper and Brothers.
———. (1912). *The butterfly house.* New York: Dodd, Mead and Co.
Hoch-Smith, A. and Spring, J. (1978). *Women in ritual and symbolic roles.* New York: Plenum Press.
Huf, L. (1983). *A portrait of the artist as a young woman.* New York: Frederick Ungar Publishing Co.
Joyce, J. (1916/1966). *A portrait of the artist as a young man.* In H. Levin (Ed.), *The portable James Joyce.* New York: Viking Press.
Kelley, M. (1984). *Private woman, public stage.* New York: Oxford University Press.
McNall, S. A. (1981). *Who is in the house?* New York: Elsevier.
Moers, E. (1976). *Literary women.* Garden City, N.Y.: Doubleday.

O'Brien, S. (1984). 'The thing not named': Willa Cather as a lesbian writer. *Signs, IX*, 576–599.

Sahli, N. (1979). Smashing: Women's relationships before the fall. *Chrysalis, VIII*, 17–27.

Showalter, E. (1985). Toward a feminist poetics. In E. Showalter (Ed.), *Feminist criticism* (pp. 125–143). New York: Pantheon Books.

Smith-Rosenberg, C. (1985). *Disorderly conduct*. New York: Alfred A. Knopf.

A Jewish Woman in Academic America

5

FRANCES DEGEN HOROWITZ

This is an essay about identity—about identity as an academic, as a woman, and as a Jew. It is formed by memories that, like all memories, are selective of the past to serve the present; memories of experiences that seem to have shaped development. This development is still evolving; in years hence some aspects of memory will fade, others to become more salient, the present to become memory—all in turn forming the organizing principles of the definition of self at a particular time.

From conception to death the biological organism is in developmental process. Age demarcations signifying the achievement of the status of childhood, adolescence, adulthood, or old age are only signposts along a course of evolving being—each segment of which may have its own dynamics and intrinsic characteristics. Nevertheless, it is reasonable to give prominence to the formative experiences of early childhood and adolescence in trying to understand the dimensions of development that contribute to the evolution of identity. The psychological underpinnings typically emphasized in exploring the experiences of childhood and adolescence are generally those of family relationships, particularly parent-child relationships. For reasons that should become clear, however, in this essay on identity, the initial focus must be on culture and on the cultural milieu of growing up. Only after describing the cultural ambience of growing up Jewish in the Bronx, New York, will it become possible to turn to the issues of gender and then to academic and professional identity.

A Cultural Context of Jewish Identity

Much has been written about the immigrant groups that flocked voluntarily to America's shores in the latter part of the nineteenth and early part of the twentieth centuries. Bunched in homogeneous groupings, settling into neighborhoods and towns, they brought and kept, for many years, patterns and rhythms and ethnic depths that defined them as Italian, as Irish, as Polish, as Jewish. Over time, assimilating into the "American way of life," individuals would move, through education and upward mobility, into the more undifferentiated streams of life in the United States. Many, however, moderated their assimilation and reinforced ethnic rooting by maintaining neighborhood settlement patterns in the larger cities or by living in distinct areas of smaller towns and cities. Some of the features of an ethnic Bronx, Jewish experience to be described here are common to lives lived in the Italian, Polish, and Irish neighborhoods of New York; others are peculiar to the Jewish experience and some aspects are particular to me, to my own family, and to my perceptual screening of experience. All are circumscribed by time in history—the 1930s and early 1940s; a time of economic depression and of impending and then actual war.

Many of the particulars and positive dimensions and elements of New York in the 1930s have been lovingly recalled in various personal memoirs evoking in time and place the kind of experiences that envelop childhood from the focusing range of the child's eye. My child's eye was filled with the visions of Bronx tenements, first on Walton Avenue, then on Eastburn Avenue—Eastburn Avenue just off the Concourse, that great orienting thoroughfare familiar to every Bronxite. On Eastburn Avenue the buildings seemed to form a cavernous overhang to the street that was hospitable to trickles of traffic—to the milk delivery truck, the occasional private car, the bell-jingling ice cream man in the summer, and to stick ball games for good parts of the year. My block was home as much as the fifth floor walk-up apartment on Eastburn Avenue, where I and my parents, sister, grandmother, and aunt lived. If the neighborhood was not exactly an extended family, there was a sense of extension in the easy, familiar relationships born of common heritages, common values, common patterns of living, and shared traditions.

Patterns and rhythms of life dominate some aspects of memory. In my entirely Jewish milieu, specific religious practices varied from strongly Orthodox and observant to relatively secular. The question of "belief" was hardly ever an issue since in Judaism belief and the necessity of belief are private matters. Practice and observance were considerably more public and shared. Despite wide variances, the meat and chicken would typically be gotten at the kosher butcher, and the neighborhood was dominated by the way in which time regulates Jewish life. If not everyone observed the Sabbath in the manner of the Orthodox, there was the inevitable bustle of Friday afternoons, a sense of getting ready for the Sabbath, "Shabbos" in Yiddish: preparing the chicken for Friday night dinner, buying the challah at the bakery. The light of the Shabbos candles marked the weekly cycle. Though many of the fathers worked on Saturday, some did not. The fre-

quency of Bar Mitzvah celebrations meant an amount of Saturday synagogue going whether or not this was one's personal pattern of observance.

There was also the distinct recurrence of the air of "yom tov"—literally
"good day," figuratively "holiday." There are many holidays in the Jewish
calendar compared to the Christian calendar. In the fall are the "High Holidays"—Rosh Hashonah (the New Year), Yom Kippur (the day of Atone-
ment), Succoth (the Festival of the Booths), Simchat Torah (rejoicing in
the Torah)—a period spanning almost three weeks of the cycling from
summer to fall, of the Jewish New Year, of celebration, of observance. On
the High Holidays the neighborhood took on a special ambience. It was a
time for family gathering, it was festive and thoughtful, it was a time of
transmittal from generation to generation. Almost everyone cared that they
were Jewish. They identified as Jews and wanted their children to be Jewish.

There is, in Judaism, a relentless intensity about the importance of educating children, of passing on traditions, of bringing along the next generation to carry on whatever Jews define, in various ways, as the essence
of their Jewish identity. Education was understood to be more than the
formal schooling of the public schools. It was to permeate the atmosphere
with experience and with opportunities to emulate; it was to teach by
recounting the stories of the past, by embedding meaning in food, by
reemphasizing ritual within the family. The weekly recurrence of Shabbos,
the cycles of the holidays—these organized time and set the occasions for
teaching. In the spring there was Purim (celebrating the events of the Book
of Esther), and Passover and then Shavuot (recalling the receipt of the tablets
at Mt. Sinai). Purim, a bloody story in its final episodes, was not perceived
as such. Rather, in the enactment of the heroism of Esther and in the treat
of eating "hamentaschen" (a special three-cornered poppy seed or prune-
filled cookie), the emphasis was on the service to one's people, on the
concept of peoplehood, on the triumph of justice. And at Passover, with
the majestic gathering of family around the Seder table, there was the annual
retelling of the story of the Exodus with an enduring and powerful influence
on memory and on the formation of identity. Many who were to become
almost entirely secular Jews in the future would observe Passover though
they might transmute its message to more directly focus on the importance
of social responsibility. Each year, in the Passover Haggadah it is said:
"*Becol dor ve'dor hayav adam lirot et atzmo kiloo hoo yatza me'mizraim.*" "In
every generation, every Jew must feel as if he himself came out of Egypt."
In every generation, every Jew must take it as responsibility to feel what
it means to be enslaved and to act to remove the bonds of enslavement, be
they the bonds of poverty, of racism, of injustice, of powerlessness.

Halloween, Thanksgiving, Christmas, Valentine's Day, and Easter were
holidays celebrated in school, in P.S. 70. They were as much American as
they were Christian. They involved the child's experience of being a stranger
in a strange land, jumping into the fray of celebration to be part of that

strange land. The menacing sense of being a stranger in a strange land was somewhat vague, more insistent in the minds of our parents' generation than in those of their children. The immediate sense of reality in the family and in the neighborhood was of an entirely Jewish world. Since there was no television to bring vivid images into the home portraying how other lives were lived, the concept of "stranger in a strange land" was theoretical at best and communicated mainly in stories of pogroms in the old country, of adversities faced by Jews when and if they ventured beyond the Jewish experience—quotas in colleges, discrimination in housing, the anti-Semitic radio ravings of Gerald L. K. Smith.

To the child's sensibility these were distant. Much nearer and more vivid in the memory of growing up Jewish on Eastburn Avenue in the Bronx was the centrality of being a child, of the importance of children, of the almost lavish commitment to children that one felt in and out of the family, on the block, in the neighborhood, in the candy store, in the butcher shop, in the appetizing store, in the bakery. Some of its elements have been caricatured in the stereotypes of the overprotective, oversolicitous, over-intrusive Jewish mother. It is an essentially unfair, if often humorous, characterization for it ignores the underlying sense of safety engendered in a child who is the object of encompassing concern. It ignores the possibility that it provides a source of compensatory resilience in what may sometimes have been difficult individual circumstances. It ignores the many positive residuals of being cared about, of being protected, of being cherished. In the milieu of a Jewish neighborhood a child was child to everyone and there was a communal sense of caring, of cherishing, of protecting. Even the nameless adult in the next building was a potential haven for safety and for help. All the more curious because the neighborhood was essentially crime free and had a visible absence of any portent of danger.

This picture would rightly be accused as idealistically overdrawn if there were no mention of the dynamics of individual families, of arguments, of unhappiness, of particular personal psychological circumstances, of poor marriages and difficult alliances, of families beset by the stresses and strains of normal and sometimes not so normal living. Mine was not a neighborhood of poverty but neither was it one of affluence. Few owned a car, many did not have a telephone. Coming out of the shocks of the depths of the Depression left scars, debts, and insecurities. Nevertheless, the cultural context of my growing up years was one of healthy values, strong identity, a celebratory rhythm to life, a sense of aspiration and of hope. There was the background of World War II and the knowledge of what was happening to Jews in Europe, of the concentration camps, of Jews being dismissed from jobs, humiliated, attacked. These images acted as point-counterpoint to the daily routines of life in a Jewish environment—a situation common to Jews throughout many periods of history, but for an American Jew the ominous possibilities were somewhat more distant and less imminent or personally threatening. A stranger in a strange land yet anchored safely in a harbor, for the moment, perhaps.

Along with the overriding element of hope that so characterizes Jewish life there was, too, the component of purpose and of seriousness. It would have been foreign for someone to have rationalized an activity because it was "fun." One did things because they were important, they were educational, they were of service, they contributed to being a people, they helped. Children were known to play, of course, but children's play if valued (and it was not always clear it was valued) was more symbolic of the safety of America for Jews than considered as having intrinsic importance to childhood. There may be some exaggeration in this as a function of my own particular history and experience but, by and large, fathers worked very hard, some mothers worked, children were expected to take on responsible roles in the family, and there was always the understanding that life had larger, historical dimensions and that we were a part of a continuing heritage and had a role to play in that continuity even if this were never made explicit or was never the focus of didactic instruction. There was a deep valuing of analysis, of discussion, of argument. The Talmudic model of always considering "on the other hand" was typical of many interchanges between adults and tolerated and encouraged with children. Obedience, docility, and politeness were less valued in children than were spirited challenge and the ability to see and understand complexities.

There are, to be sure, few absolute characterizations to be made. Family and individual experiences varied greatly. Nevertheless, Judaism is considered a "way of life," a "way of living." What I have described is the cultural context of my growing up experiences. It provided the overriding parameters that organized, selected, and regulated many aspects of my daily experience. I carry them with me to this day though my adult years have been spent largely in non-Jewish, nonethnic environments that stand in sharp contrast to the cultural environment that helped shape my sense of identity. That identity is sometimes compatible with the ambience of nonethnic America, of academic and professional America, sometimes profoundly different.

The Question of Gender

Growing up female and growing up Jewish, two sources of identity. For me, Judaism was dominant, gender secondary. This is strange in some ways when one considers how much psychic energy has been rendered up in service of women's liberation, feminism, and gender equality in modern America. It has been typical to portray the 1930s, these years of my growing up experiences, as saturated with gender stereotypes in the movies, on the radio, in idealizations of life lived happily ever after.

Yet, that saturation was secondary to Jewish culture and its preoccupations with the patterns of Jewish life. To be certain, there were the traditional perspectives of female as nurturing, as playing with dolls, as being more protected, as being concerned with the nature of one's figure and appearance. These aspects were prominent and significant factors in gender identity and significant determinants of the life fantasies of many a young Jewish girl. The traditional roles of wife and mother, of helpmate and enabler were and are highly valued in Jewish culture. And in the Orthodox Jewish tradition, which was strongly present in my life history, women sat separately from men in the synagogue, women lit the Shabbos candles, women were responsible for observing the laws of Kashruth (keeping the house kosher). Women did not typically receive formal Jewish education and were not given the experience of Bat Mitzvah.

Boys were a distinctly different breed. They not only were more likely to go to Hebrew school after regular school and to study for Bar Mitzvah, but they always seemed to have more freedom, to have more independence, to have been set on life courses that had a job, an occupation, and a profession as goals. I was completely aware of these distinctions especially as I chafed under overprotective parents. I always believed that if my mother had raised a son instead of two daughters, if I had had a brother, that my mother would have been different and would have been forced to an allowance of freedom that I was not permitted. Yet, the only male in my household was my father. A mother, a sister, an aunt and a grandmother—we were female dominated and female structured.

Many have noted the inherent contradictions in traditional Judaism regarding women and the woman's role. Revered, yet circumscribed, cherished, yet relegated to seemingly lesser ritualistic duties despite the rhetoric that renders a woman to exalted status of the keeper of the home—the home being more important than the workplace or the place of worship. Embedded in these contradictions are the ideals of Judaism—learning and scholarship—then for men only, or mainly. In the European shtetl this often resulted in the woman taking on the role of homemaker, breadwinner, functional head of household while the husband studied and learned. In fact, the instrumentality of women in all areas of Jewish history and the generational transmission of a belief in the inherent strength and endurance of women is more characteristic of the experience of Jewish women than not. Partly because the Jewish experience is so thoroughly shot through with the sense of hope, of possibility, of making things right that are not right, independent of gender and differential roles, the Jewish milieu of growing up was, in my experience, for women as well as men, one that fostered a sense of efficacy and the possibility of being instrumental in making things happen. The artfulness of the Jewish way of life is that it reinforced an inherent sense of competency while seemingly relegating women to superficially lesser status—supposedly in the service of bolstering the Talmudically acknowledged biologically weaker male member of the species. Because argument and analysis were not gender specific and were highly valued, women as well as men were free to engage the issues of the day with vigor and independence if they chose. Moreover, it was often the source of much parental pride if children engaged in these activities.

In this context my own experience of growing up female as a dimension of growing up Jewish was mixed. While this is neither the time nor place for a more candid, personally revealing discussion, it can be said that a diverse set of elements contributed to forming a gender identity that was perhaps a bit atypical. The atypicality was born of a confluence of personal circumstances that were unusual only in how they functioned in the aggregate. I lived in a largely female household with a father who was not a strong patriarchal figure. He was in the garment industry, first as a designer and cutter, then as the part-owner of a blouse manufacturing company. He sewed and made many of my and my sister's clothes in our younger years. He was dominated by his wife in most matters and rarely typified the stereotypical male. Yet, he cared deeply about being the provider for his family and would not consider the possibility that his wife might work. He aspired to the values of the middle class and eventually achieved them while at the same time retaining a healthy distrust of the airs of affluence and of pretension.

More than these characteristics, though, he was always one of his six brothers and sisters, and the closeness of the Degen family and the hours and hours I spent in the company and homes of my aunts and uncles and cousins extended my nuclear family considerably. Whatever conflicts I faced with an overprotective mother, a difficult woman at best, were moderated by those aunts and uncles and cousins, some of whom—one aunt in particular—served as alternate models, as close-range optional exemplars.

Because of the strong personalities among my uncles and aunts, because of the relatively weaker males compared to the females, there were always contradictions of the stereotyped social expectations of being female and the nonstereotyped roles actually enacted. Whenever we gathered, and we gathered weekly or more often, the men might separate to play cards and the women to talk of clothes and hairdos and to prepare what was to be eaten. But, invariably, there would form, without regard to gender, the talking group—hard-hitting, no punches pulled arguments and fights over issues social and political, including combative discussions of recent novels and books. The range of opinions went from conservative right to liberal left socialism. The range of intelligence was more constricted and skewed toward the high end. Yet, only one of my aunts and none of my uncles nor my parents had any education beyond high school; most of them had dropped out during high school to work and help support the family. They were not "intellectuals" in any sense of the term but they were intensely and emotionally committed to ideas and to ideals as these played out in the everyday events of the social and political issues of the day: unions, national and local politics, Zionism, the war, changing social patterns and expectations were topics of discussion and debate along with the more mundane issues such as the superiority of the cake from one bakery over another.

My mother was a particularly strong figure in these discussions, often the initiator, often the seemingly victorious one, always highly opinionated and persistent in her views. She was a woman who was at one and the same time extremely materialistic and very much the spokesperson for traditional values, yet intensely resistant to being cast into some female roles. She often elected not to go to the synagogue because she did not appreciate having to sit in the balcony in the days when even Conservative synagogues had separate seating for men and women. Yet, she set high value on the slender female figure, the pretty face, the proper clothes. While aiding and abetting the education of her daughters (my sister and I were, eventually, as my father's situation became more affluent, sent to a private boarding school in Connecticut), she regarded a good marriage (defined in materialistic terms) as the ultimate triumph and goal to which her daughters should aspire. On the other hand, she admired achievement and instrumentality and believed deeply in the efficacy of formal education. These contradictions played themselves out lifelong, offering a strange panoply of options and models, filled with inconsistencies. They offered me, inadvertently perhaps, a more androgynous model than was typical of that era but perhaps more likely in a Jewish cultural setting.

There was no absence of gender distinction in my experience. I knew the stereotypical expectations of female as nurturer. Yet, inconsistencies and contradictions may offer choices that are not as obvious under more monolithic circumstances. The experience of growing up Jewish was much more homogeneous than the one of growing up female. There were few inconsistencies and contradictions concerning my identity as a Jew; there were many for identity as a female. Not only was it a matter of mixed role models, even contradictions within a given model, but there was, subsequently, a co-educational progressive boarding school for two years, a nontraditional work-study college experience at Antioch College that fostered strong patterns of independence, and then, marriage to a man who eschewed stereotypical female role expectations for a wife.

Identity is the result of a set of complex, subtle and not-so-subtle influences. In the formation of identity as a Jew and in the formation of identity as a female the forces at work devolve from different realms of concerns. In the early years gender identity may be a matter of some biological inclinations heavily influenced by external definitions and the reinforcement of particular behaviors in the home, in the neighborhood, and in the school. The development of traditional Jewish identity, on the other hand, of the kind that I experienced, may have more complex roots because it is embedded in patterns of generational transmission, in a cosmic belief system, in a pervasive set of patterns of thinking and doing that are at once extremely subtle and boldly obvious. It was, for me, and for many who grew up in the kind of environment I have described, an all-encompassing, day-to-day saturated experience communicating not so much a set of beliefs as a set of values, a set of practices, as relating to time, to food, to relationships—matters that can be made simple and concrete for a child, that can grow with the individual into matters of abstract philosophical and cosmic import and thereby shape a life-long mentality for relating to life.

I thus took a strong sense of Jewish identity with me into my years of adolescence and adulthood; I also took an understanding of expectations for females into adolescence and adulthood. But my identity as female was much less coherently formed.

The Academic and Professional World

When identity as a female and identity as a Jew confront identity as an academic an interesting swirl of compatibility and incompatibility results. The academic world, like other professional worlds, has a culture of its own. It is characterized by a set of values, a set of expectations, rhythms, and forces. It is a fast track culture for those desirous of achieving success—especially in the era of academic careers marked by commitment to teaching, research, publication, specialization, and professionalism. The fullest development of academic identity makes heavy demands on time and energy, a dedication to the pursuit of ideas, to a seriousness of purpose, to the visions of making a lasting contribution. When the academic milieu is also constituted as a physical university community there are matters related to a world of social relations and colleagueship, to a world of shared responsibilities for the mini-culture of a research group, a department, a school.

One might expect that the essential elements of Jewish identity would be more easily fitted to the academic culture than the elements of female identity. After all, the values of Judaism and the socialization of Jewish culture instill a love of learning, a commitment to intellectual aggressiveness, a tolerance and expectation of the kind of dogged persistence of Talmudic argument and analysis that very much underlies the tradition of fine scholarship and skeptical inquiry. In contrast, the ideals of female socialization, emphasizing nurturance, subtle social manipulation, compliance, submission to established structure, and nonassertiveness ought to portend greater conflicts with the role demands of the academic world. Indeed, the feminist literature is replete with analyses that address these issues while, interestingly, there is an absence of analysis concerning Jewish identity and its fit to the academic world.

Historically, the academic world was relatively closed to both women and Jews and other minorities over the same epochs of time—opening slightly in the 1920s, 1930s, and 1940s. The gates opened more widely in the post–World War II era when enrollment booms demanded increased numbers of academics, when the civil rights movement battered discriminatory practices, and when the feminist movement finally raised consciousness and conscience to new sensitivities. By the 1960s these effects were felt in the large public universities, especially in the Midwest. In particular universities and in particular departments the gates may not have always been held open willingly but considerable progress has been made so that today there are few overt barriers to women, to Jews, to blacks, Hispanics, and Catholics, though some of the more subtle manifestations of prejudice and obstacle may still operate and, in times of crisis, will be seen to surface quite boldly.

Currently, academic women must balance the traditional socialization effects of being reared female, with inclinations to family and childrearing and their time demands, against the impetus to a full academic career. For the Jew who wishes to retain a strong identity, the balancing pressures are in some ways more subtle and more difficult to articulate. They involve the conflicting pressures of time, of cycle, of ritual, of calendar, of distinctiveness. For the Jewish academic woman her two sources of identity, female and Jewish, face off academic identity. It is obvious that in woman, Jew and academic, an interesting set of combinatorial dilemmas can result.

In analyzing my own place as woman and Jew in academia the dilemmas fall in a somewhat curious manner. The female component has been in some ways fortunate, perhaps as a result of being in the right place at the right time, benefiting from the effects of the women's liberation movement and the subsequent opening of the gates. If there have been hesitancies and concerns that made some things more difficult, I have been willfully oblivious to them on the assumption that one does what is to be done and the empirical evidence of competence and functionality will generally prevail. For those women who have not found compatible conditions and thus faced more problems than I, such an observation may well seem arrogant. And, indeed, it may be. It is not that some of the classic matters that affect women have not happened to me. They have certainly been experienced: a certain initial wariness among some men; exclusion from the "old boy club" networks; a lack of relationship with some who have a locker room mentality; an unwillingness to enter into some macho-style interactions to the discomfort of male colleagues; hearing jokes and remarks that stereotype women as sex objects and as being interested only in shopping. Some of this has happened and is to be regretted. But, from my point of view, shaped by a more androgynous socialization as female, these attitudes and events should be afforded little functionality in relation to my own behavior. To permit other people's attempts to define you is to relinquish control over one's definition of self and identity, an attitude perhaps influenced by my identity as a Jew.

In contrast, living as a Jew in an academic environment, in a nonethnic section of midwestern America, as a distinct minority, has required more effort, more reflection, and more conscious decisions. Many of the behaviors valued in the academic world are, as has been noted, extremely compatible with some of the behaviors valued in the Jewish culture. But, the patterns and rhythms of life necessary to the maintenance of Jewish tradition, to a strong Jewish identity, and to the passing of this identity to one's children are not as easily reconciled. Part of the problem lies in the practical aspects of calendar and time. And part of the problem is to be found in the threat of difference, even though tolerating difference of opinion and ideas is an academic ideal. Jews are different not only in beliefs but in behaviors, and if difference in belief is acceptable, some differences in behavior prove to be quite threatening. Moreover, some of the differences in behavior require adjustment of standard operating procedures that are not always granted gracefully.

Of relevance here, for the Jew, male and female, is the importance of time and patterns and cycles in the Jewish calendar, in the Jewish home, in the Jewish way of life: Friday evening and the beginning of the Sabbath, Saturday observance of the Sabbath as a day of rest and study, the holidays when one does not work, especially in the fall term. Living as a Jew requires behaviors that in some daily ways distinguish one as a Jew. For example, the more traditional male will keep his head covered at all times; if the laws of Kashruth are to be observed there are restrictions on what one will eat. Even Jews who do not keep the laws of Kashruth in their adult years may still find they cannot eat pork and pork products, shellfish, or mix milk and meat products. In academic settings where there are not large numbers of Jews, the sensitivity required among non-Jews on many of these dimensions will not exist, partly out of lack of knowledge, if nothing else. For some non-Jews it is sometimes a matter of annoyance to be asked to pay attention to these issues.

The problems of establishing relationships in the academic world that involve sensitivity, tolerance, and even appreciation and understanding of Judaism are compounded by the wide variance of practice among Jewish academics. Assimilation to the non-Jewish world is a strong and powerful tendency everywhere in the American-Jewish community. But it has been particularly strong among Jewish academics who find the demands for success in academia not entirely compatible with what is needed to retain identity and to practice Judaism. If there are one hundred Jewish faculty among a thousand, perhaps half of these will be absolutely indistinct from their non-Jewish colleagues except perhaps electing not to teach on the first day of Rosh Hashonah and on Yom Kippur. Maybe a third will observe Friday evening by having "Shabbos" dinner and attending Friday evening services. A handful might keep the laws of Kashruth and fewer still elect to observe the Sabbath each Saturday. Because Professor X who is Jewish does not care if the departmental honors banquet is scheduled on Friday evening, it is difficult for the department to feel concerned that Professor

Y, who is also Jewish, does care and will not attend if it is scheduled on Friday evening. Because Professor X will eat ham it is difficult for the host or hostess to understand that being sensitive about this issue at departmental or university events is important for Professor Y. The lack of consistency in practice from Jew to Jew introduces an understandable confusion among non-Jews who are not familiar with the variegated practices of all those who consider themselves Jewish.

Such matters are perhaps matters of awkwardness. The more profound aspect relates to the maintenance of identity and the price sometimes extracted for that maintenance. Judaism is, in its essence, a way of life as much as it is a system of beliefs. One can easily be a standard, believing Christian in the academic American setting without causing a ripple of inconvenience to oneself or to anyone else. There is not much difference between being a believing Christian and being an observant Christian, and the calendar is arranged to accommodate Sundays, Christmas, and Easter. In Judaism, the degree of observance defines one's Jewish identity more than the matter of whether one is a believing Jew. In Judaism it is more important to be committed to act and to do than to believe. The pressures for assimilation are as strong as they are on Jews because some of the aspects of being an observant Jew are inconvenient in modern America; for academic Jews they are inconvenient to academic America, especially where the Jewish academics constitute a small minority among the faculty and staff. To have to "regret" to attend the major departmental function because it is held on a Friday night, to have to arrange for your classes not to meet or to be taught by someone else on Rosh Hashonah and Yom Kippur, to make oneself distinct in eating practices is "inconvenient." It is difficult to say one will not attend a seminar or a meeting on Saturday when that is the only time everyone else can meet and your presence is essential. Since a Sunday morning meeting is scheduled only rarely the issue hardly ever arises for Christian faculty members. For faculty members who have no religious practices, it is a puzzling nonissue.

There is another dimension of difference that is extremely profound in its implications. It has been said that Judaism may be defined as the historical experiences of the Jewish people. In the late twentieth century central elements of that historical experience are the Holocaust and the establishment of the State of Israel. The depth of the emotional meaning and the importance of these events for most Jews is difficult to communicate to non-Jews. In the academy, where the cold and bold intellectual analysis without emotional commitment is much the ideal, non-Jews of otherwise significant sensibilities find the hesitancies, the emotional component, and the personal feelings connected with these topics among their Jewish colleagues as cause of puzzlement and perhaps suspicion. This kind of difference violates directly cherished academic values and can create an emotional distance between Jewish and non-Jewish academics.

In the American academic world tolerance is a strongly held value and in the abstract there is an acceptance of the idea that pluralism enriches America. It is not demanding to hold these beliefs and welcome Jewish colleagues who are highly assimilated and require no real accommodation or sensitivity to Jewish practices and sensibilities. The valuing of tolerance and pluralism is more severely tested in relation to less assimilated Jewish colleagues whose behavioral patterns do not entirely conform to the majority group's rhythms of life. It is as if one is expected to pay the price of acceptance by curbing the practices that reinforce one's identity as a Jew. This in order to be afforded the full tolerance of having one's being Jewish valued as contributing to the ideal of a pluralistic academic community. When one is unwilling to pay that price some academic colleagues, who consider themselves otherwise quite tolerant, become annoyed and, on occasion, hostile to the more insistent presence of Jewishness. A quiet distance develops, subtle emanations of prejudice and supposedly outmoded stereotypes may appear and find expression—one senses that one may be a stranger in a strange land. There is a sadness in this, a sadness born of the realization that the academy that so values intellectual differences can be less accepting of the differences that constitute one real definition of a pluralistic society. One comes to cherish those colleagues who do possess the emotional sensibilities related to these matters.

Woman and Jew in academic America—a personal perspective; a generic perspective. These exist only against a backdrop of history and of the present. Just as memory evolves, so does reality. The present was once future. These observations, then, are reality for now. They are the reflections of a Jewish woman in academic America who has derived significant satisfaction from being Jewish, from being a woman, from being a member of the academy—even as the values and ideals of these various sources of identity may at times conflict. Some of the generic issues will change over time as will the personal perspective. But it is likely that the broad issues of identity as a Jewish woman in academic America will endure for my lifetime and for the lifetimes of others of my generation.

PART TWO

WOMEN IN RELATIONSHIP TO OTHERS

The Virgin Mary: Mother as Intercessor and Savior of Society

6

SANDRA L. ZIMDARS-SWARTZ

Reported appearances or apparitions of the Virgin Mary, which perhaps reached a peak in the Middle Ages but have not disappeared from the modern world, have only recently begun to attract the attention of people interested in gender-specific religious imagery. One may assume that the image of Mary functions under any circumstances as a multidimensional symbol, Mary having been, for example, both mother and virgin. An examination of some typical twentieth-century apparitions, however, where Mary typically calls people to contrition, penance, and conversion so that the world may avert impending disaster, indicates that in the apparitions of our century it is Mary's role as mother rather than her status as virgin that is being emphasized. Within the realm of religious symbolism, these apparitions appeal to an idealized picture of motherhood and give to this ideal mother a role in the events that most apparition devotees believe will constitute the end of the world.

Marian Apparitions: General Background

From August 19–23, 1985, two young boys in the Republic of Ireland claimed that the Virgin Mary appeared to them for nearly two hours on each night. According to the boys, she showed them scenes from the Bible and gave them messages to be conveyed to the public. Mary said she wanted "peace and prayer and no more fighting in the world" and she asked the Irish people to be her messengers (Ryan, 1985, p. 4). In Medjugorje, Yugoslavia, four girls and two boys reported seeing the Virgin on June 25, 1981, and began to have daily visits from her, which have continued now for more than five years. Here too Mary is said to have given her visionaries messages destined for the public, and here too her message might be sum-

marized as "peace." According to both the Irish and Yugoslavian visionaries, Mary has recommended prayer as the means for effecting peace, and
at Medjugorje she has stressed fasting and suggested that "Christians have
forgotten that they can prevent war and even natural calamities by prayer
and fasting" (Miravalle, 1986, p. 71).

Such apparitions of the Virgin Mary are of concern primarily to Roman
Catholics, although the events are often attended, observed, and studied by
others. Within Roman Catholicism apparitions are considered private revelations, that is, they may serve as an aid to faith but they do not add
anything to Roman Catholic doctrine. Few of the hundreds of apparitions
reported to Catholic authorities are ever investigated by episcopal com-
missions, but when such investigations are made it is usually decided that
nothing prohibits belief in the divine origin of the apparition, or that the
genesis of the apparition is to be sought elsewhere, for example, in auto-
suggestion. Because the apparitions often include messages destined for the
public, they can generate immediate and intense interest, and the gathering
of crowds of the devout and curious renders them public events. In Ireland,
for example, the two boys were surrounded each evening by thousands of
people. A loudspeaker system was set up and during the last three days of
the apparitions the boys held microphones and broadcast their reports of
biblical scenes and messages to the assembled crowd. In Yugoslavia, the
children receive the apparitions in the parish house in the presence of a
handful of people while hundreds and sometimes thousands wait outside,
watching the window for the light that signals the beginning of the apparitions or filling the nearby church to pray during the presumed presence of
the Virgin. Several of the children have ceased seeing the Virgin, but as of
June 1986, two were still going into the parish house to receive their daily
visit from Mary.

Events such as these have come to be known as "public apocalyptic
apparitions." The hallmark of an apparition is the bodily appearance in the
physical environment of someone or something not normally expected
within one's immediate perceptual range. But while the events are public,
that is, the visionaries are generally in the presence of a crowd, only the
visionaries report seeing the apparition. The term "apocalyptic" conveys
the sense of immediacy and urgency that accompanies the apparitions. The
themes of an apocalyptic worldview are sometimes explicit in the messages,
or are called upon by believers to achieve a fuller understanding of those
messages. Here God is understood as being so angry with the world over
its unrepented sins that his justice demands immediate retribution. Disasters
such as famine, war, earthquakes, and persecution of the Church are understood to be both punishments for sin and exhortations to spiritual and moral
reformation; and Mary is understood as intervening in order to warn the
world, to effect the necessary conversion in sinners, and thus to avert or
forestall the chastisements that threaten. The means for this conversion are

usually seen as prayer, fasting, and other special devotions, for example, those to the hearts of Jesus and Mary. The Virgin's intervention is perceived to have cosmic significance, for in the battle between good and evil, the heavenly forces and Satan, her warnings call humanity back from the brink of eternal disaster, and her admonitions to prayer, fasting, and special devotions provide humanity with spiritual weapons with which to fight the devil.

Such an apocalyptic worldview pervades the recent messages of Mary both in Ireland and in Yugoslavia. "God is angry with the world," Mary told the boys in Ireland. "We have ten years to improve and pray," she said. "If not, this is what will happen." The boys then experienced themselves in the midst of the activity surrounding the building of Noah's ark and witnessed the destruction wrought by the flood. If the world should not improve, Mary further warned, the devil would take over God's church in ten years. But she also offered hope. "With our faith and prayers," she is reported to have said, "we can overcome the devil" (Ryan, 1985, p. 4).

In the messages conveyed by the visionaries in Yugoslavia, the twentieth century is a testing period for humanity. One visionary, Mirjana Dragicevic, reported a personal encounter with Satan, after which the Virgin appeared to her to assure her that the devil was indeed real. Mary then recounted a conversation between God and Satan in which Satan asked for permission to test the Church, and God agreed to allow such a testing for one century. Mary told Mirjana that the twentieth century is this period of testing, but at its end the power of Satan would be broken. Mirjana also reported that Mary said these appearances at Medjugorje were to be her last on earth. According to Mirjana, the Virgin's concern is the conversion of the whole world before it is too late (Miravalle, 1986, pp. 13–14, 19).

Nineteenth-Century Apparitions: An Emphasis on the Immaculate Conception

Barbara Corrado Pope (1985) suggests that apparitions of the Virgin serve to reinforce Roman Catholic belief, and she stresses the role of the Church in this effort. As virgin and mother, Pope argues, Mary perfectly realizes the only two roles deemed appropriate for good women by patriarchal institutions. Moreover, maternity and virginity are states of being that confer power on a person. In Roman Catholic doctrine it is the fact that Mary was the mother of Jesus that gives her a special role in the drama of salvation and that is the basis for the special privileges she is accorded: Mary is "preredeemed" in her Immaculate Conception so that she is never touched by the guilt of original sin; she is virgin before, during, and after the birth of Jesus and, in popular tradition, she is even exempt from the pains of childbirth; she has been physically assumed into heaven. Pope argues that these special privileges remove Mary from the realm of physical corruptibility and enhance her perceived powers on behalf of humanity. Through these powers she can abrogate the harsh demands of divine justice and offer relief from the laws of nature to those suffering from physical ailments.

Pope provides a sustained analysis of Mary as symbol in two of the nineteenth-century apparitions that received approval from the Roman Catholic Church, Rue du Bac (Paris, France, 1830) and Lourdes (France, 1858). In these two series of apparitions, reported respectively by Catherine Laboure and Bernadette Soubirous, Mary identified herself with her Immaculate Conception. She appeared to Catherine standing on a globe, her feet on the head of a snake, with rays radiating downward from the gems of the rings on her hands. Surmounting her image, in an oval shape, was the saying, "Oh Mary, conceived without sin, pray for us who have recourse to you." She told Catherine to have a medal struck with this image. Mary appeared to Bernadette eighteen times during the spring of 1858, at first without identifying herself. At the request of local clergy, however, Bernadette asked the woman of her vision to identity herself by word or sign, and on March 25, the Feast of the Annunciation, she obliged with the startling phrase, "I am the Immaculate Conception."

Pope argues that in these two apparitions, as well as those at La Salette (France, 1846) and Pontmain (France, 1871), Mary comes to give warning and offer hope. She offers maternal concern for her children, warning them of coming trials, showing them ways to soften divine judgment (penance, prayers, pilgrimage), and offering help and hope for relief from spiritual and physical suffering. But in the two most popular and best-known of the nineteenth-century apparitions, Rue du Bac and Lourdes, the iconography of the Immaculate Conception predominates. The implications of this iconography are most striking at Rue du Bac, where Mary in her sinless state treads on the head of the snake, which represents Satan. Since Mary has long been understood as a symbol of the Church, her victory here can be seen as representing the eventual triumph of Christians over sin. Pope argues that the militant message of this iconography contributed to its popularity, particularly with church authorities. The Roman Catholic Church of the nineteenth century was a church under intellectual and political siege, menaced by numerous national revolutions, and Catherine's image of Mary, struck as a medal and distributed worldwide within ten years of her vision, "projected a militant and defiant message that through Mary the Church would defeat its enemies" (Pope, 1985, p. 177).

Contemporary Apparitions: An Emphasis on Maternal Imagery

Although the imagery of the Immaculate Conception appears to overshadow the maternal imagery in the most popular Marian apparitions of the nineteenth century, it is the imagery of Mary's motherhood that clearly dominates her reported appearances in the twentieth. The apparitions at San Damiano, Italy, and Garabandal, Spain, will serve to illustrate the roles associated with Mary as mother that are typical of recent apparitions.

The apparitions of Mary reported by Rosa Quattrini (1909–1981) at San Damiano, Italy, are replete with powerful maternal images in which the seer herself participates. While many accounts speak of Quattrini's "childlike simplicity," she is affectionately referred to in the literature as "Mama Rosa," for when the apparitions began she was a mature married woman with three grown children, and she seems to have taken a motherly role in her dealings with pilgrims to San Damiano, consoling, advising, warning and exhorting them on both spiritual and personal matters (Gabriel, 1968, pp. 26–28). The Virgin is reported to have appeared to her first in 1961, on a Feast of Saint Michael the Archangel (September 19), and to have healed her from a serious illness (Gabriel, 1968, pp. 14–15). But it was not until the fall of 1964 that the apparitions took place on a regular basis (Fridays and certain feast days) and began to attract public attention.

"Do you not see that the world goes to its destruction hour by hour?" was Mary's message to Mama Rosa on December 17, 1967 (Gabriel, 1968, p. 86; the translations from the French are my own). Sins, especially those of the flesh, have brought the world to the edge of an abyss. These sins wound Jesus more than he was wounded on the cross, Mary said, and cause her to weep tears of blood both for her suffering Son and for her human children who are in danger of being eternally lost. But the danger to humanity is temporal as well. God, usually called the "Eternal Father" in the messages, wants to do justice, Mary warned, and terrible punishments threaten the entire world because of its sins. These punishments may take familiar forms such as earthquakes and wars, but they are unimaginably terrible. The Virgin exhorted people to pray that the Eternal Father will have pity and mercy, that he will give peace and love to the world, and that the chastisements will be postponed (Gabriel, 1968, pp. 87–90).

Mary told Mama Rosa that in heaven she herself had been beseeching the Eternal Father to have pity on humanity. It is her motherhood that leads her to intercede with the Eternal Father on humanity's behalf and to come to earth to warn people of their danger, call them back to safety and salvation, and offer them help and hope. Indeed, the diminutive "mama" often appears in the messages, evoking an intimate bond between mother and child and appealing to a presumed relationship of familiarity. Mary identifies herself, for example, as the "Mama of Mercy, Mama of Pardon, Mama of the Afflicted, Mama of Sinners, Mama of All" (Gabriel, 1968, p. 19), and she is most often referred to by Mama Rosa as the "Heavenly Mama." The call in the messages which Mama Rosa reports is a universal one. "I love all my children," Mary said, "and I want you all to be saved, all close to me in Holy Paradise, that we would all be united close to the

Father . . . " (Gabriel, 1968, p. 19). To this end Mary has promised that she will not abandon her children in the battle against Satan and that her "heart of a Mother" will triumph in the world (Gabriel, 1968, p. 97).

These messages stress that Mary has been issuing her maternal call to humanity for decades in various places on earth, and they present this as part of the divine plan to prepare for the Second Coming of Jesus. According to the message of November 22, 1967, the Trinity has placed Mary on earth because of her desire to save all her children. She has the task of instilling in her children love, knowledge, and affection for her, their Heavenly Mother, and setting their hearts on fire for the coming to earth of the Universal King (Gabriel, 1968, pp. 100–101). A rejection of this maternal call compounds the danger to humanity; this is humanity's last chance for mercy before Christ's Second Coming and to fail to heed Mary's call intensifies God's anger. "The Eternal Father wants to do justice," Mary told Mama Rosa on May 12, 1967. "He is tired of the entire world because it does not hear my word as a mother" (Gabriel, 1968, p. 87). Mary's suffering and frustration over recalcitrant humanity's lack of response to her is apparent in a message later that same month (May 25). "I have come onto this earth to carry peace into hearts and into nations, and they have not accepted it" (Gabriel, 1968, p. 87).

For Jean Gabriel (1968), who defends the supernatural origin of the apparitions at San Damiano, Mary's maternal concern for humanity at this supposed crucial juncture in the divine plan of salvation becomes an argument in defense of her real presence in the apparitions. He accepts the grave portrayal of the contemporary era in the messages, and he appeals to an understanding of motherhood that would demand a response in such a situation from a truly loving mother. Could a mother, seeing her children in danger of being forever lost, not do everything to try to save them? he asks rhetorically. No, for a mother would prefer to die a hundred times rather than lose her child. In support of this position, Gabriel cites the message of January 5, 1968, in which Mary tells Mama Rosa that a human mother does all to save her child, for even if that child is the most ungrateful and sinful, it is still hers. How could she, Mary, not do all to save her children of the whole world, who are standing on the edge of an abyss? For Gabriel, Mary, having seen her children engaged in a battle with Satan and in danger of being lost, could not remain in heaven, apart and unmoved. If she would, she would not be a mother. But Mary is a mother, Gabriel argues, and has made her real presence felt on earth. Believing that there is an innate response in people to this motherhood and that each one knows within the heart that Mary is his or her mother, Gabriel holds that these appearances of Mary are but a part of the divine plan in which the ultimate triumph of the Mother of God and Mother of humanity is willed (Gabriel, 1968, pp. 18–19, 104–119).

Another apparition of Mary was reported by four young girls in Garabandal, Spain. Between 1961 and 1965, Conchita Gonzalez, Mari Loli Gonzalez, Jacinta Gonzalez and Mari Cruz Barrido claimed to have seen the Virgin more than two thousand times. The first three girls, who are not related, were twelve years of age when the apparitions began, and the fourth was eleven. Here too the messages of the apparitions are apocalyptic in content. On October 18, 1961, the Virgin told Conchita that people needed to make a lot of sacrifices and that it was necessary to be very good for "the cup is already filling up," and if people did not change a very great chastisement would follow (Daley, 1985, p. 36). Four years later, on June 18, 1965, Conchita reported that the Archangel Michael had appeared to her at the behest of the Virgin and had warned her that since people had not heeded the earlier warning, the cup was now overflowing. Mary also outlined a scenario of final events that included a warning in which people would see their sins and the results of those sins, followed by a miracle of such an order that the whole world would see it. A permanent sign would be established at the site of the majority of apparitions, a grove of pine trees near the village. If people did not convert with the warning and the miracle, the Virgin told Conchita, the chastisement would be imposed (Daley, 1985, pp. 36–45).

The maternal imagery of Garabandal is conveyed through Mary's relationship to her young seers. According to observers, she appeared as a mother concerned to educate her children in spiritual and moral matters. During the course of the four years of the visions, Mary taught the girls both how to pray and specific prayers, for example, modifying the prayer "Holy Mary, Mother of God, pray for us" to include the phrase "and our Mother" after the second phrase. She taught them how to confess their sins before communion and the importance of such values as obedience to parents. More striking, however, are the reports of the seers and their observers that during their ecstasies the Virgin played games such as hide-and-seek with the children. The girls felt free to ask questions such as whether there is snow in heaven and where the infant Jesus was when the Virgin appeared without him. They reported that Mary allowed them to try on her crown and that of her infant Son, and she permitted them to hold the baby. Observers seem to have been impressed with those scenes, reporting that the girls cradled their arms as if holding a baby with infinite caution. Like Gabriel's view of the events at San Damiano, those who defend the apparitions at Garabandal have taken such maternal solicitude as an argument for their divine origin. Guy Le Rumeur, for example, argues that at Garabandal the Virgin is shown not as a distant queen but as a loving and nearby mother who is interested even in her children's smallest deeds (Le Rumeur, 1979, pp. 54–61).

Neither the apparitions reported by Mama Rosa at San Damiano nor those reported by the four girls at Garabandal have been accepted by Roman Catholic authorities. Rather, the local bishops have acted so as to discourage cult development. In February, 1968, the Bishop of Piacenza attempted to discourage public devotion at San Damiano by forbidding Mama Rosa to appear in public during the apparitions. In obedience, she remained inside her house during the apparitions but transmitted the messages to those gathered outside by loudspeaker! In June, 1970, the Bishop forbade Mama Rosa to transmit the messages either publicly or privately and forbade her to receive pilgrims and speak to them in the name of the Heavenly Mother (Osee, 1977, p. 62). From that time until her death in 1981, Mama Rosa apparently continued to receive apparitions and to record the messages but without publishing them. Church action has not, however, prevented pilgrims from going to San Damiano or from making donations toward the chapel and hospice they believe Mary wished to have built there.

The reaction of Church authorities to the apparitions at Garabandal has been similarly negative. On August 26, 1961, Monsignor Doroteo Fernandez, then bishop of Santander, appointed a commission to investigate the reported apparitions and on October 7, 1962, Monsignor Eugenio Beita Aldazabal, successor to Monsignor Fernandez, issued a statement reporting that the commission had judged the phenomena at Garabandal as lacking in supernatural character, a position reaffirmed by the successive bishops of Santander. Despite this discouragement of belief on the part of the supervising bishop, believers have flocked to Garabandal as they have to San Damiano, and there is now an international network of devotees working to spread the message of Garabandal. Supporters of the apparitions both at Garabandal and at San Damiano see them as consonant with other reported appearances of Mary, including those officially recognized by the Roman Catholic Church such as Lourdes and Fatima (Portugal, 1917), and they continue to urge their cause to Roman Catholic authorities (Le Rumeur, 1979, pp. 127–128).

Contemporary Apparitions: The Apocalyptic Context

The social significance of the maternal imagery of the twentieth-century apparitions can best be assessed in relation to the terrible sins that are understood as provoking the threat of imminent chastisement and apocalyptic judgment. For the majority of apparition devotees, the very apex of evil, which has reached the height of its development in the twentieth century, is atheism. They see at Fatima, Portugal, in 1917, Mary's initial attempt to warn humanity of this evil. Here three shepherd children reported that on July 13 Mary requested that Russia be consecrated to her Immaculate Heart. If her request was heeded, Russia would be converted and the world would have peace, but if her request was not observed, she warned, Russia would spread its errors throughout the world, creating wars and persecuting the Church. Her message, however, ended on a note of hope. Her Immaculate Heart would triumph: the Pope would accede to her request, Russia would be converted, and there would be a period of peace. For devotees of Fatima, Russia is the exporter of communism, which for them is virtually synonymous with atheism, and Russia thus becomes a symbol for what they believe is now wrong with the Western world. William Christian (1984) and Thomas Kselman and Steven Avella (1986) have noted the influence of Fatima on recent Marian apparitions and the role these apparitions have played in the anti-communist concerns of many Roman Catholics.

Closer to home, however, the apocalyptic scenario associated with the triumph of atheism, which for the typical devotee is the context of Mary's intervention in the twentieth century, is characterized by a breakdown of the divinely ordained moral, social, and spiritual order. A good example of how this may be understood is Guy Le Rumeur's *La revolte des hommes et l'heure de Marie* (Human revolt and the hour of Mary, 1981). In the section of his book devoted to "the great apostasy," Le Rumeur takes up the concept of women's equality and the issues of abortion and contraception. He argues that God created women and men to found a family: women were created with the physical ability to nurture children while men were created and ordained to provide the physical sustenance of the family. Although the two sexes may be complementary in their natures, for Le Rumeur they are not equal. Indeed, social order demands that the family have a voice of authority and that that voice be the man's. Le Rumeur sees the efforts of modern women to gain equality with men in all domains, including the priesthood, as an abandonment of the moral order created by God. Although Le Rumeur does not state so explicitly, he would presumably believe they have also abandoned God.

Le Rumeur understands decisions favorable to contraception and abortion to be manifestations of an atheistic materialism. This *Zeitgeist* counsels that young marrieds should establish themselves financially before having children and take into account their earning capacity when deciding on the number of children to have. Le Rumeur is especially bitter that such advice can be given even by members of the Roman Catholic clergy. The decision to impede or interrupt pregnancy is made too often, he believes, on "the law of numbers," that is, limiting population out of concern for materialistic resources and personal comfort. For Le Rumeur, it falsely pits the present, which humans can judge only subjectively, against the future, which God alone can know.

Le Rumeur sees Mary's apparitions, so frequent in recent years, as constituting a revelation of the final events of the world consonant with the scenario described in the Book of Revelation (1979, p. 162). This scenario provides him with a way to understand why so many Roman Catholic clergy appear to be forsaking their spiritual vocations in favor of making concessions to the world. Messages reported in several Marian apparitions underline the warning at Garabandal that "many cardinals, many bishops and many priests are on the road to perdition and taking many souls with them" (Daley, 1985, pp. 44–45). The Church, then, is in a time of persecution and suffering, even at the hands of her own priests. But Le Rumeur believes that when this time of suffering has ended the Church will emerge purified and triumphant (1981, p. 262). Mary's so-frequent appearances in recent years indicate to him that this time is near. Indeed, Le Rumeur goes so far as to say that, according to elements in the apparition messages, there should be only two popes after Pope Paul VI. For Le Rumeur, then, the present era anticipates the Second Coming, and the immediate recognition of and response to the messages of the Marian apparitions is thus all the more crucial (1979, pp. 162–165).

In the context of such an apocalyptic scenario, typical for devotees of recent Marian apparitions, the significance of the maternal imagery in these apparitions becomes clear. Scholarly observers of Marian devotion and apparitions have acknowledged the psychological appeal of Mary as mother. Many believe with Jean Laurenceau (1973–1974) that Marian imagery has its point of departure in an unconscious and deeply felt image of one's own mother. The desire to be with one's mother is intensified, Laurenceau suggests, in a time of anguish and imminent chastisement. Dáithí Ó'hÓgaín agrees and observes with regard to the recent Marian phenomena in Ireland that "the same great mother who is the refuge of the sinner at the hour of death is the refuge of the whole community when it is under threat" (1985, p. 73). The comments of these two scholars are a starting point for understanding the power attributed to motherhood in recent apparitions, both in their messages and in the apologies written on their behalf. As has been shown, the contemporary situation is understood as so grave and the future so menacing that only a mother could pull her wayward children back from the brink of disaster. The apparitions draw on and exalt to a heavenly plane a task generally assigned to mothers, that of teaching spiritual and moral values to children. The fact that recent apparitions in France, Yugoslavia, Ireland, and Italy all draw and build on this notion that mothers are the only ones who can effect moral and spiritual reformation in their children suggests that this is a belief that transcends cultural bounds. Mary appears as the Heavenly Mama to convert her children from atheism back to their Eternal Father. The mother who brought in salvation with the birth of her divine son returns at the end of time so that her "heart of a mother" may triumph and the salvation of her children before the final events may be assured.

References

Christian, W. (1973). Holy people in peasant Europe. *Comparative Studies in Society and History, 15,* 106–114.

———. (1984). Religious apparitions and the Cold War. In E. Wolf (Ed.), *Religion, power, and protest in local communities* (pp. 239–266). New York: Mouton.

Daley, H. (1985). *Miracle at Garabandal*. Dublin: Ward Rivers Press.

Gabriel, J. (1968). *Presence de la tres Sainte Vierge à San Damiano*. Paris: Nouvelles editions latines.

Kselman, T. and Avella, S. (1986). Marian piety and the Cold War in the United States. *The Catholic Historical Review, 73*, 3, 403–424.

Laurenceau, J. (1973–1974). L'importance psychologique de l'image maternelle dans les messages de San Damiano. *Bulletin de la Societe e Française d'Études Mariales, 30–31*, 57–66.

Le Rumeur, G. (1979). *Notre-Dame du Carmel à Garabandal*. 79290 Argenton l'Eglise: Guy le Rumeur.

———. (1981). *La revolte des hommes et l'heure de Marie*. 79290 Argenton l'Eglise: Guy le Rumeur.

Miravalle, M. I. (1986). *The message of Medjugorje*. Boston: University Press of America.

Ó'hÓgaín, D. (1985). A manifestation of popular religion. In C. Toibin (Ed.), *Seeing is believing* (pp. 67–74). Dublin: Pilgrim Press.

Osee, J. (1977). *Call of the Virgin at San Damiano*. North Quincy, Mass.: Christopher Publishing House.

Pope, B. C. (1985). Immaculate and powerful: The Marian revival in the nineteenth century. In C. W. Atkinson, C. H. Buchanan, and M. R. Miles (Eds.), *Immaculate and powerful* (pp. 173–200). Boston: Beacon Press.

Ryan, A. (1985, December 25). The Melleray phenomena. *The Cork Examiner*, pp. 1,4.

Turner, V. and Turner, E. (1982). Postindustrial Marian pilgrimage. In J. Preston (Ed.), *Mother worship* (pp. 145–173). Chapel Hill: University of North Carolina Press.

Feminist Issues in Intimate Relationships between Women and Men

7

SHARON S. BREHM

Social scientists have recently documented the existence of an association between feminist beliefs and divorce. When divorced women and men are asked about reasons why the divorce occurred, "gender role conflicts" (Kitson and Sussman, 1982) and, to a much lesser extent, "women's liberation" (Cleek and Pearson, 1985) are included among the various factors cited by both sexes. The cause for such citations is, however, unclear. Some investigators believe that married women holding nontraditional beliefs about gender roles are more likely to encounter conflict in the marriage and, therefore, seek divorce (Finlay, Starnes, and Alvarez, 1985). Other researchers have emphasized the effects of divorce, demonstrating that women become less traditional in their gender role attitudes during the course of the divorce process (Brown and Manela, 1978). This latter view coincides with massive evidence that the outcome of modern divorce, American style, offers marked financial (Weitzman, 1985) and social (Guttentag and Secord, 1983) advantages to men and disadvantages to women. At present, divorce seems far more likely to create feminist beliefs among women suffering its hardships than feminism among married women is apt to increase their chances of divorcing.

On the other hand, it does seem reasonable to expect that discord between men and women, especially men and women involved in intimate relationships, will increase in the coming years as our society moves closer toward gender equality. The basis for this expectation lies in those psychological motives that are produced by and serve to maintain patriarchal society. Although unquestioned acceptance of male authority has been se-

An earlier version of this chapter was presented at the Mellon Seminar for Faculty Development, University of Kansas, Spring 1985.

riously eroded in the Western world over the last twenty-five years, all of us, women and men, still have a difficult time discarding many of the psychological needs and desires that support male supremacy. Because these motivations are increasingly inconsistent with more egalitarian social structures, we can anticipate experiencing more turmoil within ourselves, as well as between women and men who have arrived at different ways of resolving this inconsistency. It is the goal of this essay to expand our understanding of some of these motives, with the hope that their influence can be diminished.

Men's Need to Perceive Women as Inferior

The long and dreadful history of misogyny has been described in detail by a number of writers (e.g., Daly, 1978; de Beauvoir, 1949/1974; Hays, 1964; Phillips, 1984; Warner, 1976). What I want to address here is *why* men take such a negative view of women. My interest is in the psychological benefits that come from this belief and, therefore, maintain the need for it. I will not dwell on the obvious practical benefits men derive from relegating women to a servant caste.

From a social psychological viewpoint, there is nothing at all mysterious about why men have subscribed to misogynist beliefs for so long across so many different cultures. These beliefs make men feel better about themselves; by identifying women as inferior, they can regard themselves, in comparison, as superior. This process of elevating one's own self-esteem by focusing attention on the deficiencies of others is called "downward social comparison" and appears to be a common way to cope with feeling bad about the self (Wills, 1981). Indeed, all forms of invidious comparison with another individual or groups of individuals can be considered as meeting the need for enhancing self-esteem through the process of downward social comparison. This commonality in need and process may account for why negative stereotypes about "the other" are so similar in basic content. Whether we examine sexism, racism, nationalism, or religious conflicts, the "ingroup" members always seem to characterize the "outgroup" members as dirty, morally and intellectually inadequate, and treacherous. Sexism is distinct only in its breadth of application. No matter what his color, nationality, religion, or social class, any man can believe that he is superior to every women—inherently superior, as a matter of birthright. This ever-present availability of someone to benefit from comparison with is an extraordinarily useful prop for the male ego.

Of course women too use downward social comparison vis-à-vis the opposite sex. Among themselves, women bolster their self-esteem by discussing how men are slovenly, childish, and untrustworthy. But there is a certain ambivalence in downward social comparison as practiced by women that does not hold true when it is exercised by men. After all, until quite

recently the vast majority of women were legally controlled by and financially dependent on the men (fathers, brothers, husbands) in their lives.
One hesitates when so vulnerable to regard the person one depends on as
a complete imbecile. When women derogate men there is usually a mis-
chievous or spiteful quality to it quite unlike the flat, brutal statements that
men make about women.

Indeed, such statements can be so brutal that one has to question whether
downward social comparison offers a sufficient explanation for their occurrence. It seems likely that the more grotesque flights of misogynist
rhetoric reflect a second source of motivation for men to perceive women
as less than fully human, a motivation that while it runs in the same direction
as downward social comparison is separate from it. This motive, compatible
with especially terrible images of women, is men's need to reduce an especially terrifying fear.

Most writers (Hays, 1964, remains the most comprehensive) who have
suggested that misogyny reflects men's fear of women have failed to distinguish between what are two related but distinct aspects of this fear. First,
there is the fear of sexual involvement. The sexual drive, which can have
a distressing independence from rational decision-making, threatens a man's
desired sense of control over his body and his actions. Moreover, fear can
be produced by sexual acts themselves. It is not surprising if a man feels
anxious when he places his vulnerable penis (or thinks about placing it)
inside a, to him, unfamiliar orifice. It is just as unsurprising that women
have the same fears: women too can experience sexual desire as a threat to
self-control; a woman can feel anxious when she allows (or thinks about
allowing) a, to her, unfamiliar protuberance to be placed inside her. Obviously, sexual fright is not restricted to males. What has been restricted is
the economic, political, and social power that permits males to indulge,
publicly as well as privately, in their anxious sexual fantasies and that gives
them the ability to control female sexuality in order to reduce this anxiety.

Men are also motivated to keep woman in her inferior place because they
fear the power of women. Part of this power is related to the fear of sex;
it has been easy for men to convince themselves that their sexual impulses
are pulled from them by seductive women rather than pushed by their own
internal psychological and physiological needs. The fear of women's power,
however, involves more than sexuality. In and of itself, a woman's body
must seem enigmatic and awesome to men. She bleeds without having been
injured, and she stops bleeding without any external interference. Most
significantly, she gives birth. One's response to these remarkable events
could be worship or fear, and men have engaged in both. When fear predominates, men can comfort themselves with theories about women's
"lower" nature, and use these theories to justify their control over women.

Thus, men are motivated to perceive women as inferior beings because
this perception allows for the fulfillment of some basic psychological needs:

the need to enhance self-esteem, the need to reduce the fear of sex by controlling the other's sexual expression, and the need to limit the power of others. All these needs are shared by men and women. Only men, however, have had sufficient power to be able to adopt and enforce that perception of female inferiority that so efficiently provides satisfaction. Accordingly, it will be difficult for men to give up such a convenient invention. They will have to arrive at a state of mind where the guilt and anxiety they experience from their own misogynist thoughts outweigh the distress they feel from not being able to use women's presumed inferiority to raise their self-esteem, reduce their sexual anxiety, and counter their fear of women's power. Moreover, they will have to have the courage to seek new, non-misogynist ways of meeting these needs at the very time that the authority of man qua man is disappearing, that women are being more assertive about their sexual desires, and that more individual women are assuming positions of power. Particularly in their intimate relationships with women, where the opportunities for sexual and personal conflict are maximal, men's progress toward a genuine egalitarian regard for women may be extremely slow.

Men's Need to Control Their Emotions

In their classic study of marital satisfaction, Blood and Wolfe (1960) concluded that "responsive husbands produce satisfied wives" (p. 203). It was evident in the same study that many wives are far from satisfied and often perceive their husbands as distinctly unresponsive. Numerous other investigators (e.g., Dosser, Balswick, and Halverson, 1986; Doyle, 1983; Lewis, 1981; Pleck, 1982) have also noted the lack of emotional responsiveness among men, and some have suggested that this deficiency may play a central role in marital dissolution: "If men need so much and are so underdeveloped in the skills of interpersonal sharing and emotional expressiveness, they may ask too much and give too little to support marriage" (Veroff, Douvan, and Kukla, 1981, p. 24).

Although there appears to be substantial agreement that extreme control over emotionality characterizes many males of today's American middle class, there is disagreement about how pervasive such a characteristic is among the male population in general (across cultures, in different historical eras). Feminist writers who suggest that emotional overcontrol is the inevitable result of the patriarchal dualism between mind/male/rationality and matter/female/emotionality (Ruether, 1983) as well as those who attribute male discomfort with emotionality to their attempts to separate from the emotionally gratifying mother (Chodorow, 1978; Dinnerstein, 1976) imply that lack of emotional responsiveness among males is widespread and perhaps universal. In contrast, William J. Goode (1983) has argued that the John Wayne ideal (strong and silent) is peculiar to the modern American middle-class ethos, and that much greater emotional and affectional expressiveness can be found among men of other cultures and earlier historical periods.

Goode, however, does not attempt to explain why being "strong and silent" has become so valued for males in American society. In her discussion of this issue, Marilyn French (1985) emphasizes two factors that may influence the range and freedom of males' expression of emotion. According to French, men are more likely to be emotionally expressive in those cultures where male control over women is unquestioned and where, therefore, mem do not need to prove their distinctiveness from and superiority over women by avoiding all "feminine" behavior. French also proposes that the modern world of work (where the place of work is separated from the intimacies of home, and where emotional suppression is required of those in subordinate positions) serves to institutionalize emotional constriction. Indeed, the requirement that women adopt the masculinist values—including the suppression of emotional response— prevailing in current economic and political structures in order to gain access into those structures has generated one of the central dilemmas of modern feminism.

To understand the ramifications of that dilemma, we must consider the psychological, interpersonal, and moral costs of an extreme suppression of one's emotional responsiveness. Such extreme suppression is necessarily based on fear and develops through a process of avoidance learning. That is, when emotional expression is severely punished, it can happen that just having feelings (even if they are not acted upon) can make the person anxious, and this anxiety may lead the individual to try to avoid emotional response altogether. By promoting the ideal of the strong and silent supermale and derogating males who express traditional feminine emotions (such as love, compassion, kindness), our society ensures that many boys grow up with a generalized anxiety about these emotions and teaches them to control, inhibit, and deny their own feelings.

The fear-avoidance sequence described above constitutes the development of a phobia, and it is appropriate to characterize many adult men as being feeling-phobic. As one would expect in such a phobic state, men are often stupid about emotions. They are so concerned about controlling/avoiding emotional reactions that they never learn about the full range of emotional experience—in all its different kinds as well as degrees of intensity. This very stupidity then serves to increase men's fear even further. As long as the closet door is kept firmly closed, one can never find out that the monster in there was only imagined.

The single clear exception to the premise that men are phobic in regard to feelings supports the more general rule. Many men are quite comfortable with feeling angry and expressing this feeling through aggression. But anger is a "manly" emotion. Men are permitted to feel it, so they do not fear it, do not avoid it, and learn to discriminate its varieties. Women, on the other hand, are often phobic in regard to anger; they go through the same learning process with anger that men do with the "softer" emotions. It is in no way accidental that women who are angry often cry and men who are sad often hit something, or someone.

Thus, the price for becoming phobic about any emotion is very high. We become stupid about that feeling and deprive ourselves of the opportunity to learn that it can be experienced without destroying us. In addition, making any emotion into a monster can poison our relations with others. The woman who does not know when she is angry may become bitter and malicious. The man who flees in terror from love and vulnerability lives in a desert of emotional dryness and social isolation.

Most important, these men in flight from feeling pose a threat to all of us. We are all prisoners of egocentrism; we see all things and all people through the distorted lens of our hopes, fears, and beliefs. Emotional closeness to another is perhaps the only sure way to break out of the jail of self; that break is necessarily incomplete, but it is also extremely powerful. If we never have this experience of connection with at least a few people, then all people are objects to us. We can set up rules for how we deal with various classes of objects, and for men, morality consists of rule-bound behavior (Gilligan, 1982). Rules, however, can be broken or modified; as rational creations, they are subject to competition from other rational considerations. Throughout human history, far more people have died from the deliberate, rational, principled decisions of their killers than as victims of someone's uncontrollable frenzy. In our own time of peril, rules emanating from the strong and silent are unlikely to save us.

Women's Need to Be through Men

The notion that we discover ourselves through the reactions of others has a long history in American social science (e.g., Cooley, 1902; Jones and Gerard, 1967; Sullivan, 1953; Duval and Wicklund, 1972). What none of these theorists (all male) ever considered, however, is that men and women may differ in how much of themselves they find in this way. In fact, every woman has what Cooley called a "looking-glass self" because every woman has been trained since childhood that major life goals (marriage, children, socioeconomic position) depend in large part on figuring out how to be an attractive object for a man. As Simone de Beauvoir put it, "For the young girl, erotic transcendence consists in becoming prey in order to gain her ends. She becomes an object, and she sees herself as an object . . . " (1949/ 1974, p. 378).

Though this finding of the second self (the self as sexual object) may typically take place in adolescence, it has a long life afterwards. I agree with Mary Daly (1984) that we can assume the existence of "a widespread low-grade multiple-personality disorder among women" (p. 370), but I would locate the cause for this disjunction of personality in women's adoption of a man's view of them rather than in women's suppressed anger. Many women are quite literally two different people depending on whether or not a male is present (usually a male in whom the female has an erotic interest). Women are themselves in action, and they are other selves in terms of what they imagine to be the male response to them.

Sometimes, of course, the latter persona is simply a pose—a calculated way of getting her way that is experienced as false but necessary. More often, the male-defined self has a vividness and intensity not experienced in other, more task-oriented contexts. When the male-reflected self emerges, it can feel like a metamorphosis, the coming alive of one's better, truer, more fulfilling self. Doris Lessing (1958) has described the outer limits of this phenomenon with great precision:

There is a type of woman who can never be, as they are likely to put it 'themselves' with anyone but the man to whom they have permanently or not given their hearts. If the man goes away there is left an empty space filled with shadows. She mourns for the temporarily extinct person she can only be with a man she loves; she mourns him who brought her 'self' to life. She lives with the empty space at her side, peopled with the images of her own potentialities until the next man walks into the space, absorbs the shadow into himself, creating her, allowing her to be her 'self'—but a new self, since it is his conception which forms her (pp. 48–49).

The reason for the power and pervasiveness of the male-defined self rests ultimately on idolatrous attitudes toward men. Not only are women informed that their attractiveness to men is a central, necessary component in their worth as individuals; not only are most women financially dependent on men's earnings; but the religions of the world rely predominantly, often exclusively, on male images of the divine. At all levels—the normative, the practical, and the spiritual—women have been inculcated with a specific hunger for male approval. Therefore, the burden of the second self can only be lifted through profound changes in socialization practices, economic arrangements, and religious imagery. Only when males are no longer granted the godlike status of unearned power will women move out from under the shadow of the second self.

Future Directions

During the present time of transition, the contrast between the motives described in this essay and the egalitarian beliefs of many women is particularly sharp and discomforting. More and more women are outraged at being treated as inferior to men. Women have begun to recognize that the strong and silent masculine ideal wreaks havoc in their intimate relationships with men as well as in national and international decision-making. And many women are waging the long, hard, and lonely struggle to reduce their psychological dependency on male approval. Men too have begun to voice more egalitarian attitudes, and for many of them these attitudes are more than mere fashionable rhetoric.

Thus, despite the likelihood of greater difficulties between the sexes in the immediate future, the more long-term prospects for heterosexual interactions may be quite favorable. If men and women become more egalitarian in their outlook, and the discrepancy between their commitment to gender equality diminishes, tension and conflict in heterosexual relations could also decline. I doubt that such a change would reduce the rate of divorce, but divorce itself might then become a more amicable process. When there is economic justice for women (which will necessitate the sharing of childrearing), when men become able to acknowledge their feelings and respond to the feelings of others, and when women's fundamental sense of identity is not torn apart by being without a male partner—under these conditions, parting will still be sorrowful but not so devastating as it often is now.

Unfortunately, I am not at all optimistic about the prospects for a feminist revolution *throughout* our society. My concern here stems from what might be called the "Margaret Thatcher syndrome." In many ways, Ms. Thatcher is a laudable model for twentieth-century women: she is not perceived as inferior to men; she seems to have a firm sense of self independent from male approval; she is a mother as well as a partner in an enduring marriage. Much of her political success, however, appears to be based on her extraordinary embodiment of traditional masculine values: Ms. Thatcher is more confrontational, less compromising, and more hard-driving than any of her male peers (e.g., Newhouse, 1986).

The example provided by Ms. Thatcher suggests the possibility of a new development in patriarchy. In such a society, there would be gender equality in employment and women would not be any more dependent on male approval than men on female approval. Privately, men and women would share the roles of provider and homemaker, and there would be no gender difference in their emotional responsiveness to each other. In contrast, the public forum of this version of patriarchy would remain dominated by traditional masculine values, possibly even exaggerated in order to compensate for men's greater acceptance of traditional feminine values in their private lives. Furthermore, the essential principle of hierarchy would remain undisturbed, though it would be based on attributes other than gender: the face of the new god would simply be gender-free materialistic success.

No one can foretell the future, but this particular speculation does not seem so far-fetched and it raises some fundamental questions about love and evil, and about men and women. It is arguable that over the course of human history, men have contributed more than their fair share of evil and women more than their fair share of love. If, then, we succeed in obtaining parity between the genders while leaving traditional masculine values supreme in public life, will we have broken the gender dimorphism of love and evil without having reduced the level of evil? It is my own belief that the *human* tendencies to seek superiority at the expense of others, to stifle empathy and compassion toward others (especially those perceived as different), and to worship false gods will not automatically be eradicated by the advent of gender equality. Creating ways to oppose these human evils, and the societal structures they spawn, constitutes a necessary and fundamental objective of the larger moral vision of feminism.

References

Blood, R. O. and Wolfe, D. M. (1960). *Husbands and wives: The dynamics of married living*. New York: Free Press.

Brown, P. and Manela, R. (1978). Changing family roles: Women and divorce. *Journal of Divorce, 1*, 315–327.

Chodorow, N. (1978). *The reproduction of mothering: Psychoanalysis and the sociology of gender*. Berkeley: University of California Press.

Cleek, M. G. and Pearson, T. A. (1985). Perceived causes of divorce: An analysis of interrelationships. *Journal of Marriage and the Family, 47*, 179–183.

Cooley, C. H. (1902). *Human nature and the social order*. New York: Scribner.

Daly, M. (1978). *Gyn/Ecology: The Metaethics of radical feminism*. Boston: Beacon Press.

————. (1984). *Pure lust*. Boston: Beacon Press.

de Beauvoir, S. (1974; original publication in French, 1949). *The second sex*. Trans. and ed. by H. M. Parshley. New York: Vintage Books.

Dinnerstein, D. (1976). *The mermaid and the minotaur: Sexual arrangements and human malaise*. New York: Harper and Row.

Dosser, D. A., Jr., Balswick, J. O., and Halverson, C. F., Jr. (1986). Male inexpressiveness and relationships. *Journal of Social and Personal Relations, 3*, 241–258.

Doyle, J. A. (1983). *The male experience*. Dubuque, Iowa: Wm. C. Brown.

Duval, S. and Wicklund, R. A. (1972). *A theory of objective self-awareness*. New York: Academic Press.

Finlay, B., Starnes, C. E., and Alvarez, F. B. (1985). Recent changes in sex-role ideology among divorced men and women: Some possible causes and implications. *Sex Roles, 12*, 637–653.

French, M. (1985). *Beyond power*. New York: Ballantine Books.

Gilligan, C. (1982). *In a different voice: Psychological theory and women's development*. Cambridge, Mass.: Harvard University Press.

Goode, W. J. (1983). Why men resist. In A. S. Skonick and J. H. Skonick (Eds.), *Family in transition* (pp. 201–218). Boston: Little, Brown and Co.

Guttentag, M. and Secord, P. F. (1983). *Too many women? The sex ratio question*. Beverly Hills, Calif.: Sage.

Hays, H. R. (1964). *The dangerous sex: The myth of feminine evil*. New York: G. P. Putnam's Sons.

Jones, E. E. and Gerard, H. B. (1967). *Foundations of social psychology*. New York: Wiley.

Kitson, G. C. and Sussman, M. B. (1982). Marital complaints, demographic characteristics, and symptoms of mental distress in divorce. *Journal of Marriage and the Family, 44,* 87–101.

Lessing, D. (1958). *A ripple from the storm.* London: Michael Joseph.

Lewis, R. A. (1981). *Men in difficult times: Masculinity today and tomorrow.* Engelwood Cliffs, N.J.: Prentice-Hall.

Newhouse, J. (1986, February 10). Profile: Margaret Thatcher. *The New Yorker.*

Phillips, J. A. (1984). *Eve: The history of an idea.* San Francisco: Harper and Row.

Pleck, J. H. (1982). *The myth of masculinity.* Cambridge, Mass.: MIT Press.

Ruether, R. R. (1983). *Sexism and God-talk: Toward a feminist theology.* Boston: Beacon Press.

Sullivan, H. S. (1953). *The interpersonal theory of psychiatry.* New York: W. W. Norton.

Veroff, J., Douvan, E., and Kukla, R. A. (1981). *The inner American: A self-portrait from 1957 to 1976.* New York: Basic Books.

Warner, M. (1976). *Alone of all her sex: The myth and the cult of the Virgin Mary.* New York: Alfred A. Knopf.

Weitzman, L. J. (1985). *The divorce revolution.* New York: The Free Press.

Wills, T. A. (1981). Downward social comparison principles in social psychology. *Psychological Bulletin, 90,* 245–271.

Women, Dependency, and Depression

8

CAROL E. FORD AND *MIRIAM BERKMAN*

Depression represents one of the most significant mental health issues associated with women's lives. Recent findings from the Epidemiologic Catchment Area program of the National Institute of Mental Health, a comprehensive study of the prevalence of mental disorders, indicated that approximately 5 to 9 percent of women experience an episode of major depression at some point in their lives; consistent with earlier epidemiologic findings (see Weissman and Klerman, 1979, for a review), the lifetime prevalence of major depression was significantly higher for women than for men (Robins, Helzer, Weissman, Orvaschel, Gruenberg, Burke, and Regier, 1984).

A number of authors have discussed the role of sociocultural factors in women's apparent vulnerability to depression (e.g., Cox and Radloff, 1984; Repetti and Crosby, 1984; Weissman and Klerman, 1979). In the present chapter, we will explore a link between situations involving interpersonal dependency and depression. It is our contention that the assumption of a dependent role can, under specific circumstances, lead to depression; moreover, some aspects of women's traditional and contemporary roles in interpersonal relationships appear especially conducive to those conditions of dependency that may result in depression.

It should be noted that the conclusion that women experience more depression than men is not accepted universally (see, for example, Hammen, 1982; Repetti and Crosby, 1984). The debate on this matter centers around

We are grateful to Sharon Brehm for many valuable discussions related to our topic as well as for very helpful comments on an earlier version of this chapter. We are also grateful for suggestions regarding the ideas in this chapter provided by Robert Arkin, Denise DeBarre, Miriam Rubin, Nancy Whitney, and Rex Wright.

two issues. First, disagreement arises from the complexities and uncertainties in our current understanding of the construct of depression (e.g., Hammen, 1982); this issue is unlikely to be resolved in the near future. In addition, there is the question of whether it is gender that is responsible for the differences in men and women, or some other factor(s) that happen to be associated with gender. Taken to its extreme, the argument in this essay could fall into this category; if interpersonal dependency is critical for the development of depression and women have been constrained by socio-cultural forces to be more dependent than men, then it would be correct to say that there is a dependency difference in depression, not a gender difference.

Many of the circumstances that are associated with depression point to the possible importance of interpersonal dependency in the origins of the depressive state. Perhaps the most compelling indication is found in the differential association between marital status and depression in men and women. According to Radloff (1975), for example, the number of reported symptoms of depression among married individuals were higher for women than men; however, no gender difference was apparent among the never-married. Although there are numerous ways in which spouses can be dependent on one another, women are far more often financially dependent on their husbands than vice versa. Even when women work, their earnings usually account for considerably less than half of total family income. The possibility that a relatively large independent income may serve to reduce the risk of depression among women is suggested by Cox and Radloff (1984), who found more depression among women than men in all the employment subgroups that they examined *except* among high-level professionals.

Other demographic risk factors for depression include youth, low education, low income, low-status employment, and recent or current physical illness (Cox and Radloff, 1984). Although there are a number of conceivable explanations for the association between these factors and depression, it is notable that each of these circumstances is conducive to, perhaps even necessitates, reliance on others.

In their research, Warren and McEachren (1983) obtained findings that are consistent with the idea that dependency is an important psychological aspect of some of the life circumstances associated with depression. Surveying a sample of adult women, they found that education, employment, and marital status were associated with perceptions of life control and of derived identity (i.e., the extent a sense of self is based on relationships with others). Lower ratings of life control and higher ratings of derived identity were also associated with a greater number of reported symptoms of depression; perceived life control, in fact, accounted for more variance in depression scores than any other psychological or demographic variable.

The dual propositions that depression is related to interpersonal dependency and that this link is particularly relevant for women are not new. Most of the previous work on this topic, however, defined dependency in terms of a personality characteristic: an extreme need to associate with and rely on others, particularly for interpersonal outcomes such as support or affection (e.g., Hirschfeld, Klerman, Gough, Barrett, Korchin, and Chodoff, 1977). Classical psychoanalytic theories, for example, emphasized the role of *characterological* dependency in the development of depression; although only recently linked together explicitly, this formulation can be seen to overlap with psychoanalytic theories on the psychology of women (Weissman and Klerman, 1979). In a related vein, Blatt (1974) theorized that the *phenomenology* of depression is related to either dependency or self-criticism. Blatt and his colleagues (e.g., Chevron, Quinlan, and Blatt, 1978) suggested that depression in women is associated with feelings and concerns about dependency, while in men it is connected with self-critical thoughts and feelings.

Our focus here on the psychological effects of dependent *situations* is thus a departure from previous formulations. Moreover, we begin with a more general definition of a dependent condition than has been used previously. From our perspective, dependency occurs whenever one individual consistently obtains a desired commodity through the actions of another. A woman who typically relies on a particular co-worker to write the first draft of their reports is in a dependent position, as is a woman who counts on a special friend for emotional support. This approach has several advantages over earlier treatments of dependency and depression. One obvious benefit is that a situational analysis avoids the unproven assumption that dependent behavior is consistent across relationships. In addition, while some people may be more generally dependent than others across a variety of situations, this tendency presumably would cause depression only when it leads people into dysfunctional situations. Thus understanding dependent situations provides a necessary link between any personality tendency for dependency and depression.

Another distinct advantage of our perspective on dependency comes from the view of psychological health it entails. First, we do *not* assume that dependency is inherently maladaptive. Second, we do *not* assume that the locus of the problem when dependency-inducing situations do go awry is invariably the person who is relying on another. In contrast, the typical definitions of dependency in the personality and phenomenological traditions implicitly implicate pathology in the dependent individual. If dependency is viewed as an *extreme* need for others, then, indeed, it seems probable that conflicts surrounding dependent relationships will occur and will be caused by the individual with the excessive needs; the absence of conflicts, in fact, might stimulate speculation regarding the psychological health of a partner who attempts to satisfy inordinate demands. If, on the other hand, dependency is defined simply as a stable relationship in which desired outcomes are obtained through the actions of another person, then it is possible to delineate when such relationships are maladaptive (when, for example, they may lead to depression), and to explore antecedents other than the extent of the needs of the dependent individual that may contribute to this maladaptive situation.

From Dependency to Depression

Insufficient Reinforcement

In considering the potential consequences of dependency, clinical and social psychological research suggests two possible pathways to depression. The first pathway begins with the most obvious problem that can occur when relying on someone else: he or she does not come through. Put more formally, the dependent person may believe the reinforcement he or she is receiving is inadequate. Such a perception can occur because the individual who is relying on another wants an unrealistically high amount of reinforcement; alternatively, the amount of reinforcement received may be objectively low.

Assuming that the individual who is relying on another had some expectation that reinforcement would be forthcoming, the failure to obtain adequate satisfaction should initiate a search for the causes of that failure (cf. Wong and Weiner, 1981). If someone on whom we are relying fails to meet our needs, we are likely to try to understand why. When there is a reasonable explanation involving a temporary state of affairs (e.g., my husband didn't hug me because he's tired tonight), the psychological impact will most likely be temporary as well. Such explanations may, of course, appear sensible at first, only to be disconfirmed later (e.g., my husband can't be tired *every* night). In such instances, however, the psychological impact will most likely be delayed until a further failure to receive adequate reinforcement suggests that the best explanation is a more enduring one.

When the most convincing reason is a stable and enduring one (e.g., my husband didn't hug me because he is uncomfortable with physical affection), failure to receive reinforcement should also be viewed as stable and enduring. Upon becoming convinced by such an explanation, the dependent individual faces a decision, perhaps a dilemma. If the relationship involves only one outcome, a consistent failure to obtain adequate reinforcement should result in a relatively uncomplicated search for alternative means of satisfaction. Other options would include obtaining the outcome for oneself, finding someone else who can provide it, or identifying a reasonable and available substitute for the outcome itself. Reevaluating the standards for adequate reinforcement also may be possible, including perhaps a genuine decision that giving up the outcome altogether is acceptable.

Many relationships, of course, are not simply a matter of one outcome provided for one person by another. We may rely on our friends or sexual partners for emotional support, material aid, and entertainment. Moreover, seeking an alternative for one outcome may impact on other aspects of the initial relationship. A woman who is not receiving sexual satisfaction from her spouse, for example, may risk the benefits she *is* deriving if she seeks another sexual partner. Before pursuing other courses, then, she must balance the lack of sexual satisfaction and any other sources of disappointment against the outcomes she does obtain from her spouse. An individual should be motivated to pursue an available alternative only when the benefits from obtaining the alternative are perceived to outweigh the costs to the existing relationship (Kelley and Thibaut, 1978). For present purposes, such a decision to seek reinforcement elsewhere is considered a step off the path toward depression.

Thus, the critical situations for our analysis are those in which either no alternative means of procuring satisfaction are apparent, or the cost of leaving the relationship appears too great. Given that it is possible to give up the outcome altogether, the belief that there are no alternatives should only occur if the outcome is seen as too valuable to go without. In both instances, therefore, the net result is that the individual continues to rely on someone for an important outcome that is not forthcoming.

This situation of continued and unrewarding dependency bears a close resemblance to the conditions that have been suggested by a number of psychological theories to lead to depression. Behavioral theorists, for example, argue that depression occurs when an individual receives inadequate reinforcement (e.g., Lewinsohn and Hoberman, 1982). Behaviorists have not, however, specified the social circumstances that may affect the connection between inadequate reinforcement and depression. Our model serves to provide a social context for the behavioral perspective.

Alternatively, the circumstances we have delineated here could be viewed as an example of the conditions described by the learned helplessness model of depression. The basic premise of the helplessness model is that depression may ensue when individuals come to expect that there is nothing they can do to control an important negative outcome (e.g., Abramson, Seligman, and Teasdale, 1978). Since the circumstances we have identified include the perception that the lack of reinforcement will endure, individuals confronted with what we might call failed but unavoidable dependency might well feel themselves to be helpless.

Other cognitive theories suggest that a pervasive negative view of the self is one of the central beliefs that cause depression (e.g., Beck, 1967). The potential impact on self-esteem of relying on someone for an outcome that is not forthcoming thus may be another mechanism leading to depression (cf. Birtchnell, 1984). A loss of self-esteem may occur if the outcome itself is linked to how the dependent individual feels about him or herself.

For example, a woman who bases her self-concept on the approval she garners from others may suffer a loss in self-esteem if caught in a relationship in which she receives few overt expressions of respect.

In addition, we believe that people only *feel* dependent if circumstances make the contingent relationship between another person's response and an outcome salient. Obviously an acute awareness of this contingency is likely when one cannot obtain what one needs and wants from another person, and no viable alternative is in sight. It is important to note that the perception that one is dependent may in and of itself be highly detrimental to self-esteem. The personality theorists discussed earlier are not unique in holding a viewpoint on dependency that seems implicitly derogatory to the individual; we live in a culture that places great value on self-reliance. Thus, it is not surprising that people perform poorly under conditions designed to induce perceptions of dependency (e.g., Langer and Benevento, 1978). Lowered self-esteem may contribute to poor performance when dependency is salient; conversely, poor performance may well lead to further reductions in self-esteem.

Taken together, there are several ways in which insufficient reinforcement in a dependent relationship ultimately may result in depression. Does this mean that the dependent individual who is receiving adequate reinforcement is not susceptible to depression? There is reason to suggest that the answer to this question is not necessarily "no," and that there may be detrimental conditions in a dependent relationship in which reinforcement is sufficient.

Role-Conferred Disadvantages and Dependency

Consider a wife and husband who are employed, respectively, as a clerical worker and a partner in a prominent law firm. The man's job involves challenging tasks, while his wife's work is more menial. Moreover, because her husband provides the majority of their income, the woman often feels she should defer to his preferences. She is a facile bridge player, for example, but rarely plays because her husband, who is decidedly bad at bridge, selects more athletic leisure activities.

This wife and husband are in a situation that illustrates how contextual constraints can interfere with or facilitate people's opportunities to present themselves in the best light. Ross (1977) has labeled those external factors that bias people's display of their abilities as role-conferred disadvantages and role-conferred advantages. In our example, the husband's job enables him to exhibit the full range of his abilities, the wife's does not; furthering his advantage, the husband's dominant role in structuring their activities permits him to avoid ones in which he is less proficient.

Objectively, any inference about the relative competence of these spouses should include consideration of the situational constraints that affect their performance. Research on role-conferred inequities, however, suggests that evaluative judgments are relatively insensitive to such contextual factors, even when one partner clearly can structure the situation to his or her advantage (Ross, 1977). The wife and husband in our example thus are likely to neglect the part role-constraints play in the capabilities each manifests and believe that the husband is in fact the more competent of the two partners.

More generally, when an outcome is contingent on someone else's response and the dependent individual does not have the opportunity to engage in an equivalent response, both people are likely to believe that the dependent individual is less competent in the arena in question. The fact that one person is providing an outcome for another may contribute to perceptions of differential abilities. That is, it might be reasoned that one individual relies on another *because* the other person is more capable. Objectively, of course, differential competence is only one of a number of factors that may lead to a dependent relationship. Personal priorities or societal constraints, for example, also influence decisions about who will provide certain outcomes. Over time, however, the display of competence by one person and not the other may foster potentially inaccurate backward reasoning that the dependent individual is in that position precisely because he or she is unable to perform equally well. Finally, to the extent that the dependent individual has less power in the relationship, the person on whom he or she is relying also can structure their interactions in ways that enhance his or her own presentation, producing further perceptions of differential competence.

Clearly a link between a loss in self-esteem and depression is relevant to this situation. The critical issue is whether the arenas in which dependent persons are disadvantaged are relevant to their self-esteem. A woman who is not invested in her average athletic skill may be unaffected if her spouse, who played on his college tennis team, arranges weekly doubles matches. A woman who places great value on her intellectual achievement and who works in a menial job while her husband works in a more challenging one may, however, suffer a severe loss of self-esteem and become depressed.

Dependency and the Maintenance of Depression

Thus far we have identified insufficient reinforcement and a reduced chance to show competence as specific conditions of interpersonal dependency that may produce depression. The occurrence of depression in this social context also may increase certain interpersonal factors hypothesized by Coyne (1976) to maintain and exacerbate depressive responses.

Coyne depicted a "chronic depressive cycle" in which depression causes an individual to seek support and reassurance from significant others. Having sought these responses, the depressed person is in a dilemma; is the reassurance received genuine or was it given because it was solicited? Any ambiguity in the manner in which comfort is imparted (e.g., with a critical tone of voice) will increase the interpretative dilemma. Unsure of the meaning of what he or she has received, the depressed individual repeatedly solicits support and reassurance. Sooner or later, these persistent requests produce a negative affect in the other person, and this response only serves to heighten the depressed individual's uncertainty and insecurity.

An individual who becomes depressed in a dependent relationship may be particularly susceptible to the cycle Coyne described. The depressed individual may be seeking support in a relationship that has itself led to a loss in self-esteem. If there was insufficient interpersonal sustenance in the first place, repeated efforts to solicit it are not likely to succeed. Indeed, Coyne explicitly noted that when relationships are "stable yet low in support and validation, they may encourage a chronic depressive cycle" (p. 37).

Women, Dependency, and Depression

The dependent individuals in our illustrations have all been women. This is, of course, a book about women and, accordingly, our focus is on how dependency may affect our sex. We do not intend to imply, however, that the effects we described are gender-specific. A man who relies on someone who is not providing adequate reinforcement should be as susceptible to depression as a woman. A man who experiences role-conferred disadvantages surrounding essential aspects of his self-image should be no less vulnerable to a loss in self-esteem than is a woman in the same situation.

Although the effects of specific conditions of dependency should be the same for men and women, in many ways the likelihood of experiencing these conditions in our present society appears strongly related to gender. As noted earlier, married women may be at risk for depression associated with dependency simply by virtue of the fact that they are often reliant on their husbands for material goods.

In addition to the possibility that sufficient material reinforcement will not be received, to the extent that money is power, women are at clear risk for role-conferred disadvantages in their relationships. Women in lower paying, less prestigious jobs also may be at risk for role-conferred disadvantages relative to their husbands in their sense of professional achievement. The latter issue may be especially acute for contemporary women who incorporate the increasing societal value given to women's professional accomplishments into their personal standards, while at the same time, genuine opportunities for role-equity lag behind.

Both sexes have needs that are inextricably linked to the response of others (e.g., emotional support and affection), and in heterosexual relationships, men and women turn to each other for many such needs. Men, however, seek support and affection from persons who traditionally are socialized to be nurturing, while women are turning to persons who typically have been socialized not to express emotionality. Thus traditional sex roles increase the chances that women will experience insufficient emotional support in their relationships with men. Those same traditional roles increase the value women attach to their abilities to form emotional ties, and may, thereby, increase the chances that a failure to obtain a man's support may damage the woman's self-esteem.

Men and women in dependent heterosexual relationships also may differ in their beliefs regarding the accessibility of alternatives. Women recently have been barraged by media presentations indicating they face a paucity of available male partners. On this basis alone, a woman who is confronted with a dysfunctional relationship may assume that the likelihood of a better, alternative relationship is low.

Having examined some potential negative consequences of dependency and ways in which women may be particularly susceptible to depression in this context, we would like to note briefly the positive side to our analysis. Identification of the pitfalls in dependency also suggests avenues of prevention. Avoiding dependent relationships altogether might be one possibility. We believe, however, that such an extreme measure is neither necessary nor desirable; a similar map of the costs of complete autonomy could be drawn, perhaps including consideration of the loss of all reinforcement that is inextricably tied to others, and of the threats to self-esteem inherent in trying to meet all one's needs oneself.

Instead, it seems to us that a more realistic prescription, readily derived from our analysis, as well as from the work of others (e.g., Brehm, 1987), focuses on trying to expand potential sources of interpersonal gratification and self-esteem. That is, the problem with a dependent relationship may not be that it involves dependency, but that it can too easily become the sole available source for meeting important needs. Efforts to establish and maintain an expanded social support network are not, however, without cost. Additional sources of gratification and esteem carry with them additional burdens, as contemporary women who juggle their personal and professional goals know only too well. Despite this knowledge, our analysis of dependency and depression has led us to conclude that the price to be paid for an expanded social network is, in the long run, worth paying.

References

Abramson, L. Y., Seligman, M. E. P., and Teasdale, J. D. (1978). Learned helplessness in humans: Critique and reformulation. *Journal of Abnormal Psychology, 87*, 49–74.

Beck, A. T. (1967). *Depression: Causes and treatment.* Philadelphia: University of Pennsylvania Press.

Birtchnell, J. (1984). Dependence and its relationship to depression. *British Journal of Medical Psychology, 57*, 215–225.

Blatt, S. J. (1974). Levels of object representation in anaclitic and introjective depression. *Psychoanalytic Study of the Child, 29*, 107–157.

Brehm, S. S. (1987). Coping after a relationship ends. In C. R. Snyder and C. E. Ford (Eds.), *Coping with negative life events: Clinical and social psychological perspectives* (pp. 191–212). New York: Plenum Press.

Chevron, E. S., Quinlan, D. M., and Blatt, S. J. (1978). Sex roles and gender differences in the experience of depression. *Journal of Abnormal Psychology, 87*, 680–683.

Cox, S. and Radloff, L. S. (1984). Depression in relation to sex roles: Differences in learned susceptibility and precipitating factors. In C. S. Widom (Ed.), *Sex roles and psychopathology* (pp. 123–143). New York: Plenum Press.

Coyne, J. C. (1976). Toward an interactional description of depression. *Psychiatry, 39*, 28–40.

Hammen, C. L. (1982). Gender and depression. In I. Al-Issa (Ed.), *Gender and psychopathology* (pp. 133–152). New York: Academic Press.

Hirschfeld, R. M. A., Klerman, G. L., Gough, H. G., Barrett, J., Korchin, S. J., and Chodoff, P. (1977). A measure of interpersonal dependency. *Journal of Personality Assessment, 41*, 610–618.

Kelley, H. H. and Thibaut, J. W. (1978). *Interpersonal relations: A theory of interdependence.* New York: Wiley.

Langer, E. J. and Benevento, A. (1978). Self-induced dependence. *Journal of Personality and Social Psychology, 36*, 886–893.

Lewinsohn, P. M. and Hoberman, H. M. (1982). Depression. In A. S. Bellack, M. Hersen, and A. E. Kazdin (Eds.), *International handbook of behavior modification and behavior therapy* (pp. 397–431). New York: Plenum Press.

Radloff, L. (1975). Sex differences in depression: The effects of occupation and marital status. *Sex Roles, 1*, 249–265.

Repetti, R. L. and Crosby, F. (1984). Gender and depression: Exploring the adult-role explanation. *Journal of Social and Clinical Psychology, 2*, 57–70.

Robins, L. N., Helzer, J. E., Weissman, M. M., Orvaschel, H., Gruenberg, E., Burke, J. E., and Regier, D. A. (1984). Lifetime prevalence of specific psychiatric disorders in three sites. *Archives of General Psychiatry, 41*, 949–958.

Ross, L. (1977). The intuitive psychologist and his shortcomings: Distortions in the attribution process. In L. Berkowitz (Ed.), *Advances in experimental social psychology* (Vol. 10) (pp. 173–220). New York: Academic Press.

Warren, L. W. and McEachren, L. (1983). Psychosocial correlates of depressive symptomatology in adult women. *Journal of Abnormal Psychology, 92*, 151–160.

Weissman, M. M. and Klerman, G. L. (1979). Sex differences in the epidemiology of depression. In E. S. Gomberg and V. Franks (Eds.), *Gender and disordered behavior: Sex differences in psychopathology* (pp. 381–425). New York: Brunner/Mazel.

Wong, P.T.P. and Weiner, B. (1981). When people ask "why" questions and the heuristics of attributional search. *Journal of Personality and Social Psychology, 40*, 650–663.

The Art and Science of Contemporary Counseling Psychology: The Dilemma of a Caring Relationship

9

DIANE McDERMOTT

The purpose of this essay is to explore the therapeutic and professional implications of how conventional feminine attributes interact with the current practice of counseling psychology. It centers on one therapist's efforts to translate traditional feminine nurturing and care giving skills into client oriented therapeutic caring. Drawing on my own experience as a counselor and counselor educator, I will describe some of the paradoxical consequences generated for contemporary women constrained to work within the male dominated theoretical structure and methodologies of the discipline. I will also sketch out some suggestions for how some of the inherent contradictions between disciplinary demands and the needs and strengths of women may be resolved.

Natural and Cultural Factors in Sex Role Caring

The simplest way to begin is to employ some stereotypic assumptions about the differences between men and women. As a general rule it seems safe to conclude that many women are better at processing subjective interpersonal information than are men. This is not the same as asserting the perjorative oversimplification that men are more rational and objective than women. It simply argues that whether as a result of biological inheritance, normative influences such as culturally and socially prescribed gender roles, or some combination of internal and external factors, many women appear to have unique strengths in processing the subjective affective content of human communications. How could this have come about?

Visualize if you will a group of Australopithecine hominids crossing open savannah three or more million years ago. If we could observe such a trek, we would undoubtedly see divisions of labor between males and females. Each gender would contribute specialized skills necessary for the survival of the species. We know from observing modern primates moving across open ground that males would be ranged around the perimeter so as to detect danger, such as an approaching predator, at maximum distance from the group. As hunters, attention in early males would have been directed outside themselves and subjective feelings would have had no utility in achieving the goal of the hunt. In the center of the group, pregnant females and infants, the group's genetic future, would move with relatively greater security. As the caring and nurturing center of the reproductive process, females would devote more visual attention to proximal stimuli— the care of infants. As the gatherers in the hunting and gathering way of life, early females would spend much of their time collecting vegetables, seeds, nuts, fruits, and tubers which have always made up the bulk of the human food supply; by definition such activities occur close to the self, within reaching distance.

It seems plausible, therefore, that nature created a relationship between women and near or proximal experience; this relationship, especially its core focus on the needs of offspring, may well have promoted an affectively oriented subjective style of processing information. Concomitantly, the more distant experience characteristic of men may have favored a more objective habit of mind. What is self-evident is that nurturing, and loving, involve processing the information of close or near experience. One can fantasize or adore at a distance, but to take care of someone one has to be close enough to know the needs of the other person. Although one could argue that basic human needs are common to all and, then, that it is not necessary to know another well, the fact is that effective nurturing comes from responding to the specific nuances of specific needs in a unique individual. To nurture effectively one must be not only close but perceptive.

Whatever the hypothetical and problematic contribution of biology to caring and nurturing in women, there can be no doubt about the influence of learning traditional sex role skills. Women learn, from the time they are very small, that they must be able to respond to the needs of others. Not only do we learn from our observation of our mothers' role, but the bulk of society's messages promote such skills for women. While the recent women's movement has certainly served to reduce stereotypic sex role portrayals, there continues to be considerable reinforcement for the traditional values of womanhood. Women of all ages still receive messages that caring is what they do best and that nurturing is their primary role. Much has been made of the double day that many women find they must live; one day at a job outside the home and another day's work waiting for them when they return to their families. On balance it seems safe to conclude that society is yet dominated by traditional sex role stereotypes. Stereotypes exist, however, precisely because they do characterize so many people.

While there are always exceptions to any rule, for the most part counseling students reflect these stereotypes. Demographic and attitudinal research reveals that the average counselor trainee is white, middle class, Protestant, and from an unbroken home where the father worked and the mother was a homemaker (McDermott and Stadler, 1985). The implications of these findings are that counselors most probably have learned traditional values with respect to male and female ways of caring and nurturing. It is also true that at the master's level the average counselor is likely to be female, while at the doctoral level (although this trend is changing) the counselor is more likely to be male. Because of this, counselors may also learn traditional views of the appropriate status differential between men and women.

Such a status difference in the past accounts for the paradox that even though counseling, as with many helping professions, is a field open to women, its theoretical underpinnings have been largely developed by men. Given our admittedly stereotypic assumptions that women tend to be better at processing near affective interpersonal information whereas men prefer to deal with the more distant information of things, this fact creates some unique problems for many women. Male-generated objective theories of counseling at best passively ignore and at worst actively discriminate against a major talent or skill of women: namely, developing nurturing and caring relationships. What happens when a female disciple of objective cognitive theories find out that what really works in counseling is her ability to form caring bonds with clients? She collides with a world of male distinctions about objectivity and subjectivity, a world that often contradicts her own experience. At best, this confrontation takes one down a confusing road of counseling relationships before finding a comfortable, workable style that incorporates both the objective/distant and subjective/near habits of mind that respectively often mark male and female approaches. At worst the stress of this confrontation can lead to burnout and disillusionment.

One of the most unfortunate consequences of being a caring woman confronted with objective theories and techniques that leave little room for intuitive nurturing relationships is that one can begin to doubt the value of these skills. In contrast, I would argue that while certain aspects of cognitive and affective distance have definite adaptive value for women in the field of counseling psychology and life in general, it is also possible and desirable to effectively use those elements of caring and nurturing, which women know so well. It is time for women to stop devaluing their best attributes and to start learning to use them judiciously and with confidence.

The Emergence of Counseling Psychology

In light of the early history of counseling psychology as a discipline, the contradictions facing the caring, nurturing woman today are even more paradoxical. (Although the specific emphasis here is on counseling psychology, these remarks would also apply to pastoral psychology, clinical psychology, social work, and psychiatry.) Eric Fromm's popular *The Art of Loving* first appeared in 1956 and illustrates the caring affective context of both early counseling and traditional feminine attributes. Fromm described motherly love as unconditional and fatherly love as conditional, thereby giving expectations and demands over to father while creating mother as an all giving source. He said about unconditional love: "I am loved for what I am, or perhaps more accurately, I am loved because I am. This experience of being loved by mother is a passive one. There is nothing I have to do in order to be loved—mother's love is unconditional bliss, is peace, it need not be acquired, it need not be deserved" (p. 39).

These are powerful messages and they shaped many of us of that generation. Whether or not it was Fromm's intention, women who read *The Art of Loving* internalized the image of a woman/mother who is all giving, all forgiving, a constant spring from which caring and nurturance flow. And in Fromm's view the mother would teach, or pass on to, her daughters the ability to provide unconditional love, while the father would teach his sons about the real world, the world in which one has a right to expect others to meet expectations and demands in order to receive favor. In the 1950s view, not only was mother's love passive, so was the mother. But what happened if a woman was not a wellspring of love and tenderness, if she had needs of her own to meet? What usually happened was guilt—a sense of being bad or wrong, and at the very least different.

The roles were clear and strong. We were the primary caregivers of children, we were the mainstay and backbone of the home, and it was our role and responsibility to nurture all who lived there. It was vital to our very survival that we learn to apprehend the needs of others, to become so sensitive and perceptive that we could always be there when they wanted us. We learned to meet our own needs by meeting the needs of others, when, that is, we admitted we did have needs.

The 1950s was a period of extreme traditionality. Yet in my contact with young women clients and students, women born in the 1960s and 1970s, there is still the assumption that the primary role of women is to care for others. Although women recognize needs of their own and assume they have a right to have those needs met, the central focus on the personal gratification derived from meeting the needs of others remains. The focus becomes evident when young women express guilt for not being what the partner (or employer, professor, child, parent) wants them to be. It is also apparent when these young women express resentment or anger at demands, which may or may not actually have been made, but which they feel are their responsibility to meet. When women shoulder the sole responsibility for the failure of a relationship or the misbehavior of a child, this points out the weight women still place on caring and nurturing of loved ones. While this kind of hyperresponsibility is, in fact, not conducive to what we now recognize as healthy caring, its presence, along with extreme feelings of guilt and anger, demonstrates that women still respond to a social conditioning that heavily emphasizes caring and nurturing roles.

Another influential counseling theorist of the 1950s was Carl Rogers. Rogers, like Fromm, was concerned with caring and saw it as vital to the growth of humanity. In his work (e.g., 1951), he attempted to uncover the conditions necessary for effective psychotherapy and formulated these "core conditions" under the headings of congruence or genuineness, unconditional positive regard, and accurate empathy.

Rogers considered these three core conditions necessary before clients could experience an atmosphere warm and accepting enough to permit freedom of expression and, hence, through gradual gaining of self-acceptance, movement toward self-actualization. Other early figures went even further in stressing the need for warmth and caring as core conditions for successful counselor-client relationships. A Scandinavian psychoanalyst named Trygve Braatoy (1954) described the therapeutic process as follows.

Psychotherapy is an exquisitely human enterprise. It is a deeply personal encounter—wherein a trained professional attempts to assist a suffering fellow human to resolve the psychosocial problems and conflicts that place unacceptable limits on the quality of subjectively experienced living. Beyond issues of formal training, theoretical orientation, and technical skill, the effective practice of psychotherapy will be seriously hampered unless the therapist's relation to his [*sic*] patients is first and foremost determined by love (p. 53).

Thus, for Braatoy, the essential core condition of therapy is love.

The Rise of Reductionistic Skill Training

In contrast to the affective context of much of counseling theory in the 1950s, our postmodern culture values what is technological and scientific; it places far less value on tenderminded and subjective perspectives and actions. Since its inception, psychology has increasingly attempted to bring scientific objectivity to what many feel is essentially subjective, because, increasingly, any discipline must become as objectively and scientifically replicable as possible if it is to survive. Although fields such as physics and medicine can afford to take risks into the subjective now and again, counseling psychology, a relative newcomer, and one whose basic subject matter is elusive, sticks strictly to the tough-minded code it has adopted. In striving to become a respected discipline, counseling psychology has moved more and more in the direction of science and technology and left behind the poetic. The art of the 1950s has fallen into disrepute, as science reigns.

Our training programs now stress the acquisition of skills, a grounding in theoretical and methodological issues, and the ability to conduct original, rigorous research. Very seldom are there opportunities for deeply moving human interactions between individuals; when they do happen they occur by chance rather than as an integral part of the training program. It would almost appear as if deep human encounters are viewed as unmanageable and uncontrolled; who knows what could happen to the student-professor relationship if those kinds of experiences were encouraged? Students continually express surprise and disappointment that they do not experience significant affective human encounters in a program training people for what is, by definition, a significant human encounter.

This reductionistic focus on skill training has been a primary tenet of counselor education since shortly after Rogers formulated his core conditions for psychotherapy. Thus, what began as a rather ephemeral and poetic view of the counseling process became heavily technicalized. Among others, Ivey (1971) and Kagen (1975) reasoned that if one could identify the behaviors comprising Rogers' core conditions, then these behaviors could be taught to budding counselors. Soon there was a massive body of research to demonstrate just exactly what the core conditions were and how they could be measured. For example, the Accurate Empathy Scale (Truax and Carkhuff, 1967) was devised, stimulating prodigious amounts of research. This scale reduced empathy to responses that could be rated on a scale from one to nine, independently of the actual content of the statements themselves or the context of the session. As research on and classification of responses reflective of the essential core conditions proceeded, concrete skills were specified which could be taught to students. Such skills included open-ended questions, paraphrasing, labeling of affect in the client, the ability to draw conclusions about the client's assumptive frame of reference, clarifying the client's responses, and making comments reflecting back to the client his or her statements.

Training programs in such skills are effective in producing better counselors. Students often come into counseling programs full of a desire to help but with no idea how to get past their own social conditioning in interacting with others. Beginning students are typically full of advice and problem-solving strategies, which they use before having heard the client out. In fact, listening is the most basic skill many students must learn. Within just one semester of skills training, important changes occur in the way these students are able to hear their clients and how they respond.

Thus skills training programs are invaluable, but what is missing is the link between the efficacy of these skills and who the counselor is as an individual. So often students feel that they are being lost as individuals and that what they initially believed they had to contribute is of no value. More specifically, women students often feel that their nurturing qualities are being censored and that they will be ineffective, poor counselors if they allow themselves to enact them. Indeed, when women demonstrate a mothering quality in counseling, many supervisors would be quick to admonish them for it. When, however, men exhibit the same or a similar quality, supervisors may be surprised and attribute it to their positive ability to be in touch with their "emotional side."

The sense of individuality that has been lost is what I have come to define as "therapeutic caring." This affective approach to psychotherapy stresses the generation of intuitive insights through becoming emotionally close with clients. There is nothing spiritual or mystical about why this process succeeds. Therapeutic caring works because carefully constructed hypotheses are consciously applied for the benefit of the client. Therapeutic potential is demonstrated by effectiveness, as hypotheses are tested and either rewarded or refuted. Such insights or hypotheses originate from an avowedly subjective process, rather than being the result of the more distant and supposedly objective methods favored by males.

The very act of empathizing on a deep level is energy intensive. It means allowing oneself to feel what a client is feeling, to be truly touched by the client's story. It means not staying away from the client's emotions, but rather allowing the feelings to happen with the intent of more fully understanding the client's needs. It is true that empathy always has a certain "as if" quality to it; however, everyone at one time or another has experienced vicarious, but genuine and intense, emotion. If this were not possible, then thriller movies would not be box office hits. Unfortunately, when faced with a live human being who is telling us a part of his/her life, we may pull back and increase our distance in an effort to be objective, and refuse to let ourselves understand on all the levels available to us.

The Dark Side of Caring

As a counselor and educator I have seen both sides suffer when caring was not done in a judicious, replicable, and professional manner. My own personal journey into and out of burnout illustrates the negative consequences for the caregiver. My early years as a professional were lonely and socially isolated. What was not lonely and isolated was my work in counseling. I loved the feeling of connection with other adult human beings and found that in these relationships I was valued and needed. I saw many more clients than necessary, but the satisfactions I gained made it worthwhile. After several years, however, the emotional energy it took to maintain such a high level of caring for these clients began to take its toll. All the classic symptoms of burnout—distancing, blaming, fatigue, and boredom—began to appear.

I was fortunate to have the opportunity to leave counseling for several years to administer my institution's Women's Studies Program. This was totally rejuvenating and allowed a new perspective on the burnout process and on caring in counseling. When I returned to counseling it was with an approach that was far more careful in expending a great deal of emotional energy. I made conscious decisions about when to expend a great deal of emotional energy in nurturing and caring and when to be somewhat more distant with clients. I also recognized that it was not possible to see great numbers of clients and continue to do a good job with them. Thus, a balanced work load incorporating counseling, teaching, and writing became another way of preventing burnout.

How does what I have described as "therapeutic caring" accelerate the burnout syndrome? While the positive side of nurturing and caring lies in its effectiveness as a counseling technique, and there is also a positive quality to being needed by clients and colleagues as well as the sensory gratification of vicarious emotional arousal, the dark side of caring is strain, drain of energy, and emotional and professional burnout. For many women it simply feels so good, so natural, to be caring for someone that it is easy to convince ourselves that we are doing something worthwhile with our lives. But frequently, caring goes into a bottomless pit of need and does not, in fact, help others. The main result, then, of unjudicious caring may be an ineffective counselor.

Another aspect of the dark side of caring is that it is usually "other directed," that is, the caring woman frequently cares for everyone except herself. To care for oneself, for many women, has come to be associated with selfishness to such a degree that the intensely nurturing woman may suppress her own needs almost entirely. Not only is burnout an almost certain consequence of this, but so is resentment and anger with the consequence that the person may become cynical and manipulative. When this occurs, the individual has reached a point of entanglement in a double bind between society's messages to be a caring person and the psyche's desire to be a whole person. One not too infrequent response to this entanglement is to cut the Gordian knot and simply leave whatever situations seem to be causing problems. Divorce or changing careers are two examples of this reaction.

Yet another facet of the dark side of caring and nurturing is the fact that nurturing can go so far as to actually disempower those for whom one cares. Just as the mother can do so much for her children that they never learn to take care of themselves, so the overly nurturing counselor can prevent the client from learning through the healthy struggle of personal anguish and decision making. We are taught that pain is bad, and that as women we should prevent hurt as much as possible. Yet growing is often a painful process and the counselor who must always make things better is doing a great disservice to his or her clients. Caring, then, can be a powerful therapeutic tool, but it can also be a dangerous force that must be used wisely and appropriately.

In what direction, then, can we revise our views of caring to be healthier for our loved ones, our clients, and ourselves? What is needed is a recognition that our ways of caring have been learned through social conditioning and are maintained by tacit assumptions of the validity of cultural sex role stereotypes. If we can accept the premise that women are not necessarily genetically determined to meet the needs of others, any more than are men, we can allow for the possibility of change. On the other hand, even if we have been admirably equipped by nature for our reproductive niche, our cultural functions and attainments remain unlimited. We left behind the need for biological specialization of function when, long ago, we left the state of nature behind and staked our future on cultural mechanisms.

It is not in the direction of caring less, only differently, that I believe change is needed. We must learn to discriminate which needs to meet and when it is better to remain distant. A really good therapist learns to trust his or her inner reactions to clients and to use them to bring about better understanding. Good therapy need not be devoid of the therapist's emotions; because one can understand on a deep emotional level does not imply agreement or loss of objectivity. It also does not mean becoming an emotional sponge. Our patriarchal culture has given us the dualism of emotion and reason; that dualism is reinforced whenever counselors hide therapeutic caring behind closed doors while talking publicly about therapy in the objective way that was taught during their training. If counselors are to learn to use therapeutic caring effectively and to avoid the risks of the dark side of caring for themselves as well as their clients, it will be necessary to develop theories and techniques that articulate how to use that potential safely. If caring is an intrinsically rewarding feminine experience as well as a potentially dangerous female trap, women will need to play the predominant role in shaping these theories and techniques.

References

Braatoy, T. (1954). *Fundamentals of psychoanalytic technique*. New York: Wiley.

Fromm, E. (1956). *The art of loving*. New York: Harper and Brothers.

Ivey, A. (1971). *Microcounseling: Innovations in interviewing training*. Springfield, Ill.: Thomas.

Kagen, N. (1975). *Influencing human interaction*. Washington, D.C.: American Personnel and Guidance Association.

McDermott, D. and Stadler, H. (1985, July). *Attitudes of counseling students in the United States toward minority clients*. Paper presented at the annual meeting of the International Congress on Counseling Minorities, Utrecht, The Netherlands.

Rogers, C. R. (1951). *Client centered therapy*. Boston: Houghton Mifflin Co.

Truax, C. B. and Carkhuff, R. R. (1967). *Toward effective counseling and psychotherapy: Training and practice*. Chicago: Aldine.

PART THREE

WOMEN IN PROFESSIONAL ROLES

The Compassionate Professional: Historical Notes on the Woman Physician's Dilemma

10

REGINA MORANTZ-SANCHEZ

Sixteen years ago Dr. Estelle Ramey, then as now one of the few top ranking women in academic medicine, noted that the stereotype of the woman doctor was still the "horse-faced, flat-chested female in supphose who sublimates her sex starvation in a passionate embrace of the New England Journal of Medicine and cyclic AMP" (1971, p. 425). One might argue that such typecasting has finally disappeared; after all, in 1982, the *New York Times* Sunday Magazine published an advertisement depicting a woman surgeon doing rounds with her male colleagues dressed only in her ruby-red Maidenform bra and panties. Certainly increasing numbers of women medical students—now roughly one-third of the total—suggest that something has changed. Yet as the Maidenform Company's tasteless ad poignantly demonstrates, women physicians still face the difficult dilemma of forging a female professional identity in a world dominated by and primarily responsive to men and the male life cycle. While all medical students share the task of learning to feel and act like physicians, women must confront their own and others' confusion about how to remain "feminine" as well. Ironically, these doubts may only increase as young women become more comfortable as professionals. Such problems among women physicians are clearly more subtle than they were fifty, even twenty, years ago; nevertheless, they still exist.

In addition, some young women are aware that the private struggle to remain "feminine" may be vitally connected to a larger and more philosophical question: the problem of their "role" in medicine. Are women doctors supposed to act like men, or are they somehow different? If different, how so and in what ways? Should women physicians rejoice in, or bemoan that fact of difference? Should they strive harder to overcome their alleged "limitations"? Or does that difference, if it exists, enhance their abilities as professionals? And further: Do women have the right to pursue professional goals, usually considered "masculine," with the same vigor as their male colleagues and for similar reasons of self-interest and personal fulfillment? Or does their fundamental connection with children and family life necessitate additional justification for the pursuit of individualistic goals traditionally deemed at odds with the demands of wifehood and motherhood? Is the object really equality between men and women, and is that end legitimate enough, or must women contribute as well to some higher female social mission? For example, what obligations do women professionals have to other women, or to the promotion of feminist values? Should they emulate the professionalism of men, or seek to temper prevailing norms by asserting uniquely female concerns?

The Medical Profession in the Nineteenth Century

None of these questions are new; women physicians have struggled with such problems since they entered medicine over a century ago. But in 1850, the profession was still immature, lacking most of the identifying characteristics that would be taken for granted seventy years later. It shared no common intellectual base and was plagued by competing sects with contending theories on the causes and treatment of disease. Educational standards were haphazard except in one respect: they were uniformly low. Generally unable to control entry into the field, physicians were forced to stand by as women and other "undesirables" were licensed to practice. Weak and ineffectual professional societies had yet to develop either a strict professional ethos or a set of shared ethical assumptions.

In addition, the role of the physician was shaped by a traditional system of belief and behavior shared by doctor and patient alike. Central to this system was a holistic approach to the body and disease which viewed sickness as a total condition of the entire organism: the body in disequilibrium with the environment. Moreover, individual body parts were believed to be integrally connected: thus a sour stomach could cause emotional stress, while emotional distress could curdle the stomach. The dictates of such a system demanded not only that the physician's therapy display a visible physiological effect—an effect that could be witnessed by the patient and his family—but that the physician know his patient well. The "art" of medicine lay with the doctor's ability to select the proper drug in the proper dose to bring on the proper physiological changes. The best practitioners were familiar not only with the patient's history and unique physical identity, but with the family's constitutional idiosyncrasies, all of which must be assessed along with relevant environmental, climatic, and developmental conditions. It should come as no surprise that the locus of practice and treatment was primarily the patient's own home. Indeed, doctors most often treated entire families, and in emphasizing the sacredness of personal ties between doctors and patients, early medical ethics merely echoed on another level a medical theory that stressed the relevance of family history to clinical judgments.

Though this rationalistic framework was labeled "scientific," no physician in the nineteenth century would have denied the importance of intuitive factors in successful diagnosis and treatment. "The model of the body, and of health and disease," Charles Rosenberg has observed, "was all-inclusive, antireductionist, capable of incorporating every aspect of man's life in explaining his physical condition. Just as man's body interacted continuously with his environment, so did his mind with his body, his morals with his health. The realm of causation in medicine was not distinguishable from the realm of meaning in society generally" (1979, p. 10–11). As Professor Henry Hartshorne put it to the graduating class of the Woman's Medical College of Pennsylvania in 1872, "It is not always the most logical, but often the most discerning physician who succeeds best at the bedside. Medicine is indeed a science, but its practice is an art. Those who bring the quick eye, the receptive ear, and delicate touch, intensified, all of them, by a warm sympathetic temperament . . . may use the learning of laborious accumulators, often, better than they themselves could do" (1872, pp. 6–7).

Moreover, at midcentury, when advances in the laboratory began increasingly to discredit traditional heavy dosing, emphasizing instead the self-limiting quality of most diseases, the "art" of medical practice became even more important. Often skeptical of his own ability to intervene, many a physician sought merely to minimize pain and anxiety and "wait on nature." As we shall see in a moment, such a situation made some members of the profession particularly receptive to the entrance of women.

Women Enter the Profession

For their part, women entered the field by championing an extremely powerful paradigm of ideal womanhood which became so embedded in nineteenth-century American culture that one easily finds traces of it today. Though women physicians did not invent the ideal, they believed in it, helped to define it, and used it to achieve their own ends. Its features, of course, have been painstakingly explored by historians over the past decade. According to its dictates, the central organizing metaphor for women's lives—their mission in society—was motherhood. Though the Victorian sanctification of motherhood could sequester women in the family at home, it just as often served as a persuasive justification for a more integral role for women in society at large. Indeed, women did not always have to become mothers in the physiological sense. Thus Elizabeth Blackwell, a leader in the movement to train women in medicine, could speak continually of the "spiritual power of maternity" which all true physicians—male or female—must possess (1889, pp. 10, 13, 21). A generation later women physicians were reiterating similar themes. "Being women as well as physicians," acknowledged Margaret Vaupel Clark, president of the Iowa State Society of Medical Women, "we share with our sex in the actual and potential motherhood of the race. Being women we make common cause with all women. . . . And being women and mothers, our first and closest and dearest interest is the child" (1915, p. 128).

Wedding this cultural paradigm to traditional assumptions about the role of the physician, female medical leaders and their supporters fashioned a formidable argument for training women in medicine. If the doctor's responsibilities were integrally linked to the family, who better than scientifically trained women physicians could monitor family health? "Ladies," the dean of the Woman's Medical College of Pennsylvania told a graduating class in 1858, "it is for the very purpose of making home enjoyments more complete that you have been delegated today to bear health and hope to the abodes you enter" (Preston, 1858, p. 10). "Our medical profession," Elizabeth Blackwell observed, "has not yet fully realized the special and weighty responsibility which rests upon it to watch over the cradle of the race; to see to it that human beings are well born, well nourished, and well educated." Such work, she believed, was "especially encumbent upon women physicians," who better understood "the all important character of parentage in its influence upon . . . the race" (1896, p. 253).

Moreover, given the demands of medical work, women had a natural vocation for it. "They were," argued Dr. Marie Zakrzewska, "by nature sympathetic and more caretaking in sickness" (Vietor, 1924, p. 376). "The True physician," wrote Angenette Hunt in her graduating thesis from the Woman's Medical College of Pennsylvania, needed "gentleness, patience, quick perceptions, natural instinct which is often surer than science, deep sympathy." All these qualities, Hunt believed, "belong to the sex in an eminent degree" (1851).

Women physicians also had special obligations to other women who, silenced by the dictates of Victorian modesty, could bring themselves to confess neither their physical nor their emotional distress to a man. A recurring theme in Dr. Harriot Hunt's memoirs is women physicians' superior ability to diagnose female patients because they were better able to draw them out. One patient thanked heaven that Hunt was a woman, "for now I can tell you the truth about my health" (Hunt, 1856, p. 157). Even male physicians admitted that there were many women who preferred "to suffer the extremity of danger and pain rather than waive those scruples of delicacy which prevent their maladies from being fully explored" (Meigs, 1848, pp. 20–21).

Most women physicians in the nineteenth century measured themselves against their own powerful professional prescriptions which meshed traditional ideals about gender with their new occupational demands. Indeed, in 1897, when the medical students and alumnae of the Woman's Medical

College of Pennsylvania published a rather remarkable little volume of short stories and nonfiction essays entitled *Daughters of Aesculapius*, we can see that their role assumptions had changed little in the fifty years since women had entered medicine. Though not particularly an exemplar of avant garde literary achievement, the book speaks eloquently of the deepest concerns young women physicians shared at a moment in time when they contended with a profession gradually taking on its modern face.

Several of the short stories illustrate quite poignantly the variations on familiar cultural themes. In "Mater Dolorosa—Mater Felix" a sensitive, unmarried hospital resident physician draws out from a beautiful young obstetrical patient the confession that her three-day-old baby is illegitimate. Able to intuit the inner goodness in this desperate unfortunate, the doctor manages to convince the wealthy young seducer to marry her charge. The tale ends several years later with a visit from the girl—now a happy, refined, and elegant matron—requesting that the doctor see her through her second pregnancy. When the young lady thanks the woman physician for altering her fate, she responds that it was Providence who chose to do good through the "humble instrumentality of a woman doctor" (*Daughters*, 1897, p. 65). Another narrator who chooses an unmarried hospital resident physician for a heroine has her struggling to save the life of a sick slum child with whom she ultimately falls in love and resolves to adopt. A glum and sullen little girl before the gentle doctor began her ministrations, the child is gradually transformed into an angelic creature by the woman's patient devotion. Unfortunately, the child's mother inadvertently passes on to her daughter a deadly pneumonia in a goodbye kiss, and in the final paragraphs of the story, doctor and mother confront each other after the girl's death. The doctor resolves to rehabilitate the mother—who has herself been transfigured by her sorrow—in place of the child (*Daughters*, pp. 80–137).

In a story entitled "One Short Hour," a graduating student writes of a medical student forced to choose between her career and the man she loves. The hapless Rachel is confronted by a fiancé who can no longer endorse her professional aspirations. Begging her to marry him at once, he confesses that he has come to believe that a wife's place "is always beside her husband,—sheltered." The girl, refusing to relinquish her goals after years of hard work, nevertheless defends herself in the language of self sacrifice, not self-actualization: "Ah, Howard," she sighs, "if only once you could hear the fervent 'Thank God, you have come!' that springs to the lips of the pain-racked one, and could but see the gratitude in her eyes, you would realize that the tear on the hardlined face and the hope in the trusting gaze are dearer—yes, forgive me—than caresses!" (*Daughters*, pp. 80–107).

Because it also deals with marriage, Dr. Hester A. Hewling's "Dr. Honora" is in some sense a companion piece to "One Short Hour." Favorably but fancifully resolving felt tensions between marriage and work, it tells of a young woman physician on the verge of quitting the profession after three discouraging years in a small town. Almost miraculously her life is changed when she is accidentally given the chance to prove her abilities by saving the life of a small child—the granddaughter of a prominent citizen. She is rewarded not only by the respect of her patrons, but also by the love of the handsome Dr. Bragg, the family's regular physician. Admitting that he had not before approved of women doctors, he declares that "above all else" the world needs "strong, gentle women physicians." The story ends with the couple's retirement to his Virginia farm, where they open an orphanage and a hospital, practicing together in "home-mission work" (*Daughters*, pp. 133–149). As with the previous stories, women doctors' special mission forms a significant underlying theme in both these tales. In the first the medical student sacrifices her personal happiness for a higher purpose; in the second, Dr. Honora is fortunate enough to find an unusual man willing to share her mission with her. What is also clear is that she sacrifices none of her womanly charm, delicacy, or household responsibility by continuing to practice. In the end, Dr. Honora plays mother to a group of orphans and sick patients with Dr. Bragg's loving, patriarchal approval. It is earned, of course, because her professional aspirations are not selfishly motivated, but come from her dedication to a higher cause.

Daughters of Aesculapius demonstrates in a graphic way the double-edged nature of the ideology that carried many nineteenth-century women into public activity. Though women's public sphere was gradually broadened to include all those aspects of endeavor that could be improved by a feminine perspective, no countervailing role adjustments were made in the private sphere. Women were expected to remain feminine and ladylike in spite of professional training. Thus nineteenth-century assumptions about female nature remained a given. Indeed, women doctors rarely argued that women would be fundamentally changed by medical training; rather, it was medicine that would be altered by the entrance of women. Nowhere is the power of such assumptions demonstrated more clearly than in the esteem bestowed on certain "model" female educators—especially those with children. For example, Emmeline Cleveland, professor of Obstetrics and Diseases of Women at the Woman's Medical College of Pennsylvania from 1862 to 1878 and an important figure among the first generation of women physicians, was not only one of the first reputable women surgeons, but also a nurse to an ailing husband, a mother, and the sole support of her family.

Contemporaries idolized Cleveland as "a womanly woman" who, in spite of myriad professional responsibilities, never slighted her domestic duties. Dean Rachel Bodley loved to retell her own first encounter with Cleveland, one which she believed afforded the "key" to the woman's character. Carrying her small son on her shoulders, Cleveland was descending the stairs of the Woman's Hospital after doing rounds. The two were "beaming the brightest smiles each upon the other," Bodley recalled "and the laughing child and the happy mother constituted a picture fair to look upon" (*Memorial to Emmeline Horton Cleveland*, 1879, pp. 5–16). Such reports of Cleveland's womanliness were always contrasted with her reputed skill and courage as a surgeon, and no doubt both traits eased her success among prominent male colleagues in Philadelphia. Cleveland herself preached the expansion not of women's "rights," but of their "obligations" in an "enlarged" social setting (1859). Her view of herself and her role as a woman physician marks her as one of our first "superwomen." Indeed, it should be clear by now that the stereotypical superwoman was a characteristic invention of the nineteenth century and can be attributed directly to the deeply imbedded gender prescriptions women brought with them when they entered the professional world of that era.

Given the demands made on the physician throughout most of the nineteenth century—the limited range of therapeutic tools, the high valuation placed on the personal interaction between doctor and patient, the tendency to treat whole families, the locus of practice in the home—women physicians managed to make a fairly successful case for their place in the profession. Women who entered medicine, though they had difficulties with overt discriminatory barriers in the beginning, were able to adjust to a new sense of themselves as doctors with relatively little role strain, because much of what was required of them called for "feminine" sympathy, compassion, and self-sacrifice.

The Challenge of Twentieth-Century Medical Professionalism

Such has not been the case for twentieth-century women physicians. Indeed, the period after 1900 has witnessed the gradual appearance of a professional ethos fundamentally at odds with the very qualities nineteenth-century women physicians believed made them better doctors. Before this ethos took hold in the modern period, medicine, like other professions, altered significantly. With the evolution of bacteriology it expanded its monopoly over more and more specialized knowledge, creating powerful professional schools and associations that established higher standards for member admission, training, and certification. Systems of peer review to monitor and regulate practice and a code of ethics that stressed the esoteric nature of scientific knowledge and justified the profession's autonomy from lay interference were also devised. As the complicated nature of modern medical technology helped to shift the locus of medical care from the home to the hospital, doctors in the twentieth century have accrued an extraordinary amount of power, both in the supervision of the division of labor in health care and in the regulation of drugs and therapy. Today's science has given the physician powerful curative tools of which the nineteenth-century physician could only dream. Because doctors can often cure, less and less emphasis has been placed on day-to-day care. With the relegation of such tasks to nurses and ancillary personnel, and the fragmentation of medical knowledge resulting from specialization, the relationship between doctor and patient was fundamentally altered. A successful physician no longer required "the spiritual power of maternity," but the hardnosed rationality of the pure scientist. Little wonder that the stereotypical woman doctor became what Estelle Ramey described—horse-faced, flat-chested, and sex-starved.

Accompanying these changes was the development of a professional ethos that valued aggressiveness, scientific objectivity, careerism, individualism, and "altruistic" commitment to work. Professional expertise, unlike office or industrial employment, commands high status and connotes esoteric knowledge, and for this reason professionals often identify with their work in ways not common to other workers. Professionals are expected to shut out personal considerations—not only their own but their clients'—in the pursuit of rational and efficient devotion to a calling. This drastic change in the work culture of medicine has affected women in two ways. First, changes in the nature of the occupation made medicine in the first half of the twentieth century a less attractive theater for traditional female endeavor. Second, as women's interest in the profession was rekindled in the 1960s and 1970s, medicine's occupational values have ensured certain conflict for women physicians in a number of different areas.

Because most women are still socialized to function primarily in the privacy of the family, where sentiment, intuition, feeling, and interrelatedness predominate, many of those who choose a career in medicine experience uneasiness with values purported to be rational, scientific, and gender neutral, but which are in reality stereotypically masculine. Whether they realize it or not, in this discomfort they are reconnecting with the legacy of their nineteenth-century predecessors. Early women physicians were instinctive critics of the dehumanization inherent in industrialization. They feared the tendency of the capitalist order to turn people into commodities, even as they hailed the positive role of individualism in bringing about female emancipation. From their vantage point as women they quickly comprehended that the rationalization of human knowledge could be carried too far. They brought to medicine a critique of the growing primacy of cure over care, and though their values were ultimately swallowed up in the triumph of twentieth-century medical professionalism, this perception formed the basis of their criticism of the profession to which they so fervently wished to belong (Morantz-Sanchez, 1985).

Contemporary women physicians have continued to find fault with the masculine professional style. Seeking a more nurturing patient-physician interaction, Dr. Carola Eisenberg, dean of student affairs at Harvard Medical School, voiced the opinions of many when she praised women's tendency to show emotion and argued that it could be done without compromising professional identity. "Strength," she urged, "is not incompatible with compassion" (Klemesrud, 1979). "If what is epitomized as 'a good physician' embodies a masculine set of traits and ideals," agreed Dr. Carlotta Rinke, in an article written for the *Journal of the American Medical Association*, "women will invariably suffer an identity crisis in attempting to adapt their womanhood into a male professional model" (1981, p. 2419).

Women physicians who wish to marry and have a family have had to deal not only with a professional ethos at odds with female sensibilities, but a professional work culture tailored to the male life cycle. In 1965 Alice Rossi laid the blame for the shortage of women in science squarely on the inability of most women who chose to be wives and mothers to overcome familial obstacles to pursuing a fulfilling career (1965). Medical sociologists as well have connected the then static numbers of women physicians and their relatively high dropout rate at the time to the difficulty of handling a career along with family responsibilities. Though women doctors marry in the same proportion as women in the general population, they marry later and have fewer children. Twice as many women as male physicians choose salaried positions, and on the whole, they work fewer hours than men (Mandelbaum, 1981). Moreover, marital status and family size are inversely related to career success, with those who publish and achieve high academic rank tending to be single (Westling-Wikstrand, Monk, and Thomas, 1970).

Of course gender prescription has become more flexible in the second half of the twentieth century. The powerful nineteenth-century paradigm of ideal womanhood, which connected women's special mission with their role as mothers, has gradually given way to an ideology of greater equality between men and women. But shifting paradigms have not totally transformed the reality of women's lives. The structure of the American family is being altered only gradually. Moreover, women—married or single—persistently remain culturally identified with familial concerns. Successful women physicians who are mothers are still required to be superwomen, while single women, much more often than their male counterparts, feel forced to choose between marriage and their careers. Professional values have responded only marginally and selectively to female perspectives. Women are seen and still too often see themselves as potential disrupters of the routines of professional life. In truth, women physicians will continue to pay a high price for their professional and personal choices until the ethos and structure of medical education and practice can be altered to accommodate female values and needs in a more fundamental way.

References

Blackwell, E. (1889/1972). The influence of women in the profession of medicine. In E. Blackwell (Ed.), *Essays in medical sociology 2*, 5–12. New York: Arno Press.

————— (1896). *Pioneer work in opening the medical profession to women.* New York: Longman Green.

Clark, M. V. (1915). Medical women's contribution to the education of mothers. *Woman's Medical Journal, 25,* 126–128.

Cleveland, E. (1859). *Introductory lecture to the class of 1858.* Philadelphia: Woman's Medical College of Pennsylvania.

Daughters of Aesculapius. (1897). *Stories written by alumnae and students of the Woman's Medical College of Pennsylvania.* Philadelphia: Woman's Medical College of Pennsylvania.

Hartshorne, H. (1872). *Valedictory address.* Philadelphia: Woman's Medical College of Pennsylvania.

Hunt, A. (1851). *The true physician.* Unpublished thesis. Woman's Medical College of Pennsylvania, Philadelphia.

Hunt, H. (1856). *Glances and glimpses.* Boston: John P. Jewett and Co.

Klemesrud, J. (1979, October 12). Female doctors assess the problems of their profession. *New York Times,* section A, p. 18.

Mandelbaum, D. R. (1981). *Work, marriage and motherhood: The career persistence of female physicians.* New York: Tavistock.

Meigs, C. D. (1848). *Females and their diseases.* Philadelphia: D. G. Brinton.

Memorial to Emmeline Horton Cleveland. (1879). Philadelphia: Woman's Medical College of Pennsylvania.

Morantz-Sanchez, R. (1985). *Sympathy and science: Women physicians in American medicine.* New York: Oxford.

Preston, A. (1858). *Valedictory address.* Philadelphia: Woman's Medical College of Pennsylvania.

Ramey, E. (1971). An interview with Dr. Estelle Ramey. *Perspectives in Biology and Medicine, 14,* 424–431.

Rinke, C. (1981). The professional identities of women physicians. *Journal of the American Medical Association, 245,* 2419.

Rosenberg, C. (1979). The therapeutic revolution: Medicine, meaning and social change in nineteenth-century America. In C. Rosenberg and M. Vogel (Eds.), *The therapeutic revolution: Essays on the social history of American medicine* (pp. 3–26). Philadelphia: University of Pennsylvania Press.

Rossi, A. (1965). Women in science, why so few? *Science, 148.* 1196–1202.

Vietor, A. (1924). *A woman's quest, The life of Marie E. Zakrzewska, M.D.* New York: D. Appleton.

Westling-Wikstrand, H., Monk, M. and Thomas, C. B. (1970). Some characteristics related to the career status of women physicians. *Johns Hopkins Medical Journal, 127,* 273–286.

Woman and Speaker: A Conflict in Roles

11

KARLYN KOHRS CAMPBELL
AND *E. CLAIRE JERRY*

The rhetorical history of women tells the story of the nineteenth-century struggle to obtain the right to speak and to function as moral agents. The struggle demonstrates that public speaking and femininity were perceived as mutually exclusive. Because gender roles persist, contemporary women who seek leadership positions face barriers that make it particularly difficult for them to succeed. This essay examines women's rhetorical history in order to define the conflict between speaking and femininity; it also considers some of the strategies contemporary politicians have used to overcome these continuing role conflicts.

The concept of "true womanhood" (Welter, 1976) or the "woman-belle ideal" (Scott, 1970), which defined females as suited only for gender-based roles as wives and mothers and as a repository for cherished but commercially useless spiritual values, arose in response to the urbanization and industrialization that separated "home" and "work." As this concept reified in the United States between 1820 and 1850, two distinct subcultures emerged. Man's place was public, the realm of the mechanical, political, and monetary, and his "nature" was violent, lustful, and competitive. Woman's place was "home," a haven from amoral capitalism and dirty politics, where "the heart was" and the spiritual and emotional needs of husband and children were met by a "ministering angel." Woman's "nature" was defined as pious, chaste, submissive, and domestic (Welter, 1976).

As defined, woman's role contained a contradiction that surfaced as women responded to the moral evils of prostitution and slavery. Despite their allegedly natural moral superiority, women were censured for acting to remove these evils (Berg, 1978; Hersh, 1978). Women who joined moral reform and abolition societies and made speeches, held conventions, and published newspapers entered the public sphere and thereby lost their claim to purity and piety. What became the woman's rights movement grew out of this contradiction.

The prohibition against public speech and social action was justified from Scripture. Eve, it was claimed, had brought sin into the world by succumbing to the blandishments of the serpent. As a result, she was placed under the dominion of her husband and prohibited from speaking. Women felt this contradiction acutely and argued against this interpretation of Scripture (Stanton, 1892, 1895). These theological disputes reflected a more complex political reality that emerges out of woman's struggle for the right to speak, briefly surveyed below.

The nuances of the prohibition are revealed in the careers of early women speakers. Angelina and Sarah Grimké (Lerner, 1967) began by speaking against slavery to women in homes in New York in 1836, but as their audiences grew, their lectures were moved to church auditoriums. Curious and interested men began to attend. This pattern recurred in Massachusetts in 1837; soon the American Anti-Slavery Society admitted all comers. During that tour, Angelina debated two southern men who challenged her testimony about the condition of slaves in the South. Soon afterward, a "Pastoral Letter of the General Association of Massachusetts to the Congregational Churches Under their Care" was issued. It said: "We invite your attention to the dangers which at present seem to threaten the female character with widespread and permanent injury." The appropriate duties of women, as stated in the New Testament, are "unobstrusive and private. . . . [W]hen she assumes the place and tone of man as a public reformer, . . . her character becomes unnatural. If the vine, whose strength and beauty is to lean upon the trellis-work and half conceal its clusters thinks to assume the independence . . . of the elm, it will not only cease to bear fruit, but fall in shame and dishonor into dust" (Stanton, Anthony, and Gage, 1887, p. 1). Angelina responded: [W]e are placed very unexpectedly in a very trying situation, in the forefront of an entirely new contest—a contest for the rights of woman as a moral, intelligent, and responsible being" (Barnes and Dumond, 1934, p. 415).

The college careers of Lucy Stone and Antoinette Brown are also revealing. While students at Oberlin, they horrified the community by debating each other in a rhetoric class. At graduation, Brown was permitted to deliver an oration to an audience that included men; she had completed a curriculum limited to women; hence, all speakers were women. Lucy Stone was very nearly prevented from graduating when she refused to allow a male faculty member to read her oration; she had taken the regular course and would have shared the platform with males (Gurko, 1976).

These examples, while far from exhaustive, are instructive. The issue was not speaking as such, but speaking to males, speaking on an equal basis with males, speaking that challenged male authority and rationality. Women might seek to influence their families or other women on domestic issues, but when they addressed issues that transcended their immediate families or offered advice to males, women were severely censured.

Women were attacked for their moral reform efforts because rhetorical action is, as defined by gender roles, a masculine domain. Speakers are expert and authoritative; women are submissive. Speakers operate in the public sphere; women's concerns are domestic. Speakers call attention to themselves, aggressively take stands, affirm their expertise; "true women" are retiring, their influence is indirect, they have no expertise on matters outside the home. The public realm is driven by ambition; similarly, speaking is competitive, energized by the desire to persuade others. These are traditionally masculine traits related to man's allegedly lustful, competitive nature. In other words, a woman who speaks affirms her "masculinity"; more precisely, she affirms her possession of qualities that are ascribed only to males. As such, she enacts her equality, which explains the outraged reactions to women speaking to mixed audiences, sharing a platform with male speakers, and debating, even on such issues as slavery and prostitution.

A woman who speaks publicly threatens her audiences by claiming masculine attributes. To diminish this threat, audiences demand that a woman speaker be both masculine and feminine, that she fulfill the traditionally masculine requirements associated with rhetorical action and that, simultaneously, she demonstrate her femininity. Put differently, audiences refuse to accept women simply as speakers; a woman must modify that role so that it is "feminized." Moreover, women are disadvantaged because they experience particular discomfort in speaking having been acculturated to perceive rhetorical action as a violation of their gender role, as "unfeminine" (Campbell, 1983).

The successful woman speaker must fulfill the ordinary requirements of the speaking role, demonstrating expertise, authority, and rationality. But if that is all she does, she will be criticized as "unwomanly," "too aggressive," and "cold." However, if she does not meet these requirements, she will be seen as incompetent and lacking credibility, as "irrational," "sentimental," and "wishy-washy." While there is no longer a prohibition against speaking as such, the gender conflict involved in speaking demands that women continue to find creative solutions to this problem. All professional women experience these difficulties, but the problems of women in politics are particularly acute because speaking is integral to it and because politics is the public realm from which women have traditionally been excluded.

Those who study politicians recognize the special problems women face. Ruth Mandel (1981) argues that the female candidate "still must cope with centuries-old biases—with perceptions that her image is wrong, that someone who looks like her was not made to lead a city, state, or nation or to decide questions of national well-being or international security. She must still cope with her own and society's views about the intersections between private and public life for women—about whether and how to function as both a mother and a mayor, a wife and a senator" (pp. xvii–xviii).

Moreover, this conflict intensifies when a woman faces an incumbent, a common situation as women seek to enter politics: "To assume a posture as challenger, confronter, attacker, she must adopt a mode of behavior she was brought up to consider inappropriate for members of her sex" (Mandel, 1981, p. 41). If the woman candidate does not attack, she cannot win, yet if she attacks, she risks being viewed as shrill, nagging, and "bitchy." Trent and Friedenberg (1983) explain that "the traditional view of women as deferential, soft, and feminine continues to dominate public attitudes. Thus the use of vigorous attacks conflicts with accepted stereotypes of the ideal or typical woman" (p. 115).

A similar problem exists in demonstrating competence. Successful challengers ordinarily push incumbents to offer solutions, but avoid doing so themselves, because defending specific policies enmeshes speakers in details. However, women are at a disadvantage. "To avoid offering solutions may well reinforce the old 'dumb female' stereotype. But when women offer detailed solutions to evidence knowledge and familiarity with issues, they lose the offensive position crucial to challengers" (Trent and Friedenberg, 1983, p. 116).

Finally, female candidates find it more difficult to appeal to traditional values, a standard in campaign rhetoric, because their candidacy contradicts traditional values about women. A profile of the female politician reveals how women have coped with this problem. According to a study by the Center for American Women and Politics at Rutgers University (Williams, 1981), the typical woman candidate who wins office is married, holds a job in addition to running her home, and has two or more children. She is active in community organizations and has completed some graduate work. She is usually not a lawyer, but comes out of a traditional female field such as education or social service. She is forty-eight years old on average and enters politics later in life than most of her male counterparts. In other words, most women are able to run successfully for public office only after they have fulfilled the traditional female role.

Empirical researchers have only begun to study these problems, and work to date can only suggest possibilities. One study found that women speakers were more successful when they adopted noninstitutional positions, i.e., took stances that challenged entrenched beliefs (Bostrom and Kemp, 1969). Conceivably such challenges are perceived as demonstrations of intellectual competence. Another study found that when females derogated their opponents, they were perceived as more extroverted and credible than males using the same strategy (Burgoon, Wilkinson, and Partridge, 1979), a finding suggesting that the traditional notion of female moral authority may have some benefits in political campaigns. Still another study has confirmed that women must use "low intensity" language that does not confirm preconceptions of women as irrational and emotional, stereotypic views that contradict the requirements for successful speaking (Burgoon, Jones, and Stewart, 1975). At most, these studies provide minimal guidance for achieving women. However, the political careers of two well-known female politicians suggest more detailed guidelines for success in speaking.

Like most female candidates, Geraldine Ferraro was both a traditional and nontraditional woman. A wife and mother who took primary responsibility for raising her three children, she worked as a public schoolteacher, yet she kept her birth name, completed law school, and went into private practice, later becoming an assistant district attorney. In 1978 she was elected to the first of three terms in the U.S. House of Representatives and served on the House Budget and the Public Works and Transportation Committees. She was active in the House Democratic Caucus and in the Democratic party, serving as chairperson of the Platform Committee for the 1984 National Democratic Convention.

How Ferraro dealt with the rhetorical problems of being a woman can be seen from looking at speeches delivered during her 1984 vice-presidential campaign. Ferraro demonstrated competence by referring to experiences that qualified her for office. In her convention acceptance speech, Ferraro linked her past to the issue of law and order: "I became an assistant district attorney, and I put my share of criminals behind bars" (7/21/84). At St. Louis (7/19/84), she referred to "my pension reform bill," and in New York (9/24/84) she said she could talk about Congress "from an insider's point of view."

Ferraro rejected the notion that her sex rendered her unsuitable for high political office. In the vice-presidential debate (1984) she answered John Mashek's question about her competence this way:

It is not only what is on your paper resume that makes you qualified to run for or to hold office. It's how you approach problems and what your values are. I think if one has taken a look at my career, they'll see that I level with the people, that I approach problems analytically, that I am able to assess various facts with reference to a problem, and I can make the hard decisions (p. 3).

Ferraro was asserting her ability to lead. The dilemma of the woman speaker was evident in *Newsweek*'s report on the debate, which concluded: "It was as if, having breached the last male preserve in our politics, she were trying to show that she was man enough to be president" (Goldman, 1984, p. 108).

Although attacking an opponent is incompatible with the conception of women as passive and submissive, Ferraro's speeches were replete with attacks on Reagan. At St. Louis, she claimed that voters "aren't about to be fooled by an anti-feminist administration," and she called Reagan's tax policies "unfair." In New York she said: "I want a President who stops putting our money where his mouth is." Recalling Reagan's congratulatory remarks to female athletes at the Olympics, Ferraro (9/24/84) contrasted what he said with his policies toward women: "I want to help women get to the starting block, not just pat them on the back after they cross the finish line." At Vanderbilt University (10/2/84), the attack was more intense: "[T]his President had the gall to blame his predecessors for the tragedy in Beirut." In St. Louis, she challenged Reagan: "[W]ith so much at stake, I won't close my mouth until he opens up his secret plan and tells the American people exactly how he's going to bring deficits down."

While such attacks violate the traditional female role, a woman's use of this strategy may enhance her perceived credibility and competence (Burgoon, Wilkinson, and Partridge, 1979). Right up to election day, Ferraro repeatedly drew crowds of 8,000 and more; crowds came to hear her speak because they liked her style, suggesting that such attacks made her appear extroverted and attractive to audiences.

Ferraro appealed to traditional values as illustrated by her slogan, "the housewife from Queens." In her speeches, she referred to her family. Her acceptance speech began with recollections of her life as the daughter of an immigrant and ended with a reference to her husband and children. In several speeches, when discussing military policy, she asked: "What will happen to my son John and to your children and grandchildren?" In a speech in New York, she spoke of the daughter who had recently joined a brokerage house. She said: "Donna turned to me and said: 'Don't worry, Mom. I won't lose my social conscience.' I know she won't. And as a country I know we can't." She even transformed her nontraditional history into an argument for traditional American values: "Later, I taught in the New York City Public School system by day, and went to Law School by night, so that I could achieve my ambition of becoming a lawyer. That was hard work, but we had a society of opportunity that rewarded hard work" (Long Beach, Calif. 9/3/84). Ferraro's theme, "I am an immigrant's daughter and I made it," translated her ambition and achievement, violations of female norms, into validation of the American dream.

Ferraro met rhetorical requirements by using evidence, analysis, and reasoning effectively. Typically, her speeches were clearly structured; most had an overview, many included the same four points she outlined in her speech at Long Beach:

In at least four crucial ways, the choice you make in November will affect your lives, directly and personally, for years to come. First, there is the choice of war and peace. . . . Second, we need a President who levels with us about the tough things we must do to ensure our future. . . . Third, we need an economy that works for us all. . . . Finally, in the future Fritz Mondale wants to build, government stays out of our private lives.

She frequently used internal summaries to remind the audience of what she had been saying (St. Louis) and usually developed conclusions that recapped her major ideas (Seattle).

The language of Ferraro's speeches was vivid, contradicting the finding that women are more effective if their style is less intense. In New York, she labeled the deficit a "crisis [that] threatens to topple our entire banking system and take the whole financial system down with it" and the President a "profligate spender." She contended that social programs had been "decimated." In Seattle, she said: "Anyone who believes that refining the murder techniques of Central Americans will advance our national interests is gravely mistaken." She created memorable phrases, e.g., "Stop exchanging insults and start exchanging negotiating proposals" (St. Louis) and "We need a president who will stop investing so much in the arms race and start investing more in the human race" (New Jersey). Alliteration made some phrases more vivid, e.g., "Since December of last year the dust has been gathering on the diplomatic tables" (New Jersey). She asked rhetorical questions, such as "Can we take charge of our own economic future?" (St. Louis) and "The question is, will we continue to be that kind of society? Or will success become the privilege of the few?" (Long Beach). Parallelism and antitheses were prominent features. In her acceptance speech, she made seven promises, each introduced with the phrase, "To those . . . we say." In St. Louis, she gave seven definitions of patriotism, each of which took the form "When [we do x] . . . that will be a patriotic act." Ferraro's choices are those of an experienced public speaker who understands audiences and how symbols function in oral discourse.

The most severe test of the Ferraro campaign came over her tax returns. Her ninety-minute press conference (8/21/84) was a triumph that ended in a standing ovation from the assembled journalists. She demonstrated that she could answer all their questions without becoming rattled or dissolving into tears. She met a stringent political test about her competence for office; she also met an even more stringent test—whether or not a woman candidate could withstand the kind of pressure that can be generated in a presidential campaign (Ferraro, 1985, pp. 157–82).

The requirements of speaking and governing compel women like Ferraro to violate traditional norms of femininity. Commenting on their findings about such women, Kelly and Boutilier (1978) note: "We assume that, compared to traditional women, politically active women will be more assertive, competitive, concerned with social justice, and more likely to possess personality traits that have historically been considered 'masculine' " (p. 24). Research has yet to demonstrate that adopting masculine characteristics is the optimum choice for a woman speaker, but Ferraro showed that such qualities can be combined with traditional female role requirements to produce effective rhetoric.

Nancy Landon Kassebaum, the first woman to be elected to the Senate in her own right, is another case study of the successful woman speaker and public figure. Like Ferraro, she fulfilled traditional female role requirements prior to entering politics by marrying and raising four children. She violated convention by divorcing, and she holds an advanced degree in diplomatic history. She had the political advantage of being a millionaire and having a family name that is known and admired in her home state. As her campaign slogan in 1978 said, she was "A Fresh Face, a Trusted Kansas Name." She beat a male Democratic candidate who had come close to defeating Robert Dole in 1974, and she was easily re-elected in 1984.

Kassebaum's success is noteworthy because she has taken stands on issues of special interest to women, including favoring a woman's right to choose abortion and passage of the ERA. Although she represents a conservative state, she has taken positions that diverge from the Republican party line on these and other issues, favoring the Panama Canal Treaty and sanctions against South Africa, and against single-issue constitutional amendments, such as those for school prayer and balancing the budget. She told her important farm constituents in Kansas that she would vote for higher grain prices but could not support government-established parity prices. Despite her unorthodox views, her work in the Senate has been highly praised by her colleagues, a confirmation of research that women can be successful in taking "non-institutional" stands (Bostrom and Kemp, 1969).

Kassebaum faced liabilities as a woman (Ashner, 1984). During her first campaign her quiet, "feminine" demeanor was criticized on the grounds that she did not have the aggressiveness needed to stand up to men. She responded: "A quiet voice can be a decisive voice" (p. 5). She separated from her husband prior to that campaign, but she did not officially divorce until after her election. Despite her wealth and position, she dressed with extreme simplicity, and throughout her 1978 campaign she appeared in a tailored, gray, "dress-for-success" suit.

Analysis of Kassebaum's speeches during her first Senate term provides important clues about how she integrated the conflicting demands facing a woman in the "masculine" roles of speaker and Senator (Ashner, 1984). Like Ferraro, she is rhetorically adept. She tends to support her claims with large amounts of evidence, to structure her speeches clearly, and to lay out carefully developed, logical arguments, as illustrated in the speech she made opposing a naval blockade of Iran (4/21/80). She questioned whether such a move would attain its object—the release of the American hostages, and outlined reasons why such action would be irresponsible: it might strengthen Iranian resolve and increase the chances that the hostages would be executed; it would disrupt world oil markets and might provoke intense anti-American hostility throughout the Islamic world.

She uses vivid language to make her ideas memorable, but she avoids usage that might be labeled sentimental or emotional, as illustrated by her speech on Amelia Earhart day (2/24/82): "Everyone has his [sic] own Atlantic to fly. Whatever you want very much to do, against the opposition of tradition, neighborhood opinion, and so-called common sense—that is an Atlantic."

Kassebaum's speeches illustrate another resource available to women speakers. A woman can "feminize" the rhetorical role, as Ferraro did, or she can assume a rhetorical *persona* or role that is less strictly genderbound. Based on Ashner's study, Kassebaum ordinarily assumed rhetorical roles that fell within the female repertoire, most frequently that of teacher or mediator. The teaching role allowed her to speak authoritatively and to use her expertise in an acceptably "feminine" way. The role of mediator permitted her to explore controversial issues and take unpopular stands. For example, she assumed the role of teacher in her speech, "The United States in Central America: Aid or Intervention?" (6/6/83). She briefly surveyed the history of U.S. involvement in the area and then examined the suspect analogy between Vietnam and El Salvador. She pushed her audience to rethink their views as she carried the analogy to its logical conclusion. She asked: "Are we by gradually increasing our involvement responding in exactly the way the guerrillas want?"

She assumed the role of mediator in analyzing U.S. policies regarding trade with Japan (1982). After detailing the data that underlie the case against Japan, she said: "This litany infuriates many Americans and not without reason. But, as is so often the case, there is another side to the story which leaves one wondering if the glass is half full or half empty." What followed briefly surveyed the Japanese case against the United States and reminded the audience that Japan is the largest export market for U.S. goods. Her conclusion was: "We have a web of relationships with Japan which does not lend itself to simple judgments but invites false conclusions."

These are strategic choices, as audiences tend to accept women as teachers, because teachers are perceived as nurturing, and as mediators, because mothers mediate between the conflicting needs of husbands and children. These role choices were buttressed by Kassebaum's general rhetorical skill and by a coherent political philosophy. But her speechmaking was noteworthy for exploiting the roles of mediator and teacher/expert in order to resolve the contradictory demands placed on women speakers.

The examples of Ferraro and Kassebaum are both daunting and reassuring. Each has exceptional talents as a speaker and politician that are difficult for other women to emulate. Yet each has found ways to synthesize the contradictory gender demands placed on women politicians.

Lest their successes be too reassuring, the career of Jeane Kirkpatrick, U.S. Ambassador to the United Nations during the Reagan Administration, provides a cautionary tale. In a speech to the Women's Forum of New York City (1984), Kirkpatrick reflected on her experiences. She spoke of reactions to her speaking:

Now, the United Nations is an institution which specializes in talking: It's a place where people make speeches and listen to speeches. But if I make a speech, particularly a substantial speech, it has been frequently described in the media as "lecturing my colleagues," as though it were somehow peculiarly inappropriate, like an ill-tempered schoolmarm might scold her children. When I have replied to criticisms of the United States (which is an important part of my job), I have frequently been described as "confrontational.". . . In the beginning I thought that I was described as "confrontational" because we adopted a policy inside the United Nations that, when the United States was publicly attacked, we would defend ourselves. . . . I now think that being tagged as "confrontational" and being a woman in a high position are very closely related. There is a certain level of office the very occupancy of which constitutes a confrontation with conventional expectations. . . . I've come to see here a double-bind: if a woman seems strong, she is called "tough"; and if she doesn't seem strong, she's found not strong enough to occupy a high level job in a crunch. Terms like "tough" and "confrontational" express a certain very general surprise and disapproval at the presence of a woman in arenas in which it is necessary to be—what for males would be considered—normally assertive.

Kirkpatrick's experiences demonstrate the great difficulties women face in leadership positions and the obstacles they face in finding speaking roles that meet the contradictory demands of their audiences. As long as gender roles persist, women will need extraordinary skill to speak effectively, and however skillful they may be, female speakers will be trapped between criticism based on feminine stereotypes and charges of "masculinity."

References

Ashner, L. R. (1984). *Nancy Landon Kassebaum: Speaker and senator.* Unpublished honors thesis, Department of Communication Studies, University of Kansas.

Barnes, G. H. and Dumond, D. L. (Eds.) (1934). *Letters of Theodore Dwight Weld, Angelina Grimké Weld, and Sarah Grimké, 1822–1844* (vol. 1). Gloucester, Mass.: Peter Smith.

Berg, B. J. (1978). *The remembered gate: Origins of American feminism; The woman and the city 1800–1860.* New York: Oxford University Press.

Bostrom, R. and Kemp, A. P. (1969). Type of speech, sex of speaker, and sex of subject as factors influencing persuasion. *Central States Speech Journal, 20,* 245–251.

Burgoon, J. K., Wilkinson, M., and Partridge, R. (1979). The relative effectiveness of praise and derogation as persuasion strategies. *Journal of the American Forensic Association, 16,* 10–20.

Burgoon, M. J., Jones, S. B., and Stewart, D. (1975). Toward a message-centered theory of persuasion: Three empirical investigations of language intensity. *Human Communication Research, 1,* 240–256.

Campbell, K. K. (1983). Femininity and feminism: To be or not to be a woman. *Communication Quarterly, 31,* 101–108.

Ferraro, G. Transcripts of speeches: St. Louis (7/19/84), Long Beach (9/3/84), Association for a Better New York (9/24/84), Vanderbilt University (10/2/84), University of Washington at Seattle (10/17/84), remarks on nuclear freeze in New Jersey (undated), vice-presidential debate (10/11/84).

—— (7/21/84). Nomination acceptance speech. *Congressional Quarterly*, pp. 1794–1795.

Ferraro, G., with Francke, L. B. (1985). *Ferraro: My story*. New York: Bantam.

Goldman, P. (1984, November/December). Campaign '84: The inside story. *Newsweek*, pp. 32–112.

Gurko, M. (1976). *The ladies of Seneca Falls: The birth of the woman's rights movement*. New York: Schocken Books.

Hersh, B. G. (1978). *The slavery of sex: Feminist abolitionists in America*. Urbana: University of Illinois Press.

Kassebaum, N. L. (4/21/80). Naval blockade of Iran. *Congressional Record*, pp. 2952–2953.

—— (2/24/82). Amelia Earhart day. *Congressional Record*, pp. 1142–1143.

—— Transcripts of speeches: United States and Japan—A troubled partnership, University of Kansas at Lawrence (11/4/82), The United States in Central America: Aid or Intervention? Washington, D.C. (6/6/83).

Kelly, R. M. and Boutilier, M. (1978). *The making of political women*. Chicago: Nelson-Hall.

Kirkpatrick, J. (12/19/84). Remarks to the Women's Forum, New York, N.Y.

Lerner, G. (1967). *The Grimké sisters from South Carolina: Pioneers for woman's rights and abolition*. New York: Schocken Books.

Mandel, R. B. (1981). *In the running: The new woman candidate*. Boston: Beacon Press.

Scott, A. F. (1970). *The southern lady: From pedestal to politics, 1830–1930*. Chicago: University of Chicago Press.

Stanton, E. C. (1892, 1895; rpt. 1974). The woman's Bible. Seattle, Wash.: Coalition Task Force on Women and Religion.

Stanton, E. C., Anthony, S. B., and Gage, M. J. (1887). *History of woman suffrage*, I, 1848–1861. Rochester, N.Y.: Charles Mann.

Trent, J. S. and Friedenberg, R. V. (1983). *Political campaign communication*. New York: Praeger.

Welter, B. (1976). *Dimity convictions: The American woman in the nineteenth century*. Athens: Ohio University Press.

Williams, B. (1981). *Breakthrough: Women in politics*. New York: Walker and Company.

Women in Newsrooms: Pink-collar Ghetto or Brave New World? 12

DOROTHY BOWLES

Newspaper reporting and editing jobs were not readily available for women in the United States for more than two hundred years after the first newspapers were published in this country, although in 1702 in London, a woman, Elizabeth Mallet, had founded the first daily newspaper in the English language (Marzolf, 1977). By the late nineteenth century, U.S. newspapers began to cast aside their preoccupation with politics and to include human interest stories plus "society" pages designed to capitalize on department store advertising aimed at housewives. This prompted publishers to hire a few women reporters because women were considered suitable for writing "soft" stories. These new reporters were often assigned the role of "sob sisters," specializing in tear-jerking accounts of news events. In highly competitive newspaper towns, particularly New York City, a few especially daring women became "stunt" reporters in the Nellie Bly mode, undertaking all sorts of dangerous exploits and writing first-person accounts of their experiences. During the Spanish-American War, New York City newspapers had women reporters in Cuba to focus on the "women's angle" of the war (Beasley and Gibbons, 1977).

In 1910, the U.S. Census Bureau reported 4,000 women employed full-time as journalists—including all areas of journalism, not just newspapers—and by the end of World War I, this number had jumped to about 12,000. A few, such as Rheta Childe Dorr, had escaped the confines of the women's pages or sob sister reporter to work as war correspondents in Europe (Dorr, 1924) or as news reporters at home. Writing in 1936, Ishbel Ross, who had a brief but distinguished career at the New York *Tribune* during the 1920s and 1930s, said of the front-page "girls":

On the whole, newspaper women make few demands on their city editors. They would gladly work for nothing, rather than be denied the city room.... But the highest compliment to which the deluded creatures respond is the city editor's acknowledgment that their work is just like a man's. This automatically gives them a complacent glow, for they are all aware that no right-minded editor wants the so-called woman's touch in the news. The fact remains that they never were thoroughly welcome in the city room and they are not quite welcome now. They are there on sufferance, although the departments could scarcely get along without them. But if the front-page girls were all to disappear tomorrow no searching party would go out looking for more, since it is the fixed conviction of nearly every newspaper executive that a man in the same spot would be exactly twice as good (p. 13).

Relatively few reporters—male or female—had formal journalistic training during the pre-World War II era. When universities did begin to add journalism to their curricula, women students were given little encouragement to enter the field. The idea of admitting women to the Columbia University School of Journalism, for example, was met in 1912 with the response that a girl in the classroom would interfere with the learning of the boys and that any boy who could learn with a girl in the room would never grow up to be a man (*Press Woman*, 1985, December). Journalism students at Ohio State University were told in 1940 that "women don't have any more chance for jobs on newspapers than Jews have of surviving in Germany" (quoted in *Press Woman*, 1985, December, p. 4).

World War II was a turning point for women in the newspaper business. A woman who had been moved from women's news to general reporting on a Kansas newspaper wrote in 1941 (as quoted in *Press Woman*, 1985, December, p. 4):

The selective service act is giving women their long-sought opportunity to do general reporting. . . . Now taking the place of a man who has been drafted, I am working with the more drastic complications of deaths, accidents, rains, and community speakers. My conclusion is that the men have been impressing us with a false importance of their jobs.

Women reporters received help from Eleanor Roosevelt when from 1933 to 1945 she restricted attendance at her press conferences to females only, thus insuring that women reporters would have both a source of news not available to men competitors and a forum for topics that, as Mrs. Roosevelt put it, "might be of special interest and value to the women of the country and that women reporters might write up better than men" (Beasley, 1983). In 1959, women reporting Washington politics got help from, of all people, Nikita Khrushchev, who was invited to address the National Press Club, where women were barred from the newsmaker luncheons. The Women's Press Club, then led by Helen Thomas of United Press International, prodded the Soviet premier into refusing the invitation unless women were allowed to attend. The club finally admitted a few women to hear the talk.

At the time of the incident, long-time Washington presswoman Liz Carpenter sent a letter to the Senate Foreign Relations Committee: "It's a helluva note when we have to beg the Russians for our rights" (Roper, 1985, p. 44).

By the middle of the twentieth century, women in the newspaper world had made giant strides toward acceptance, but still all was not right with that world. An informant-based study (Strainchamps, 1974) provides a glimpse into the newspaper business in New York City during the late 1960s and early 1970s. Editorial employees at New York City daily newspapers work under contracts negotiated by The Newspaper Guild with no variations for sex differences, making hiring and promotion policies at those papers among the most enlightened in the industry. A few examples of discrimination faced by women on those "enlightened" newspapers give us a clue about how bad the situation was on typical nonunion daily papers across the nation.

—A woman with excellent grades from one of the Seven-Sister schools applied to the New York *Daily News* for a summer trainee position only to be told that she wasn't qualified because she wasn't a man.

—Women at the *Long Island Press*, including those with previous experience as war correspondents and other hard news reporting for other papers, were almost automatically assigned to the women's department.

—Women starting as editorial assistants in women's news were allowed to stagnate in those jobs for years while young men starting as clerks were promoted quickly through the ranks.

—Women who managed to get out of the women's department were routinely assigned less important stories than male reporters. Such practices, of course, limited opportunities for merit pay raises and for career advancement.

—From their male co-workers, women were repeatedly subjected to sexist comments, such as, "When did you get laid last?" How often do you have an orgasm?"

—At the Associated Press, one of the wire services that supplies much of the national and international news published in daily newspapers, no woman headed a single one of the 171 bureaus in the worldwide network during the 1960s and 1970s; the association's New York headquarters had never had more than one woman reporter at any one time; the general desk, which is the control center for all outgoing news, hired its first woman since World War II in 1969.

During the late 1960s and early 1970s, the numbers of women editorial employees at the "enlightened" New York City newspapers are also revealing. For example, the New York *Daily News*, the newspaper with the largest circulation in the Western Hemisphere at that time, employed only one female on its staff of seventy some photographers, and she had been hired during World War II when men were scarce. The entire copy clerk staff was male. There were no women city or suburban editors, no women on the wire desk, no women executives in any management area (Strain-champs, 1974). Of approximately four hundred reporters, editors, and photographers at the *Daily News* in 1970 only thirty-five reporters were women, twenty-six of whom worked in the women's department (Komisar, 1970). Women did, however, occupy most of the clerical positions.

Social and legal factors have forced newspaper executives to improve their hiring practices toward both women and minorities during the past two decades. The most potent of the legal factors was Title VII of the Civil Rights Act of 1964 (42 U.S.C. Sec. 2000). Armed with this legal tool and encouraged by the impetus of the re-emerging women's movement, women employees brought complaints against several major newspapers, including the *Washington Post* and the *New York Times*. In addition, women and black employees and the Wire Service Guild brought suit in 1973 against the Associated Press. Evidence of sex and race discrimination emerged from most of these suits, leading offending firms—either under court order or through out-of-court settlements—to adopt affirmative action plans (Beasley and Gibbons, 1977; Butler and Paisley, 1980; Stevens, 1985).

During the 1970s and early 1980s, U.S. newspapers hired many more women. In 1971, 22.4 percent of the journalists at daily newspapers were women (Johnstone, Slawski, and Bowman, 1976); by 1982 that figure had risen to 34.4 percent (Weaver and Wilhoit, 1986). At weekly papers, 27.1 percent of the editorial employees were women in 1971; 42.1 percent were female in 1982. By mid-decade, women journalists in all media were disproportionately clustered in the twenty-five- to thirty-four-year-old age bracket, however, and they were a decade behind in terms of the proportion of women employed in the total U.S. labor force (Weaver and Wilhoit, 1986). In the mid–1980s, university schools and departments of journalism and mass communications reported that women comprised nearly 60 percent of their students.

The recent influx of women into the daily newspaper job market led to speculation that the field might become a "pink-collar ghetto" with already low salaries being kept artificially low and leading to an exodus of men from the field (Beasley, 1985). This notion was quickly denounced by some newspaper people (Lawrence, 1986; Clabes, 1986). Women in news jobs continue to be paid less than men, but the gap is narrowing. A 1981 survey showed the median male-female salary disparity for news people in all media at 40 percent (Weaver and Wilhoit, 1986), an improvement from the 55 percent difference a decade earlier (Johnstone, Slawski, and Bowman, 1976). Part of the overall disparity can be explained by differential experience, because many of the women are in entry-level jobs where male-female salary differences have almost disappeared (Weaver and Wilhoit, 1986).

A chief concern in the mid–1980s was to move women through the newspaper ranks and into management positions. Recognizing that concern, the American Society of Newspaper Editors devoted an entire issue of its monthly magazine to the topic in January 1986, noting that only 11.7 percent of the policymaking positions on daily papers in 1985 were occupied by females, a percentage that had remained relatively stable during the previous five years. Although several large media groups have actively recruited and trained women and minorities for management positions, figures from the Bureau of Labor Statistics show that newspapers lag far behind business and industry in general, where 32.4 percent of the executives, administrators, and managers in 1984 were women (*ASNE Bulletin*, 1984, November/December).

The same factors that have worked to impede career progress for women in other occupations—sex discrimination and family demands on time and energy—have resulted in fewer women than men being prepared for management positions. Al Neuharth, chairman of the Gannett Company, which owns more than ninety U.S. daily newspapers, is quoted as saying, "Men are often promoted on the basis of their potential because they're bright young guys who are going somewhere. Women are most often promoted on the basis of their performance. They have to prove it first. Well, that ought to change" (Jurney, 1986, April/May).

In the newspaper business, movement up the newspaper ladder requires frequent geographical moves. Janet Chusmir, former assistant managing editor for features at the *Miami Herald* and now president and publisher of the Boulder (Colo.) *Daily Camera*, notes that some publishers hold nineteenth-century attitudes in assuming that a married woman would not be willing to relocate (1986). Research has shown that men and women in the 1980s are essentially the same in their attitudes about moving when the move means a promotion (Ogan, 1983). According to Nancy Woodhull, a senior editor for *USA Today*, women, like men, make job-change decisions on an economic basis, but "too often, the package offered to a woman is as though she's still practicing, not as though she has expertise" (Chusmir, 1986, p. 21).

That newspapers continue to lag behind other industries in promoting women to management positions may be attributable at least in part to conditions unique to the news business. Susan Miller, director of editorial development for Scripps Howard Newspapers, discussed some of those conditions in the January 1986 *ASNE Bulletin*. The hours that news people work was at the top of her list. Most American newspapers are written and edited in the evening hours, go to press about midnight, and are transported in the early morning hours to distribution points in time for home and newsstand delivery by 6:00 A.M. or earlier. And newspapers don't stop publishing on weekends. Not only is night and weekend work not conducive to family life, it makes it difficult to develop significant personal relationships with people who work "normal" hours, leading many newspaper journalists to socialize with their colleagues and to choose one of them as their partner (Weaver and Wilhoit, 1986). This choice, in turn, can lead to other problems if one of the partners is faced with the alternatives of either relocating or passing up a career-advancing opportunity.

The uniqueness of the newspaper business also affects decisions about relocation. Difficult as it is for any two-career family where frequent relocation is a requisite for career advancement, the problems are compounded if both people work for a newspaper because almost no U.S. city today has more than one daily newspaper. Thus, for the two-journalist household, there is only one potential employer in town. Unless that newspaper just happens to have two openings at the same time, is willing to hire both partners, and doesn't have anti-nepotism rules, one person is out of work.[1] Even if both people can secure jobs at the paper, one of them is likely to face a career setback.

While men and women journalists do not differ much with respect to education, race, religious background, or political party preferences, female journalists are less likely than male journalists to be married (42 percent versus 62 percent) and are less likely to have children (65 percent versus 75 percent) (Weaver and Wilhoit, 1986). Eileen Saunders, who teaches "Media and Gender" at Carleton University in Ottawa, Canada, points out:

Women find it very difficult in journalism to reconcile their working life and their domestic life [in a profession that has irregular hours at best]. . . . Affirmative action without some kind of adjustments in the working cycle does not do much for women. It just puts more stress on those women. . . . The thing to do is restructure the working cycle—allow women to work reasonable hours within journalism and yet at the same time have a reasonable semblance of a home life (*CDNPA/CMEC Newsletter*, 1985, p. 2).

The newspaper industry has been slow to provide or help employees secure child-care facilities or to adopt alternative work arrangements such as telecommuting, flextime, or job sharing, all of which would be advantageous to career women (Newsom, 1986). Finding safe and affordable child care is virtually impossible for mothers who report for work at about the time that most day-care centers close. Fortunately, leaders in the newspaper industry are beginning to consider child care and alternative work arrangements. By mid–1986, at least one newspaper was operating an on-site child-care facility, several papers were experimenting with nontraditional work arrangements, and the American Newspaper Publishers Association had appointed a committee to consider these issues. Changes in work arrangements may lead to more woman being able to accommodate newspaper careers with marriage and family.

Will a greater percentage of women reporters and editors change the product that is delivered to the newspaper-reading public? On the premise that society acculturates men to be more attuned to conflict, controversy, and confrontation and women to be more attuned to harmony and community, a University of Maryland study (Beasley, 1985) questioned whether the influx of women into policy-making jobs would lead to a "softening" of the news and an abandonment of the "watchdog" role of the press in favor of a "community-building" function. In fact, little systematic research has been conducted on gender-based differences among media managers, and research from other professions is inconclusive as to whether women and men differ as managers (Pearson, 1985). Some studies have suggested that women in management may hold those characteristics, attitudes, and temperaments more commonly ascribed to men (Schein, 1973, 1975). Indeed, a study of how men and women edit "women's news" suggested that female newspaper editors pay less attention than male editors to covering women's issues, perhaps because they believe that career advancement is dependent on conformity with the values of their primarily male superiors (Reich, 1983). Another study found that male and female reporters did not differ in their desire to participate in on-the-job decision-making, but that female editors were more accepting than males of a democratic work environment (Joseph, 1982).

The 1985 University of Maryland study—promptly dubbed the "pink-collar ghetto" report—drew heated criticism from newspaper editors and executives. The reaction of Linda Cunningham, executive editor at the Trenton (N.J.) *Times*, was typical: "Hogwash. Spend 15 minutes in this newsroom and then tell me the women around here are less demanding or more inclined to believe unquestioningly what their sources tell them. . . . News is news; it has no sex" (Miller, 1985, p. 32). Editor Judith G. Clabes wrote, "The idea that a female majority in a traditionally all-male domain will demean the profession is the worst kind of sexism" (1986, p. 5).

Another change among newspaper editors and publishers in the 1980s includes their traditional notions about what is newsworthy. Content analysis reveals such changes in media coverage of women and topics traditionally thought to be of greater interest to women than to men (Butler and Paisley, 1980). Veteran newsmen say that the presence of women in newsrooms has increased sensitivity to news of special concern to women and children (Weaver and Wilhoit, 1986). These content changes may be as much a reaction to other factors—society's relaxation of gender-based roles and competition from electronic media, for example—as to the influx of women into the newspaper business. Research has indicated that basic agenda patterns vary more according to age than to sex differences; women and men under age forty show few differences in attention patterns to media content (Graber, 1978). As Judith Clabes said in response to the University of Maryland study: "It is part of the maturing process in this business. . . . We are beginning to understand that social conditions, trends, background and thoughtful interpretations are part of the mix of responsible journalism. . . . This has nothing to do with gender" (Clabes, 1986, July 1, p. 4).

Newspapers, driven by their profit motive, aren't likely to move faster than society as a whole in integrating women into their news coverage or into their work force. Women managers may bring greater diversity to newspaper content, but they aren't going to abandon the traditional information dissemination-interpretation-adversary roles of the press. In fact, the importance that news people are thought to place on the adversarial or watchdog function as a determinant of newsworthiness may have been exaggerated. In the largest survey of news people ever undertaken (Weaver and Wilhoit, 1986), only 17 percent said they thought the adversarial role was most important. In addition, the factor most often mentioned as influencing journalists' concept of newsworthiness was journalistic training. More than 77 percent of the daily newspaper journalists interviewed said that their concept of what was newsworthy came from their college and on-the-job training. This finding lends support to the idea that women in newspaper management aren't likely to hold significantly different views than men about what is newsworthy because managers of both sexes have had similar journalistic training, and that training is dominated by men.[2] In short, newspapers mirror society. So long as male managers and male teachers dominate the profession, the interests and attitudes of men will prevail. Only when the society itself values women and their attitudes and interests more will the perspective of the newsroom—and the content of the newspaper—change accordingly.

Notes

1. The abandonment of anti-nepotism rules is an encouraging sign in the newspaper business. The *Kansas City Star* and *Times*, for example, abandoned such rules in 1984 when faced with the potential loss of two editors who married each other (Langley, 1984).

2. In 1972, the proportion of women on college and university journalism faculties was less than 8 percent; by 1984, that number had increased to 17 percent (Sharp, et al., 1985).

References

ASNE Bulletin (1984, November/December). Newspapers lag behind most other fields in promoting women to management, 35.

Beasley, M. (Ed.) (1983). *The White House press conferences of Eleanor Roosevelt.* New York: Garland Publishing Inc.

———— (1985). *The new majority: A look at what the preponderance of women in journalism education means to the schools and to the profession.* Report of the Women's Project, College of Journalism, University of Maryland, College Park, Maryland.

Beasley, M. and Gibbons, S. (1977). *Women in media: A documentary source book.* Washington, D.C.: Women's Institute for Freedom of the Press.

Butler, M. and Paisley, W. (1980). *Women and the mass media: Sourcebook for research and action*. New York: Human Sciences Press.

CDNPA/CMEC Newsletter. (1985, November/December). Media's working cycle holds back women. Toronto: Canadian Daily Newspaper Publishers Association, *13*, 2.

Chusmir, J. (1986, January). Women will move—if the offer is too good to refuse. *ASNE Bulletin*, 21.

Clabes, J. G. (1986, January). Pink collar causes editor to see red. *Press Woman*, 4–5.

——— (1986, January). What is an editor, anyway? *ASNE Bulletin*, 3–6.

——— (1986, July 1). Study examines "new majority." *AESMC News* 4.

Dorr, R. C. (1924). *A woman of fifty*. New York: Funk and Wagnalls.

Graber, D. A. (1978). Agenda-setting: Are there women's perspectives? In L. K. Epstein (Ed.), *Women and the news* (pp. 15–37). New York: Hastings House.

Johnstone, J. W. C., Slawski, E. J., and Bowman, W. W. (1976). *The news people: A sociological portrait of American journalists and their work*. Urbana: University of Illinois Press.

Joseph, T. (1982). Reporters' and editors' preferences toward reporter decision making. *Journalism Quarterly, 59*, 219–222.

Jurney, D. (1984, November/December). Women editors advance to 11.1 percent—but the numerical total barely moves. *ASNE Bulletin*, 32–35.

——— (1986, January). Percentage of women editors creeps upward to 11.7—but other fields continue to progress faster. *ASNE Bulletin*, 8–9.

——— (1986, April/May). The good news is progress. The bad news is not much. *The Professional Communicator*, 20–21.

Komisar, L. (1970). Women in the media. In *Sixteen reports on the status of women in the professions*. Presented at the Professional Woman's Caucus, New York University Law School, Pittsburgh: KNOW, Inc.

Langley, M. (1984, October 16). Office marriages win more firms' blessings, but problems crop up. *Wall Street Journal*, A1.

Lawrence, D. (1986, January). The myth of the pink collar ghetto. *Washington Journalism Review*, 21–23.

Marzolf, M. (1977). *Up from the footnote*. New York: Hastings House.

Miller, S. (1985, November 23). Was "Pink Collar" ghetto study deliberate sensationalism? *Editor & Publisher*, *52*, 32–33.

——— (1986, January). What women—and their bosses—should do to keep women climbing up the management ladder. *ASNE Bulletin*, 13–14, 18–20.

Newsom, C. (1986, May). Alternative arrangements for work. *Presstime*, 12–14.

Ogan, C. L. (1983). *Life at the top for men and women newspaper managers: A five-year update of their characteristics*. Bloomington: School of Journalism Center for New Communications.

Pearson, J. C. (1985). *Gender and communications*. Dubuque, Ia.: William C. Brown.

Press Woman (1985, December). Maryland study warns against "pink collar ghettos" of lower pay and status in journalism fields, 1–4.

——— (1985, December). Women's observations through the years, 4.

Reich, P. (1983). How men and women edit 'women's news.' Unpublished master's thesis. University of Missouri, Columbia, Mo.

Roper, J. E. (1985, November 30). Shop talk at thirty. *Editor & Publisher*, *25*, 44.

Ross, I. (1936). *Ladies of the press: The story of women in journalism by an insider.* New York: Harper.

Schein, V. E. (1973). The relationship between sex role stereotypes and requisite management characteristics. *Journal of Applied Psychology, 57,* 95–100.

———— (1975). Relationships between sex role stereotypes and requisite management characteristics among female managers. *Journal of Applied Psychology, 60,* 340–344.

Sharp, N. W., Turk, J. V., Einsiedel, E. F., Schamber, L., and Hollenback, S. (1985). *Faculty women in journalism and mass communications: Problems and progress.* Syracuse, N.Y.: Association for Education in Journalism and Mass Communication.

Strainchamps, E. (Ed.) (1974). *Rooms with no view: A woman's guide to the man's world of the media.* New York: Harper and Row.

Stevens, G. E. (1985). Discrimination in the newsroom: Title VII and the journalist. *Journalism Monographs.* Columbia, S.C.: Association for Education in Journalism and Mass Communication.

Weaver, D. H. and Wilhoit, G. C. (1986). *The American journalists: A portrait of U.S. news people and their work.* Bloomington: Indiana University Press.

Women and Power in Higher Education: Saving the Libra in a Scorpio World

13

MARLENE SPRINGER

Women and power in higher education. Even the title is a paradox: a recent study (Touchton and Shavlik, 1984) shows that institutions of higher education have an average of 1.1 women ranking as dean or above. As discouraging as this statistic is, women are nonetheless gradually moving into positions of power in the academy. When they get there, however, they find an atmosphere that is in many ways inimical to their personal priorities and professional perspectives. The paucity of women peers, the ambiguity with respect to their roles, the conflict with societal expectations all present dilemmas for women. Given this context, the question then becomes, how do women achieve and manage power in a way that is both professionally effective and personally satisfying, while also avoiding the schizophrenia of a debilitating division of their psyche into a public-male, private-female model? How do women save the Libra, with its call for balance, optimism, and sense of humane justice, in a Scorpio world based on a system of competition, control, and bureaucracy?

As women become increasingly visible in the power structures, scholars are turning their attention to women's use of power, their fascination with it, their aversion to it, their exclusion from it. Marilyn French, in *Beyond Power* (1981), blames the patriarchy for women's dearth of power; Margaret Hennig and Anne Jardim, in *The Managerial Woman* (1976), note that our inability to speak the male corporate language keeps us out of the boardroom. Over a decade ago Matina Horner (1972) identified a controversial fear of success, and Nannerl Keohane, president of Wellesley College, in a

I would like to thank J. Elizabeth Garraway for her constructive, insightful reading of the text, Patricia Hovis for her corrective care of the manuscript, and Prof. Sharon Brehm for being the kind of editor every scholar hopes for.

recent speech to the Cambridge Forum, cogently proposed that the "obstacles would-be women leaders face lie in at least three areas: in their own consciousness and expectations for themselves; in the attitudes of men with whom they must work, and who will work for them; and in the structures of our social and economic system" (1984, p. 11).

Unquestionably, then, the problems confronting women who seek or have power, be it in the academy or the corporation, are formidable. Marilyn Ferguson, in *The Aquarian Conspiracy* (1980), does, however, offer a challenging solution. Speaking to both sexes, Ferguson argues that "our crises show us the ways in which our institutions have betrayed nature" (p. 29), and that the time has come to liberate ourselves from our personal and collective history to find new ways of controlling our world both within and without—to develop a new paradigm for power.

Certainly Ferguson's hope for a new era of professional cooperation and personal integration in our lives is not limited to one gender; it is a consummation devoutly to be wished by all as both sexes collectively face the welter of issues surrounding the getting and spending of influence. However, her point is particularly relevant to women, especially those already in power who have achieved their positions through the old male structures only to discover that the system itself can require a major betrayal of one's nature. On the one hand, the traditionally sanctioned female role is to nurture, to reinforce, to sublimate. In contrast, positions of power, and especially those in the academy, often call for talents opposed to such life-long conditioning. In universities, the constituency one is called upon to manage is by temperament and talent stridently individualistic, private, and competitive. Tenure, for all of its assets, provides a sanctuary from cause and effect in that colleagues are not held accountable for their opinions or actions and, therefore, often have little cause for collegiality or concern. The ivory tower, in short, can be antithetical to the very values many women have been carefully taught to protect: community, interdependence, a sense of the personal as integral to the professional. Frequently finding themselves in an alien land, women in administration must find new ways to transform the games people play and to create a world that offers a modicum of harmony between their social conditioning, i.e., the view they hold of themselves, and the aggressive, principally male society in which they work.

A selective survey of women administrators currently in high level positions reveals agreement on the fact that women do view and use power differently than their male colleagues. Actually defining the nuances of difference is more difficult, though collectively those interviewed agreed that women use power less aggressively, possibly because they realize that their male colleagues react differently to women in authority than they do to men in similar positions. Women's use of power, therefore, is adaptive and reactive. However, several scholars are beginning to recognize and defend a more profound case for women's different use of authority. Carol Gilligan, in *In a Different Voice* (1982), has recently proposed that women, as a gender, have a distinctive women's reality, a way of looking at the world that constitutes a "different voice." In defining the source of our differences, Gilligan states:

The moral imperative that emerges repeatedly in interviews with women is an injunction to care, a responsibility to discern and alleviate the "real and recognizable trouble" of this world. For men, the moral imperative appears rather as an injunction to respect the rights of others and thus to protect from interference the rights to life and self-fulfillment. Women's insistence on care is at first self-critical rather than self-protective, while men initially conceive obligation to others negatively in terms of noninterference. Development for both sexes would therefore seem to entail an integration of rights and responsibilities through the discovery of the complementarity of these disparate views. For women, the integration of rights and responsibilities takes place through an understanding of the psychological logic of relationships. This understanding tempers the self-destructive potential of a self-critical morality by asserting the need of all persons for care. For men, recognition through experience of the need for more active responsibility in taking care corrects the potential indifference of a morality of noninterference and turns attention from the logic to the consequences of choice (p. 100).

Gilligan continues by arguing that in the quest for identity, male and female roles also diverge: males seek a freedom of self-expression, while females relinquish that freedom in favor of self-sacrifice to protect others and preserve relationships. Though few would argue with the merit of protecting others and relationships, Gilligan notes that the negative component, that virtue for women lies in self-sacrifice, has continually complicated and often thwarted women's development and the attainment of a fair share of social justice. A more positive view of such gender differences has been posited by Marilyn Ferguson (1980): "Women are neurologically more flexible than men, and they have had cultural permission to be more intuitive, sensitive, feeling. Their natural milieu has been complexity, change, nurturance, affiliation, a more fluid sense of time" (p. 226). More and more women are now arguing that women should eschew such self-sacrificial assimilation into a man-made world and look through gender-conscious eyes in order to transform that world into one more nurturing of happiness in work and relationships.

This need to revise the rules is clearly not a product of our time. Both history and literature provide a stark picture of how women have had to adapt to the frustrations and obstacles presented to women in power, i.e., how they have learned to cope with often paradoxical views of the self. Elizabeth I, for example, chose controlled schizophrenia. A consummate sexual politician, she successfully used her virginity and availability to manipulate her world. But Elizabeth also segregated her behavior from that of other women. The Homily on Marriage, issued by her court, prescribed marriage as the only acceptable role for women and told them that they must be subject to their husbands. Elizabeth herself reminded Robert Dudley, nevertheless, that "I will have here but one mistress and no master" (Levin, 1986, p. 43); and indeed she did not have any. An absolute monarch, she could denigrate, destroy, empower, or enable with her signature, which she signed "England." She was not just Queen, but the Nation (McGee, 1985, p. 6). Yet, no matter how powerful she was, or how effective as a ruler, the fact that she was female created insecurity throughout the realm and spawned a host of male imposters pretending to the throne. Elizabeth defeated them and maintained her power by assuming masculine, kingly characteristics, while exhibiting female characteristics when politically appropriate (Levin, p. 43). Unmarried, she was both king and queen—a role many women in power have traditionally emulated.

In contrast to Elizabeth's absolutist tactics, Harriet Beecher Stowe's great study of power, *Uncle Tom's Cabin* (1852/1963), offers another avenue open to women not so fortunate as to be born to the mace: indirection. In her novel that helped prompt a war and change the history of a nation, Stowe subversively explores how women gain power in the face of seemingly insurmountable legal and social strictures. While ostensibly writing about slavery, Stowe touched in the minds of her deliberately female audience their unspoken understanding that power can be obtained behind a mask. As she traces the history of her abject hero Uncle Tom, she repeatedly illustrates that it is the women of the novel who rescue the victims, who save the plantations, who preserve the moral self of the men, who have the power, and the responsibility, for social change—not through the stroke of a royal pen, but through moral suasion and political subversion. After her legendary leaps across the ice flow, Eliza escapes with the help of Mrs. Bird, who, though powerless to take Eliza to freedom herself, manipulates her husband into doing so through debunking his pro–Fugitive Slave Law rhetoric with convincing references to his humanity and his love for his dead child. Mrs. Shelby finally does get financial control of the plantation and corrects her husband's disastrous mismanagement. Casy's superb use of psychology and superstition does gain her freedom from Simon Legree, when any direct appeal to the law or society would have been useless. Andy says it all when he is faced with the choice of obeying his master's command to catch the terrified Eliza or cunningly abetting her escape as he knows Mrs. Shelby wants: "But Lor! She'll bring him to! I knows well enough how that'll be,—it's allers best to stand Missis' side the fence, now I tell yer." (p. 44). The unempowered in this novel join together, then, not openly to challenge the power structure, but to undermine and transform it.

But if Elizabeth is emblematic of direct power, and Stowe provides a study of its opposite, it is from George Eliot (1872/1956) that we get the best lessons on the conflicts the responsibility of power presents to women.

Rosamond, the femme fatale in *Middlemarch*, gains her power through the traditional "feminine wiles" of studied helplessness, flirtatious beauty, and ultimately, by refusing to adhere to any commonly accepted system of responsibility and candor. She promises what her husband wants to hear, and does whatever she wants—and thereby destroys him. George Eliot describes her finally as "mild in her temper, inflexible in her judgment, disposed to admonish her husband, and able to frustrate him by stratagem" (p. 610). Rosamond, then, is a Stowe heroine gone bad; she uses indirect power immorally. Eliot has little patience with her, and less sympathy.

Dorothea, the central character of the novel, reflects a more positive example of the use of power, but she is also often powerless. Through her own naivete, she chains herself to a husband who wants her mind and soul, both during his lifetime and after. Dorothea is able to extricate herself from him through her own strength of will and his timely death, but she also learns that the pulls between duty and dedication to self are often unbearable, and unresolvable. She compromises her goals in favor of marrying a man she at least loves, and George Eliot comments: "Many who know her, thought it a pity that so substantive and rare a creature should have been absorbed into the life of another, and be only known in a certain circle as a wife and mother. But no one stated exactly what else that was in her power she ought rather to have done" (p. 611). Rosamond, then, presents us with amoral subversion as a way to gain and wield power. Dorothea relinquishes her power and dedicates herself to humanitarianism and private duty to husband and family. The hollowness of the one is contrasted to fulfillment through compromise in the other. To have it all is not in George Eliot's lexicon.

These examples from literature and history, while seemingly somewhat removed from the practical reality of women in management, are helpful in discussing the dimension of our dilemma, in framing the compensating compromises women have had to make. Obviously, we are still not immune. There is little question that all of us have at some time longed for the ability to sign "University" or "Corporation," yet hoping to avoid divorcing ourselves from other women, as Elizabeth felt she had to do. So, too, have we often found it necessary to don the mask, smile, and pull on the velvet glove over what we hope will be a semi-comfortable iron fist to gain our objectives. And all too often the Dorothean sense of duty to be competent mothers, managers of households, nurturing caretakers, and supportive partners conflicts with personal need for space, reflective time, play—and with the desire just to work as late as we want. Yet more and more, as women come to recognize their right to be different, they are beginning to realize that they are perhaps uniquely capable of changing traditional approaches to power, both how it is perceived, and how it is used. If we are neurologically more flexible than men, it is this very flexibility that can temper the approach of Elizabeth, unmask the approach of

Stowe, and refuse to accept the compromise of Dorothea. Patricia Mische in her monograph *Women and Power* says it succinctly: "Instead of asking for a piece of the pie men have had all along, 'we should be trying to create quite another pie' " (Ferguson, p. 226).

The challenge is a formidable one, especially since women must recognize, as Hennig and Jardim (1976) so clearly describe in *The Managerial Woman*, that in the present male management world, we are indeed in a foreign country, with a language of its own—a language we ignore to our peril, but one that is often closed to us, because its origin is in an informal system of relationships that are based on a male life style. As women executives, we see evidence of it everyday: the informal chatter about sports before each meeting (I once was the only woman at a luncheon table of Big 8 college presidents, and the entire conversation never strayed from the prowess of Nebraska's Big Red vs. Oklahoma's Sooners), or the latest stories gleaned from the noon handball game or the previous afternoon's golf. Women, therefore, are forced into bilingualism (we read the sports page). Increasingly, however, this language requirement is regarded as an imposition, and women are seeking to translate male language into something more compatible with our experience, as well as to develop a common female language comprehensible to both sexes.

Creating a new language is extremely difficult, particularly for people whose sense of affinity and solidarity is tenuous. Anne Wilson Schaef (1981) in her *Women's Reality: An Emerging Female System in the White Male Society* states, "One of the first things I noticed when I began my intensive study of women is that we normally do not like or trust one another" (p. 23). The source of the distrust comes from a sense that "to be born female in this culture means that you are born 'tainted,' that there is something intrinsically wrong with you that you can never change, that your birthright is one of innate inferiority" (p. 27). Schaef labels this syndrome "The Original Sin of Being Born Female," and calls for its recognition, and dismissal.

There is little question that when we accept "original sin," we participate in our own destruction. Like Othello, when we cannot believe in ourselves, we fall prey to the Iagos in our world. Successfully powerful women, however, are increasingly learning to recognize the imperative of an alternative—a different paradigm of power—one that is based on a community of colleagues who engender trust, and an organizational model that is cooperative rather than competitive. This alternative paradigm has as its components networking, mentoring, and a willingness to lead in a different, personalized style.

Ironically, women in power are uniquely positioned to form networks. In the academe in particular, with less than two per institution, there are so few of us that the group is manageable and such peers are readily recognizable; nationally, the American Council on Education's Office of Women does an excellent job of maintaining a network of women administrators and helping to identify potential talent for administrative work. Moreover, women in positions of authority have a definite networking advantage in that they can have direct access to the mid-management level support services in a university. These support services—the personnel office, benefits office, admissions, etc.—are largely staffed by women who have survived by wearing the mask. Many are often reluctant to let men behind it—but they will let other women in.

My own experience in creating and using such a network has been one of the most positive aspects of my life at the university. Women peers relish the idea of an exchange of ideas in a language they often only subliminally recognize as different. We meet monthly over lunch to share enthusiasms and concerns. Not only do we ease our sense of isolation, but also the barriers between academic disciplines, and between administrators and faculty. Unspokenly, a power base relying on knowledge, trust, and friendship is solidified. The network of middle-management people is equally rewarding, though necessarily on a more pragmatic level. By calling on women who have a sense of camaraderie in helping another woman, I have protected positions when staff delays would have been fatal, have located paperwork lost in the maze of the bureaucracy, and identified and recruited competent staff for my own office.

Building networks, then, by learning to trust the female in others is one major way women can obtain power and use it effectively to influence change. More difficult, however, is to trust the female in ourselves. Long conditioned to think that the private and the public are to be forever divorced, we are often reluctant to share our concerns. Rather, we hide behind a Scorpian sense of privacy that dismisses revelation of the personal dimension as weak. I once observed a man who constantly reminded his staff that one should never bring one's personal life to the office—as if the events of the previous evening and early morning could suddenly be purged from one's psyche. His admonition was well meaning—he wanted to maintain a constant atmosphere of what he deemed to be professionalism—but it was also extremely naive. Rather than honest admissions of unusual stress, and the subsequent cathartic healing that could follow, the staff often assumed that tensions were work-related, but yet could not be clearly identified. The result was an ambiguity that created a sterile work environment at best, and at worst, a terribly debilitating one. It is in changing these situations that women's cultural permission to be sensitive and intuitive can be helpful—if we are willing to accept these qualities as positive, even in the marketplace. We must be willing to acknowledge, defend, and use confidently and candidly this power of sensitivity, a force so well defined by Harriet Beecher Stowe.

To be willing to shed both inwardly and outwardly the self-image of the Original Sin of Being Born Female, to refuse to see the enemy as us, and to assert our uniqueness even as we define our place in the power structure is, like developing a common language, admittedly difficult. Once again, some women will never do it, opting instead for the psychic schizophrenia of trying to be male, of developing a managerial style that must out-macho even the most Norman Mailer of individuals (Lady Macbeth readily comes to mind). They become, in effect, the female version of Rosamond reversed: female wiles transferred to male bravado. Others merely choose instead an equally damaging capitulation to self-abnegation. The former is easily recognizable and can only be dismissed for the sad spectacle it is. The latter role is less easy to ignore. As a way of viewing one's self, this self-abnegation among women seems strangely anachronistic—yet depressingly pervasive. All too frequently I see women who still consider ignorance of the institution's politics and bureaucratic system a virtue, and a bliss—a mistake I have seen few men make. Relying on learned helplessness, such women are resentful when the system does not assure them protection and astonished that they are responsible for their own survival. The problem is not a recent one, or limited to the academe. Hennig and Jardim (1976) noted this element of "passivity" prevalent in their subjects and found it closely linked with "an overwhelming sense of 'waiting to be chosen' " (pp. 30–31). The need to change this attitude is important, for it is often found in women of great potential, and therefore presents a major challenge to those who actually seek to change the systems surrounding women by mentoring younger colleagues and enlisting their support.

Mentoring, however, is itself difficult to define and often equally hard to do. The origin of the concept is fascinating. Mentor, one may remember, is the old man in the *Odyssey* who is the wise friend of Odysseus and his son Telemachus. He serves in the book in several ways. As an elder he gives Odysseus and Telemachus the benefit of his experience and advises them to act on their own sense of morality, their sense of justice. However, his second role in the *Odyssey* is even more crucial to women, for in it he lends himself out (he has little choice) to the goddess, to the "bright eyed Athena." In this role he urges Telemachus to search for his manhood, to find wisdom. Mentor as old man, then, gives advice; goddess as mentor demands challenge, excitement, search for self. Thus mentoring, defined in its truest form, means a bringing of wisdom coupled with a stimulation to search.

Even with Athena in our history, however, women mentoring women is, unfortunately, still too uncommon, and the rules are still quite nebulous. Given the lamentable scarcity of mentors in our own past, it is often difficult to determine what advice to proffer—especially since every formula must be flexible enough to meet the myriad complexities power structures present. Despite this complexity, there are some fundamentals for achieving and exercising effective leadership that we can offer as mentors. First of all, quite candidly, how one is perceived is basically everything. And, to be perceived as influential, women must have a positive self-perception, grounded in examined self-awareness. Second, the Biblical cliche that "knowledge is power" cannot be dismissed simply because it is obvious. To be recognized as powerful, we must have credibility based on clearly defined, individualized expertise and gain a sense of how that expertise fits into a larger pattern. Third, tenacity, and a willingness to stand firm on issues once the benefits and costs have been determined, are key components to gaining power and using it effectively. Fourth, women leaders must have a keen sense of timing, coupled with a sensitivity to both the people and principles involved. Here intuition—our "understanding of the psychological logic of relationships" (Gilligan, p. 100)—can be extremely important. Skills can be learned, knowledge acquired—but a political sense of how people and systems interrelate must be nurtured through careful observation and a trust in one's own perceptions of the way things are and the way they ought to be. Finally, in order to serve as positive, visible models, women who have positions of authority must be willing to risk revealing their own humane values and confidently acknowledge their own personal ambitions to see these values incorporated.

Serving as a model, however, raises another central issue for women: style. The parameters of the way we are become infinitely varied—and if there are few guidelines for mentoring, the available solutions to the problems of style offer little contrast. In *Uncle Tom's Cabin* Eliza can only escape to Canada by dressing like a man. Now we term it dressing for success, but the outfit both literally and psychologically is much the same. To do otherwise is often to "not look or act like an executive." The debate over what constitutes an appropriate "style" for a woman is both endless and, ultimately, unrewarding. What is more appropriate to hope for is that there will be no particular style for all—that we will not know what constitutes a CEO (though too frequently, we do know: white, male, middle age, conservatively dressed, vest optional, tone bland), and equally important, that the stereotypes of what we are supposed to be will be exposed for the inflexible, restrictive requirements they are. Stowe cleverly disguises Eliza, feeling she had no alternative. Women in power now are arguing for individuality, not willing to entertain a compromise.

To be powerful, then, women must be willing to be visible, not accepting of Original Sin; be bilingual, yet work into the male power system a more common language requirement; and be aware that they are taking on nothing short of the entire social and economic structure. One could rightly ask, why try it?

The answer to that question is, of necessity, personal. Undoubtedly Mortimer Adler was partially correct in his assertion that humans share a need for power. I hope that Nannerl Keohane (1984) is also equally correct that "women tend to have a healthier sense of humor and a sharper sense of self-scrutiny about the costs of the ruthless pursuit of power goals" (p. 11). Costs or not, power can be fun, and it is certainly more financially lucrative.

If women executives are candid, they will admit to enjoying both; there is a certain Scorpio satisfaction in signing one's name and making something happen, even if it is merely getting a project out of a committee.

But more important than the instant personal gratification one gets from power is the sense of responsibility many women have to make gender-oriented improvements. Certainly the current situation is ready for reform. Bernice R. Sandler's and Roberta Hall's (1986) recent report issued by the Association of American Colleges defines the academic climate in particular:

> The higher the academic rank, the fewer women in it. Women are less likely to receive tenure than men; 47% of women faculty are tenured, 67% of the men.

> It is uncommon for women to be department chairs or deans. At all ranks and in every field and type of institution, women still earn less than their male counterparts; and women administrators are mostly concentrated in a few low status areas (p. 2).

There is little question therefore that women in the university are still the second sex—a position that is no longer acceptable and one that politically conscious women in power feel called to change.

The statistics are important not just for the vivid picture they present, but also because we know that numbers, and particularly numbers of women, do make a difference. The shifts taking place in the American political arena are an excellent example. Ruth Mandel (1981) in *In the Running* states: "Indeed, women are making a difference. Early indications from the recent increases in women's political participation do suggest that a change in the sexual composition of the public world will bring with it changes in the public agenda" (p. 252). Women-oriented issues are now surging into the public consciousness as needs that must be addressed: day-care facilities, nursing-home care, battered wives, the problems of divorced women and displaced homemakers, equal pay for equal worth, property rights for married women, pension and insurance equity for divorced women. Most important, in order to raise the consciousness of the body politic, women in politics had to admit, Mandel argues, that in pursuing a mandate to govern they could "not shy away from the power it takes to do the job she seeks" (p. 20).

The increased presence of women, then, does bring about change—and change that is beneficial to society at large, as well as to women in particular. Moreover, though our numbers are still distressingly few, women in the academy are gradually making similar progress. Women's studies programs are a recognized part of the curriculum; sexual harassment is no longer openly condoned; child care centers are in evidence; birth control is available in student health centers; university vacation schedules coordinate with the public school system rather than football schedules—each of us can add to an encouraging list. In my twenty years as a university professor and now administrator, I can also cite personal chapter and verse: joint appointments of spouses in the same department or university are, if not commonplace, at least possible. When I became a full professor, there were two other women of that rank, and ninety-seven men; that ratio has dramatically changed. Until five years ago there were no women in central administration on my campus; now both the vice chancellor for academic affairs and an associate vice chancellor are women (though of our deans, only one, in nursing, is a woman).

Especially important, to me, is that my daughters have seen the change and have not only enjoyed it, but are not afraid of my position in it. I cherish the "Mommy Deanist" tee shirt I got as a present for that promotion, appreciative of their sense of irony, and recognition that increased power does not have to transform one into Joan Crawford.

Eventually, the shirt also became a metaphor for other issues I wanted to develop or acknowledge. In addition to reminding me of the potential for disintegration in trying to be everything—competent parent, professional woman, adult partner—it also became emblematic of how all the roles might be woven into a pattern. The constant sense of responsibility both to respect the present and plan for the future that children can give, for example, engenders a sense of enthusiasm for what a university's long term purpose must be. More particularly, the logistical skill required in scheduling several people's lives serves well for managing complex workdays. The psychic shifts that must occur as one moves from parent to provost to partner can be conditioning for flexibility in dealing with the diverse daily problems of the schools of engineering, medicine, and business. The list is expandable, and admittedly personal. Obviously, the formula does not always work. There are times when nothing can counter the numbing drudgery of the bureaucracy or dull the painful conflicts of personalities. But when perspective is regained, the personal and the private can complement, not conflict. Then the fact of being female *and* in a position of authority is invigorating, not enervating; power and gender are not at odds.

Yet to be at peace with power is a Pyrrhic victory if the definition of it is limited to Elizabeth's, or if it must be exercised through Stowe's methods at the expense of Eliot's compromise. Rather, women must be willing, through networking, mentoring, and leading, to create a climate for a new concept of power, one that goes beyond the standard definitions of an ability or authority to influence others, to allocate who gets what, when, and how. The new model must shift from, in Marilyn French's terms (1981), "power over," with its connotations of domination and aggression that are so prevalent in our organizations, to "power to," with its reference to ability, capacity, and freedom of action. Women's collective history of required indirection and socialization to nurture makes us uniquely qualified to effect such a shift. Indirection can become judicious discretion; sentimentality can become a positive desire to create a workplace amenable to the deep human needs to be nurtured, reinforced, valued. Marilyn Ferguson has said that "the power of women is the powder keg of our time" (1980, p. 226). But this force must be used to encourage the best that is in us all, and not to control creativity and spirit for aggressive, ego-centered ends. As women increasingly come to acknowledge their different voice and work collectively to create a new definition for signing "England," we will move successfully into the new paradigm of power, where the personal and professional merge, where we feel innately and morally comfortable within our power, and thus, where the Libra is saved in the Scorpio world.

References

Eliot, G. (1956). *Middlemarch*. Boston: Houghton Mifflin.

Ferguson, M. (1980). *The Aquarian conspiracy: Personal and social transformation in the 1980s*. Los Angeles: J. P. Tarcher.

French, M. (1981). *Beyond power: On women, men, and morals*. New York: Ballantine.

Gilligan, C. (1982). *In a different voice: Psychological theory and women's development*. Cambridge, Mass.: Harvard University Press.

Hennig, M. and Jardim, A. (1976). *The managerial woman*. New York: Pocket Books.

Horner, M. S. (1972). Toward an understanding of achievement-related conflicts in women. *Journal of Social Issues, 28*, (2), 157–175.

Keohane, N. O. (1984, January). On women and power. Cambridge Forum, printed in *Realia*. Wellesley College.

Levin, C. (1986). Queens and claimants: Political insecurity in sixteenth-century England. In J. Sharistanian (Ed.), *Gender, ideology, and action* (pp. 41–66). Westport, Conn.: Greenwood Press.

Mandel, R. B. (1981). *In the running: The new woman candidate*. New Haven: Ticknor and Fields.

McGee, M. C. (1985). *On feminized power*. Evanston, Ill.: Northwestern University School of Speech.

Sandler, B. R. and Hall, R. M. (1986). *The campus climate revisited: Chilly for women faculty, administrators, and graduate students* (Project on the Status and Education of Women). Washington, D.C.: Association of American Colleges.

Schaef, A. W. (1981). *Women's reality: An emerging female system in the white male society*. Minneapolis: Winston Press.

Stowe, H. B. (1963). *Uncle Tom's cabin*. New York: Bantam.

Touchton, J. and Shavlik, D. (1984). Senior women administrators in higher education: A decade of change, 1975–1983. (Preliminary Report, 1984, November 14). Washington, D.C.: Association of American Colleges Office of Women in Higher Education.

PART FOUR

WOMEN'S PERSPECTIVES

The Other Side of the Banner: Toward a Feminization of Politics

14

JOEY SPRAGUE

"The Personal is Political" has been the banner of the contemporary women's movement. It has drawn attention to the ways in which personal interaction and interpersonal struggles have political origins and political implications. Over the course of the last decade, however, there have been analyses along a number of lines that when woven together show that the feminist banner has another side: the political has been personalized—or at least parochialized. That is, what we have been taught to think of as politics, as political behavior, as sophisticated political analysis, is not in reality a universal verity. It is the expression of a particular point of view: a masculine point of view.

In this chapter I'd like to describe the ways in which politics has been a particularly masculine expression. I'd like to urge the expansion of our definition of politics to one focused less on institutions and more on the process of decision-making. Finally, I'd like to speculate on what an integrated gender politics, one that reconciles masculine with feminine views, might look like.

Feminist critiques of the literature on political attitudes and political participation boil down to the observation that, historically in this country, politics is what men do and political behavior is how they do it (cf. Siltanen and Stanworth, 1984). The recognized political arena is the state apparatus, especially the executive and legislative branches of that apparatus. The most recognized political actors are those who occupy positions in executive and legislative posts and those who dominate the two major political parties. Political behavior is conceived of as activity related to struggles for power in the sense of dominance or control. The major structural feature underlying the conventional understanding of the organization of politics is the distinction between public and private.

The Public/Private Distinction

The public/private distinction is generally understood to differentiate between a class of phenomena which is to be decided upon, regulated, protected, and supported by the group as a whole and another class which is a matter of individual responsibility and choice. It also differentiates between two standards for human interaction: universalistic, in which all are treated alike as members of the group, and particularistic, in which each is seen as having his/his own specific needs and goals. The application of the distinction corresponds with major institutions of social life: we think of the family as private and of the economy and polity as public. However, as several feminists have pointed out, the dividing line between public and private is difficult to maintain when actual life circumstances are considered.

Phenomena occuring in the public sphere impinge on and restrict life choices in the private sphere. Economic opportunities that differ by sex create inequalities within the home. Social welfare benefits that are tied to income (e.g., Social Security) increase the dependence of nonincome or low income earning women on their husbands (Dahl and Snare, 1978). Policies that direct public monies into subsidizing single family homes through loans and tax benefits, zoning laws that make the housing of unconventional domestic groupings highly restricted, and plot layouts that favor private yards over public parks all favor the proliferation of the private nuclear household (Markusen, 1980).

On the other hand, the "public sphere" is not clearly and uniformly public. Pateman (1983) has argued that the position of civil society in the distinction between public and private is ambiguous: it contains aspects of both. Structurally, she reminds us, one of the main occupants of the "public sphere" in this country is "private enterprise." The application of the public/private distinction within civil society appears in contrasts like those between freedom and force, spontaneous regulation and state coercion, voluntarism and power. Many have attested to the fact that important decisions in both the economy and polity are made in private contexts: in locker rooms rather than board rooms, at country clubs rather than in state houses. Whole social movements have been founded on concerns of the "private realm." Eisenstein (1982) has described the way in which the politics of the "New Right" are specifically and intentionally directed at redefining the terms of the private family. Feminist campaigns against domestic abuse are similarly directed, although toward a radically different goal.

The public/private distinction is an instance of what Jay (1981) has identified as a "logical dichotomy." There are many dichotomies that do involve contradiction, that incorporate the possibility of a middle ground, for example, good/bad and sickness/health. One can conceive of the possibility of being a little less good or a little more sick. The logical dichotomy, on the other hand, implies a contradiction between two categories with no middle ground. Jay offers as examples the oppositions sacred/profane and male/female. These logical dichotomies form the basis for a major cognitive structure in our culture, Aristotelian logic, which insists, among other things, that nothing can be both A and not-A and that all is either A or not-A.

Logical dichotomies "are not representative of the empirical world; they are principles of order. In the empirical world almost everything is in a process of transition: growing, decaying, ice turning to water and vice versa" (1981, p. 42). Further, the opposition of male to female conflicts with all the ways in which both sexes of a species are similar. Because logical dichotomies are principles of order that are contrived, maintaining the division between them requires a continual struggle. Jay suggests that the origin of the struggle is the need to create and maintain the logical dichotomy necessary for patriarchy: Male/Female.

We have already seen that the barrier between public and private is also difficult to establish empirically. The political impact of maintaining the distinction as a logical dichotomy begins to emerge when one considers the specific points at which the barrier is raised and lowered. Sexuality between nonmarried and/or nonheterosexual adults is publicly regulated but rape within marriage is, for the most part, a legal nonentity. The provision of transportation and education are public works, the production of meals and clean laundry are domestic, that is private, labor. The decision whether or not to have children is publicly constrained in laws about birth control and abortion while caring for those children who are born is generally defined as a private responsibility. Women's involvement in the police and military combat has been publicly limited while their subjection to assault in the home and workplace is too often considered a private problem.

The maintenance of the distinction between public and private is generally held to be necessary for the protection of individual liberties (Benn and Gaus, 1983; Elshtain, 1981). Siltanen and Stanworth (1984) note that this argument assumes the equation of private with personal and of public with impersonal, assumptions that do not hold up empirically. We also live our personal relations in the public realm, they contend, and some personal relations in the private realm are not all that intimate.

The real distinction, Yeatman (1984) maintains, is not between physical spheres of life but between two modes of social interaction, public and domestic: "between a collectively-oriented and universalistic sociality on the one hand and an individually-oriented and particularistic sociality on the other" (1984, p. 34). We have come to associate domestic sociality with the household and public sociality with the larger society because we have learned to narrow our conceptions of domestic forms of interaction to mothering, thus to women. Actually, domestic sociality represents what we understand as "the personal"; as such, it is a form of interaction engaged in by men as well as women and in all arenas of social life.

If the public/private distinction fails to correspond to the nature of our social lives, why is it so pervasive in our worldview? Or, to paraphrase a question posed by Pateman (1983), why do we emphasize the contrast between private and public rather than a contrast between personal and political?

Sources of the Public/Private Dichotomy

One set of views on the source of the distinction between public and private comes from the recognition that a division between public and private has often been functional for the perpetuation of male control over women. O'Brien (1983) argues that the basis for patriarchy is the struggle for control over the product of reproduction, the child. Women, by virtue of their biology, have direct access to control over the child. Men, whose reproductive biology does not allow them direct access to controlling whether or not a child is born or even to the surety that the child is biologically theirs, have invented the right of paternity as a means to assert their control. Because paternity is a socially created right, it requires a system of social support for it, a polity. On the other hand, having a private realm to lock women into helps assure individual men that their women are kept out of reach of other men, who are, in reproductive terms, "competing potencies."

Patriarchal definition of the public as the sphere of men and the private as the appropriate domain of women allows male dominance to continue even into the "female realm" (Pateman, 1983). Because the public is perceived as larger and more important than the private, it appears natural that the male, who participates in this larger world, should be the "head of household" as well.

When people cooperate in their own social dominance their compliance is usually underwritten by the threat of coercion. Dahl and Snare (1978) have pointed out that the sex-typing of public and private leads to a sex difference in the degree to which people are subject to social coercion. For men, social control is secondary in form, that is, public and bureaucratic. Thus, it is subject to social scrutiny and regulation. The social control exerted on women is much more likely to be primary, personal, operating through the private sphere. The privatization of the social control over women means that it is largely invisible and out of reach of social regulation, thus much more forceful than public control over men. In fact, Pateman (1983) suggests that the reason we think of the private as the domain of self-expression and creativity unchecked by social constraint is that for men this is often the case. If we considered the experience of individual women, the private domain would not appear to be as free and unconstrained.

A structural level argument has been made that the public/private distinction is maintained because it facilitates male domination over women, both collectively and individually. The question of why this dichotomous distinction appears natural or acceptable to us still remains.

Jay (1981) attributes the perception of a logical dichotomy to a fact of early cognitive development as described by Mahler. The earliest cognitive task for the infant, according to Mahler, is a process she calls "separation/individuation." The child's initial cognitions are of being at one with the mother, and the first steps of cognitive development involve being aware of itself as separate from her. The fact that the mother is a female means that differentiation from her amounts to identifying self as not-female. Independent thinking begins with the logical dichotomy me/female.

Of course, that the first and primary social tie for an infant is a (sole) woman is the outcome of a specific form of social relations, the patriarchal nuclear family. The dichotomy me/mother is socially created. In Chodorow's (1978) view, it has farther reaching implications for basic gender differences in psychic structure. For one thing, the dichotomy tends to be differentially imposed. Because sex is such an important category in patriarchal culture, the mother, like all other members of the group, relates to people differently depending on their sex.

The mother's relation to her daughter is as an extension of herself. The initial states of attachment and emotional connectedness continue for a relatively long period. This produces a psychic structure with a stronger basis for empathy in that the girl's ego boundaries are not fully defined—she is the mother and the child. In fact, her identity is constructed not as a separate entity but rather as connected, a "definition of self in relationship."

Mothers relate to their sons as sexual others which has the dual effect of genderizing their identity and of propelling them into distinct selves at a relatively early age. This dynamic leads to specific outcomes for boys' sense of self. Gender identification becomes the key issue in boys' self-identification. They develop their sense of masculinity partly through distinguishing themselves from the feminine mother, rejecting an identification with her for one with the father. They end up with more of a sense of differentiation, of individuation, of a separate self.

Chodorow describes the way these socially created sex differences are continued in the processes by which adult social roles and identifications are learned. Girls learn interpersonally defined roles through personal identification with their mothers. Boys, whose fathers are more remote, have to resort to positional identification with them. Their role learning is a combination of negative identification with the mother (denial of relationship) and an acquisition of abstract cultural notions of male identity.

Thus, according to Chodorow, the gendered character of the way we raise children creates a masculine worldview constructed around a strong separation between self and other, a self-identity that is explicitly nonfeminine, and an abstract conceptualization of the social world. This worldview is consistent with a division of the social into abstract dualities that are sexually coded: a masculine public and a feminine private. A feminine worldview, according to this perspective, is characterized by a self that incorporates multiple relationships to others and a concrete understanding of the social world. It would be more consistent with a conception of the social as a web.

A different source for dichotomous cognitive structures is offered by O'Brien (1983), who draws on Hegel's observation of the distinctiveness of human intentional action and Marx's argument that the most important human actions are those taken to meet basic imperatives of continued existence. Her analysis is centered on the ways in which social experience and consciousness are structured by the response of intentional actors to the basic imperative of biological reproduction.

Males and females, she notes, are in different biological positions when it comes to the kinds of intentional actions open to them. Males are biologically distanced from reproduction; their only connection is through intercourse. Females, on the other hand, are biologically linked to reproduction in an ongoing way through menstrual cycles and in a focused and unbroken way through pregnancy and childbirth. Because of this difference in the experience of their roles in reproduction, male and female consciousness is differentially structured. Women, whose reproductive potential is an integral part of adult life and is underscored by their reproductive labor, are connected to the continuity of the generations, experience time as continuous, and think in more integrative patterns. Because the male connection to reproduction is less complete, limited to circumstances connected with intercourse, males are separated from the continuity of the generations, have a discontinuous sense of time, and generally think in discrete elements. One outcome of the discontinuous character of male consciousness is the tendency to organize experience in terms of simple dualities. O'Brien culls examples from the tradition of Western philosophy, or what she calls "malestream thought": mind/body, City of God/City of Man, Capitalist/Worker.

Whether we read Chodorow or O'Brien the conclusion is similar: the perception of a dichotomy between public and private is an artifact of the experience of gendered patterns of reproductive labor. Chodorow focuses on the impact on children of having only individual female nurturers. O'Brien emphasizes the impact on adults of their differential involvement in the processes of biological and social reproduction. Each analysis leads to associating the development of a dichotomous, abstract distinction with the experience and consciousness of males, not females. The distinction between public and private is a construction of politics that emerges from a masculine worldview.

The Separation of Nurturance from Dominance

Having ruled out the public/private distinction as a means of distinguishing the political from the personal, we might be tempted to turn to distinctions based on kinds of behavior. A common conceptulization of political behavior is that of participation in a struggle for power. Sometimes the focus is on actions taken to help a particular person or party gain power, for example voting or working on political campaigns. Other times the emphasis is on the direct exercise of force or of the potential for force, as in the actions of political officials or the demonstrations of opposing groups. Differences in power mean social relationships are hierarchical.

Hierarchical relationships take two distinct forms (Miller, 1976). There are relationships of inequality that are organized around maintaining that inequality, for example typical working relations between managers and subordinates. I would call these relations of dominance. On the other hand, there are relationships that involve parties of unequal status but that are organized around reducing and even erasing the inequalities involved, for example those between parent and child. These relationships can be described as relations of nurturance.

Our conceptions of political behavior have been almost exclusively centered on behavior that is oriented toward relations of social dominance. What is generically excluded from notions of political processes are behaviors oriented toward social nurturance. This has happened because gender as a principle of social organization dichotomizes human experience.

Ruddick (1980) argues that childrearing requires an orientation that enables both the protection of the child and the ability to foster its growth. In patriarchal societies, women are socialized into this orientation and men are not. It includes a sense of humility toward the uncontrollability of the natural world, a rejection of excessive control over the child as a failure in mothering, a valuation of open structures over closed ones (the developing child is an open structure), and an adaptability to change. Its central organizing principle Ruddick calls "attentive love." Attention leads to a special kind of intellectual knowledge of a person. Love implies an interplay of attachment and the detachment that allows the loved object to grow free. The combination of attention and love constitutes a centeredness on the child's perspective and needs.

As Connell (1983) describes it, a very different way of relating to the world is conveyed to boys in their socialization to a male identity. Hegemonic masculinity is physically expressed as force, "the irresistible occupation of space" combined with skill, "the ability to operate on space and the objects in it" (p. 18). The process of instilling male identity is not just a matter of persuasion into a specific self-concept, Connell argues. It is embedded in the relation to one's own body built into the specific social practices into which boys are steered, especially sport. In each sport what is learned informally and formally coached is "a specific combination of force and skill" (p. 18). Involvement with sports not only encourages this orientation, it literally embodies it in the development of physical musculature and strength. The lesson is also conveyed in the engagement of young males with machine-related manual labor (pp. 22–32).

The claims of Ruddick and Connell are consistent with male/female differences in the experience of relationships found by Gilligan (1982). Men see relationships in a hierarchy, implying an order of inequality and generating conflicting rights. Women see relationships as forming a web, suggesting a structure of interconnection and giving rise to an ethic of care. The conception of morality typically developed by men in this society is a formal, abstract arrangement of rights and rules; moral problems arise out of competing rights and are resolved by applying a "formal logic of fairness." Women tend to develop a morality constituted by the responsibility associated with specific social relationships. For them, the source of moral dilemmas is conflicting responsibilities that are resolved through applying an "ethic of care."

Thus, what we have is a division of human social experience based on sex which leads to the development of distinct social orientations. Gendered paths of social experience lead to gendered distinctions in ways of relating both to the social and the physical world. One of these ways of relating, an orientation toward dominance and control in an environment of conflicting rights adjudicated by abstract laws, a worldview that is the outcome of a masculine gender path, has been institutionalized as appropriate public/political behavior.

This distortion of humanity into masculine and feminine halves is not easily resolved. Miller (1976) points out that the crucial areas of human experience that have been radically dissociated from men and heavily identified with women include feelings of vulnerability and weakness, emotionality, participating in the development of others, cooperativeness, and creativity. Because women have not been able to reintroduce these areas into mainstream discourse for discussion and resolution, they have remained repressed, socially as well as personally, and thus are even more threatening. Since these kinds of experience are integrally human, the threat is continuous. Males must be ever ready to block and stifle them, Miller says, in order to protect their identity as the opposite of womanly. In political terms, this implies that currently public masculinity is deeply vested in building images of toughness without compassion, of security as a strength that is defined in physical and technical terms rather than in terms of social bonding and caring. This kind of political behavior is bringing us all to the brink of oblivion.

Feminizing Politics

If we cannot simply reduce politics to activity occurring in the public sphere, how are we to identify what is political? One feminist response has been to identify inherently political interests. This approach is illustrated in Randall's assertion that "At a minimum, politics is about how people influence the distribution of resources" (1982, p. 7). Because our cultural bias is to interpret resources as nonhuman materials, this definition facilitates our excluding other than economic interests from the realm of the political. For example, cultural issues like the representation in educational materials of the appropriate roles for men or women might very well be excluded as nonpolitical. The problem of exclusion will always haunt a definition of politics that relies too heavily on content.

Another way that feminists have tried to redefine the political by identifying the issues that belong to its domain has been to assert that the political includes all that is public, shared, collective, common life. Pateman (1983) credits this approach with pointing to the arbitrariness of the public/private distinction within civil life but argues that it fails to do anything about the larger public/private distinction between public and domestic. I think that particular concern could be eliminated by excluding the adjective "public" from the string of referents. Domestic or personal life, after all, is also shared. The attractive aspect of this definition is that it allows conceptions of the political to expand as far as the total realm of the social, that is, into all shared or collective aspects of life. Unfortunately, this expansion is too broad. It provides no insight on the differences between political and other aspects of the social. While it may very well be that all that is social is by nature political, that identity should be argued rather than simply assumed. In my view, this approach is also limited by an overreliance on content; it overlooks the way in which politics is a specific kind of process.

Definitions that are based on content, on categorizing phenomena by subject matter, involve the application of abstract principles to divide phenomena into individual groups. This combination of abstraction and individuation has been argued to be the outcome of a traditionally male set of social experiences. The awareness of process, on the other hand, comes from a perception of relatedness, of seeing people not as isolated individuals but rather as parts of a web of connectedness so that the actions of one are the context for others to whom s/he is related. As we have seen, this kind of perception is associated with a feminine set of social experiences.

One definition of politics that employs a more feminine attention to process is that which asserts that everything is political since everything potentially can be influenced by force and the use of force is inherently political. Pateman (1983) criticizes equation of politics with power. Those who make power universal, she says, lose the chance to be critical of the concept of power. I would add that those who have chosen this tack have fallen into the trap of foregrounding process to the degree that content fades from sight. Ironically, the process that is foregrounded, the exercise of power, seems to be a construction emerging from a masculine worldview.

Power is the ability to coerce, to get one's way even in the face of opposition. It can be based on access to superior resources on a physical, financial, or symbolic plane. However, the ability to coerce implies that there is at least some range of choices to be made by the object of coercion. That is, the goal of the exercise of power is to control a process of decision-making. It is the decision-making that is the inherently political act and the exercise of power is simply one strategy for influencing it. Of course, the fact that politics is, in our culture, so widely conceived of as an exercise of power speaks to the degree to which we have historically experienced decision-making as a coerced process.

I am suggesting that a conceptualization of the political that integrates masculine and feminine worldviews will integrate a sense of content and an idea about process. The content of the political will be conceived of in such a way that it attends to those aspects of life that are open to social construction or socially produced change. The description of political process should allow for options other than domination. These criteria begin to be met in the approach of Siltanen and Stanworth (1984), who propose that the political includes any relationship that can be shaped or altered by human action.

But there is a third aspect of a conceptualization of politics to which even this definition does not respond and that is a model of structure. In my view, feminists have had major difficulties in redefining the political because it is so difficult for all of us to escape the dominant dichotomous conceptualization of politics. Each of these models, in the absence of a specific argument to the contrary, calls up an image of a dividing line separating the political from the nonpolitical. I would like us to explore the possibility that a better model for structuring our understanding of politics is one of concentric circles.

At the heart of the concentric circles, the heart of the political, will be a decision, a choice among options for action. Parties to the decision are arrayed along the widening rings in terms of their degree of influence on the decision-making process. In a noncoerced process, people's positions in relation to decision-making will reflect their fundamental interests, their basic stake in the decision at hand. A good way of assessing people's stake in a particular decision is by considering how much they could lose from it. Thus the highest stake is that of those whose own physical and emotional security is on the line. The next highest stake is that of people who have made the greatest personal commitment, in physical and emotional labor, to those who have the most to lose, and so on.

A model of concentric circles recognizes that there are varying spheres of interests corresponding to different social choices. From this it follows that the size and composition of the group who should participate in a decision will also vary. At one extreme are decisions that directly impact only one person. The choice to maintain or to end a pregnancy in its early stages is one example. At the other end are decisions that have life and death implications for everyone on the planet. Decisions about the use of nuclear energy and other less dramatic but no less threatening environmental hazards are the most urgent examples.

Defining politics in terms of participation in decision-making invokes questions about ways in which people are currently excluded from such participation. These exclusionary mechanisms operate at the levels of both structure and process. The most obvious way that people are "structured out" of participating in decisions in which they have an important stake is through the establishment of centralized and authoritarian decision-making agencies. Thus, many policy decisions are made without even the awareness, much less the participation, of those most concerned with their outcomes. Decentralization of most decision-making processes is an important goal for a noncoercive political strategy.

Decentralization alone, however, would not remove the structural barriers to political participation. Many others arise from the way that the political has been organized against, rather than integrated with, the personal. The timing and location of meetings, the level of time and energy commitments required for participation, the failure to routinely provide childcare all are symptoms of the ways in which we have failed to take into consideration the fact that political actors have personal lives. The ironic result is that those who have taken most social responsibility in their personal lives have been excluded from the opportunity to exercise social responsibility politically.

Beyond the structural mechanisms that include some and exclude others from any involvement in decision-making, full participation in the process can be constrained by lack of necessary resources. There are at least three kinds of resources necessary to free and adequate participation in decision-making: physical, cultural, and social. A lack of physical resources can convert what appear to be choices into demand situations. For example, the lack of adequate income, social support, and affordable quality childcare can make it very difficult for a woman to feel free to choose being pregnant. If feminists really want to support the "right to choose," we must have as a goal giving women the freedom to choose to have a child.

Making decisions involves a choice among options. Thus, real participation in decision-making requires an awareness of options and the full information required to compare them. To the extent that this knowledge exists somewhere in a social group, it is part of a storehouse of cultural resources that is potentially available to all members. The lack of knowledge turns a decision into a ritual act, a sham. Perhaps it is awareness of this fact that has led potential voters to increasingly withdraw from a decision-making process in which political campaigns have increasingly replaced discussion of real issues with media hype and empty images.

Any individual's reading of an issue and interpretation of relevant information is necessarily grounded in a perspective that owes much to personal experience. Simply relying on individual perceptions, then, is being subject to biases of which we may not even be aware. An important source of corrective insights is the perspective of others. These other points of view are important social resources that can only be gained in an environment of free and open discussion of issues. The fear of dissension and debate is a major obstacle to a noncoercive decision-making process.

In summary, the bifurcation of human experience and consciousness produced by the social construction of gender has led us, of both sexes, into incomplete, thus distorted, views about what politics is and how it can be conducted. A reintegraton of masculine with feminine perceptions would lead us away from the distraction of an unrealistic dichotomizing of the public and the private to a focus on the real heart of political activity, the choice among social options. Centering on the process of decision-making makes the structural and processual possibilities for its coercion clearer. A political agenda that gives priority to striking down barriers to full and appropriate participation in decision-making is the best strategy for removing the political from the personal domain of a few powerful people. When that goal is finally accomplished we will finally be able to say that the political is truly social. That will be a banner day for feminists.

References

Benn, S. and Gaus, G. (1983). The public and the private: Concepts and action. In S. Benn and G. Gaus (Eds.), *Conceptions of the public and the private in social life*. New York: St. Martin's Press.

Chodorow, N. (1978). *The reproduction of mothering: Psychoanalysis and the sociology of gender*. Berkeley: University of California Press.

Connell, R. W. (1983). Men's bodies. In *Which way is up?* (pp. 17–32). Sydney: George Allen and Unwin.

Dahl, T. S. and Snare, A. (1978). The coercion of privacy: A feminist perspective. In C. Smart and B. Smart (Eds.), *Women, sexuality and social control* (pp. 8–26). Boston: Routledge and Kegan Paul.

Eisenstein, Z. R. (1982). The sexual politics of the new right: Understanding the 'Crisis of Liberalism' for the 1980's. *Signs: Journal of Women in Culture and Society, 7*, 567–588.

Elshtain, J. B. (1981). *Public man, private woman*. Oxford: Martin Robertson.

Gilligan, C. (1982). *In a different voice: Psychological theory and women's development.* Cambridge, Mass.: Harvard University Press.

Jay, N. (1981). Gender and Dichotomy. *Feminist Studies, 7,* 38–56.

Markusen, A. R. (1980). City spatial structure, women's household work, and national urban policy. *Signs: Journal of Women in Culture and Society, 5,* suppl. to 3d issue, S23-S44.

Miller, J. B. (1976). *Toward a new psychology of women.* Boston: Beacon Press.

O'Brien, M. (1983). *The politics of reproduction.* Boston: Routledge and Kegan Paul.

Pateman, C. (1983). Feminist critiques of the public-private dichotomy. In S. Benn and G. Gaus (Eds.), *Conceptions of the public and the private in social life.* New York: St. Martin's Press.

Randall, V. (1982). *Women and politics.* New York: St. Martin's Press.

Ruddick, S. (1980). Maternal thinking. *Feminist Studies, 6,* 342–367.

Siltanen, J. and Stanworth, M. (1984). The politics of private woman and public man. In Siltanen and Stanworth (Eds.), *Women and the public sphere* (pp. 185–208). London: Hutchinson.

Yeatman, A. (1984). Gender and the differentiation of social life into public and domestic domains. *Social Analysis: Journal of Cultural and Social Practice.* Special Issue Series No. 15, 32–49.

Mollup's Mutations: A Study of the Growing Pains of a Feminist Imagination

15

ELIZABETH SCHULTZ

This essay, which will be autobiographical as many studies by feminist writers have come to be, begins with two childhood memories.[1] In both instances I was confined to my bedroom for an afternoon nap and conscious of a window in a room framing possibilities. In the first instance, a shade had been drawn over the window and the afternoon light was sifting like pollen into the room, laying patterns over the patterns of oriental carpet and oak floor. I was small and in my crib, desperate to push down its side bars, desperate to go out the closed door, desperate to go down the stairs I knew were behind the door and to go out into the golden light. I stood at the bars screaming and screaming. In the second instance—three to four years later—I was in a new house and lying in my big bed. It was a pink and white girl's room and the light came through dimity curtains pink and white. But through the curtains, through the windowpanes, I could see boughs burdened with pink and white apple blossoms thrashing, tossed up to be dashed down. And I was exhilarated.

For out among the apple blossoms was my playmate, Mollup, the one who could go anywhere, do anything that I could imagine. There was my playmate, swinging from the boughs, kicking up the whole pink and white storm. My playmate was not only a little girl like me made to take afternoon naps; she was a free spirit. She conducted the symphony orchestra on the top of the radio tower; those were her lights winking and blinking up there as well as her music coming out of the radio in the kitchen. She raised her arms and a cape of cobalt blue appeared to lift her off the roof ridge and to float her into the tops of the great pines in the park between my home and kindergarden. She set up housekeeping in the woods to care for animals wounded by hunters in the great annual autumn slaughter. Where, I ask myself forty-five years later, is Mollup now? What has happened to my imaginary playmate? It occurs to me that in changing guises she has always been with me—my muse—the projection of my imagination.

I realize now, however, that she became subdued when I started going to school all day, when the bars of the crib and the frame of the window became constricting social conventions and distorting gender stereotypes. Perhaps my imagination was never again to be as wildly liberated as it was during those remembered naptimes. Mollup seemed self-generating then, free to fling forth into the unknown with no sense of limitation, either natural or social. Beyond androgyny, she was capable of activities assigned by social convention to either gender, indeed capable of activities undreamed of by social convention; but free of all social context, she wasn't yet human. She would have to change and so would I; we would have to become social without being socialized, human without being homogenized. My two childhood memories reflect my early awareness of opposition between self and society, freedom and limitation, nature and culture, imagination and convention. Opposition, which, if exacerbated, could produce a peculiar schizophrenia. This essay is an attempt to trace the growth in myself and my imagination through reading, writing, and teaching literature. As I trace that process, it is apparent that the life of my muse, adventuresome and subversive, wild and creative, shrank in relation to my submission to patriarchal patterns of reading and writing and pulsated in relation to my increasing consciousness of fully human and feminist possibilities in reading and writing. The former intensified oppositions; the latter healed oppositions and fostered synthesis.

The misogyny of nursery rhymes did not trouble Mollup. It might have been interesting to live in a pumpkin, to live in a shoe. If the boys' lot—"snakes and snails"—sounded more interesting than the girls'—"sugar and spice"—I knew that the little girl with the curl, after all, had it in her to be "HORRID." Mollup might have been troubled by the fact that Little Bo Peep and Mary were relegated to sheepish activities, but then so was Little Boy Blue. And although Jack could jump over the candlestick, I knew my friends Diana and Barbara and Joyce could jump higher than that as we did every afternoon playing "High Water, Low Water" out on the driveway. I also knew that I could change the patterns of the words ("Diana, be nimble/Diana, be quick..." "One, two/Who are you?/Three, four/Ask me no more...") and in so doing, cast a singsong spell over reality. Best of all, hovering over these early days of word play was the figure of Mother Goose, astride her great bird, her high black hat set firmly on her head, her eyes screwed on a distant goal, her skirts billowing, her pantaloons showing, flying high above the chimney pots: the very incarnation of Mollup herself.

The constricting implications of the fairy tales I read after I'd put aside nursery rhymes were less easy for me to dismiss. The images of those golden girls—Snow White, Cinderella, Rapunzel, and the Sleeping

Beauty—rose before me in the day, and I was charmed. Although subjected to years of sleep, incarceration, or demeaning labor, they were given new life by the arrival of their prince and assurance of marriage. I accepted this status as an ideal and wondered if someday my prince would come. In the meantime, the images of the wicked step-mothers, vengeful god-mothers, nasty, nasty witches tormented me at night, and I was repulsed. And fascinated. They seemed all-knowing, casting spells, and predicting the future; they seemed all-powerful, looming so ominous in my dreams, rising up from crowds, caves, cauldrons. By comparison with the good and golden girls whom they sought to destroy, they embodied evil and ugliness; by comparison with these girls, they were women who acted. Their knowledge and their activities intrigued me. Except for their endless domestic chores, the girls had little to do. Ride off to a ball in a pumpkin-coach drawn by a team of mice! Tend to dwarfs and a variety of woodland creatures (Mollup liked this angle) in a forest cabin! But, then, with the arrival of the prince, even these activities had to be sacrificed.

The differences between the lives of these fairy tale girls and the witch women were made more clear to me by the tales of "The Littlest Mermaid" and Baba Yaga. The littlest mermaid had been perfectly content, swimming in her fabulous, iridescent seas and sunning beneath the azure skies, until the day her prince came along. Then, distraught with love, distracted by the promise of marriage, she changed from carefree mermaid to suffering woman. Anticipation of puberty: I felt the infinite tiny pinpricks girdling my waist in a paralyzing band where my wondrous fishtail—a creation out of Mollup's repertoire—had once been. The littlest mermaid's antithesis was Baba Yaga, the Russian witch who lived in the woods, in a marvelous house elevated on chicken's legs. To enter her house, she addressed it by name, saying "Bow down, Izbushka, bow down," and slowly, awkwardly, the house would lower itself so that Baba Yaga could step in. Accompanied by her great cat, Stika, she also traveled through the skies in a mortar, steering herself with the pestle, humming all the while. Many's the trip Mollup and I took with her. She also controlled three horsemen: he of the white horse who brought her day, he of the red horse who brought the red sun, and he of the black horse who brought her moonless nights. Her words of wonder and command—and her name (none of the other wicked women were dignified by a name) reinforced my sense of the potential magic and power of language that would be the means for Mollup's becoming social. Moved to sympathy by the littlest mermaid and to wonder by Baba Yaga, I began to see women's ways, but I had yet to encounter the treacherous romance tradition which would show me my "proper" place: marriage to a prince among men (Brownstein, 1982).

In pre-TV America, fairy tales were followed by comics. A communal activity, my friends and I spent whole June days reading them sprawled on the back-porch glider. The derring-do of Superman and Captain Marvel was balanced by that of Wonder Woman, and the dangerous detective work of Dick Tracy was balanced by the risky investigative reporting of Brenda Starr. But men—Joe Palooka, Terry and the Pirates, Mandrake, Popeye, Flash Gordon, Jungle Jim, Steve Canyon—had so many more adventures than women. Even in the Disney and Warner Brothers cartoons, the guys— Donald and Mickey, Bugs and Elmer—had all the fun. As Judith Fetterley claims women must do in reading much American literature written by men, I had to "identify against myself" (Fetterley, 1978, p. xii), for the girls—Little LuLu and Little Orphan Annie, Minnie Mouse and Olive Oil— seemed silly. I scrunched into the corner of the glider, taking on macho gore: Batman, Spider Man, Plastic Man, Frankenstein. "SHAZAM" had been a magic word, but it was transformed into "BAM" and "POW" and "SPLAT" as fists crashed against my skull, as blood spurted, as sparks darted and stars went out of orbit. Despite tidy frames enclosing pictures and balloons containing words, this was terror.

Determining to read no more comic books, I turned to another genre: romance, in the form of swashbuckling sagas and *Modern Love* magazines. Baba Yaga was reduced to devious spinster or silly old maid whereas the girls of the fairy tales became full-fledged, long-suffering heroines or ravishing beauties before whom the world bowed. As the object of men's desire or scorn and betrayal, they achieved validation. Their stories seemed irresistible. Against odds, Mollup maintained a life during my association with romance, for my friend Barbara and I would spend our Saturday evenings leaping about our beds and bedrooms, our rapiers (sticks fitted with elegant Dixie-Cup cuffs) raised high, pillow-case capes flying. We intoned and exclaimed and extemporized the speeches of those dashing heroes out of Alexander Dumas, Rupert of Henshaw, Thomas Costain, and Samuel Shellebarger. Biographies—of Madame Curie, George Washington Carver, Abraham Lincoln, Florence Nightingale, Benjamin Franklin, Harriet Tubman, Sacajawea, Barbara Fritchie, Amelia Earhart—images of men and women resolving real problems—stymied encroaching schizophrenia, myself divided between the imaginative, life-enhancing Mollup and romantic, life-stultifying gender stereotypes.

In order to strengthen and save Mollup, I needed to bring her out of the closet and give her voice. Embodying my imagination in words, I could give her a social context. I could share her free-wheeling spirit. Responding to rhyme and incantation, to "SHAZAM" and "Bow down, Izbushka, bow down," I had recognized the power of words to cast spells, to change reality. But learning the techniques of junior- and senior-high school journalism, I came to perpetrate the moral absolutes and gender stereotypes of romance in the name of truth. I became committed to choosing a prom queen and applauding football victories, to selecting those most favored (with popularity, looks, wit, and the likelihood of success) and those worthy of mention in the gossip column ("The Vacuum Sweeper: We Pick Up All the Dirt"), which, like the lists of those most favored, featured only the white, middle class, and college-bound. But it was class consensus (the class in 1954; the white, middle class; the ruling class that always abided by school policies), not mad magical Mollup, that chose who presided at the top; the rest were lopped off just as the concluding sentences in any journalist's article could be lopped off. My newspaper words did not liberate; they cast binding spells, blinding spells. Mollup's existence was being smothered, her zany ways snuffed out, lopped off. She was being socialized, my words and I homogenized.

But two friends—I bless them to this day—breathed life back into her. They countered romance and extended imagination, expanding my perceptions of gender, race, and humanity. Because we shared our lives through words, Mollup learned to speak in several tongues. Jim, the only black who worked for the high school newspaper, first made me conscious of justice and of the suffering of others. Not in an abstract fashion, for his hurt was on a daily basis. We had four-hour-long telephone conversations several times a week, yet he would not go to the prom with me. Jim's intensity, his anguish, his loneliness, his quick sense of beauty stretched my imagination toward the complex life of another. I began to write editorials on civil rights, on the United Nations rather than on prom decorations, and on attendance at sports events. Because of Jim, Mollup shed her cape of cobalt blue and took up the coat of many colors.

Because of Esther, Mollup shed her solitary ways and discovered first friendship and then a community. When the girls of the fairy tales and of romance, the real-life prom queens, rejected me, Esther asked me to come and spend the day. Before Esther's quicksilver intelligence, Mollup seemed a pale waif, but for Esther we became company, and for five years we shared all our summer days. I took up her word games, and she took up my interest in newspapers, and together we found words that entertained our summer community. We devised singing swimming games for kids age six to sixteen, a newspaper with features on all phases of human and natural life along our shore, a club with elaborate rituals, and several theatrical extravaganzas. Esther dictated the scripts; I typed, occasionally inserting a metaphor from Mollup. We engaged most of the young folk in performing in the productions and called in most of the adult summer community to watch. Romance figured into most of these dramas, but, perhaps, through our linguistic high jinx, we discovered the means of conjuring away our personal need to be sleeping beauties. If most of our characters were stereotypes (starving artists, domineering mothers, honky-tonk singers with good hearts), astonishingly, we often cast girls as boys, boys as girls. Anyone could be a pirate. Thus Mollup did not fade. With Esther in the summers, my imagination, suppressed during the school months by consensus and romance, flourished.

In the years of schooling following high school—four of college and six of graduate school—Mollup led a subversive existence. I read the great books, the classics, the canonical texts of European, English, and American literature, and I learned to write about them in critical, analytical prose. The subjects of my study were the actions, emotions, convictions, and destiny of such complex human beings as Odysseus, Don Quixote, Hamlet, Heathcliff, Lambert Strether, and Jake Barns; yet oddly my reading and my writing about them seemed to occur in a rarified sphere. My personal experiences with Jim and Esther, the personal modes of expression I'd developed through them in editorials and dramas, were not nullified, merely reduced to shadows. Through these later years of schooling, I was consistently identifying against myself. Certainly, identification with the mad King Lear committed me to the study of literature forever; his progress from vanity to humility, from anger to love, from ignorance to wisdom seemed humanity's prototypical path. Yet, I see now, in the process of his growth, Lear rages against all womankind. And his daughters—Cordelia, whose virtue aligns her with those lovely ladies of the fairy tales, and Goneril and Regan, whose viciousness aligns them with the wicked witches—seem stereotypes from romance. Emerging from the catharsis of the play years later, I realize that all the women are actually lopped off at its conclusion, leaving men alone to try to rule.

In retrospect, I (as well as other feminist literary scholars who begin their work with similar autobiographical observations[2]) can recognize that in our academic training we were immersed in a Great Tradition that had been established by men; in principles of humanism that had been determined by men; and in concepts of universality that excluded half the human race. (Black critics, I would discover later, realized these concepts also invariably excluded blacks.) Such positions, asserted as realities, were illusions as powerful as those of romance. We women students accepted the authority of the faculty (in college, almost all male; in graduate school, all male); we accepted the interpretations of the critics (also largely male). We accepted the authority of the word as spoken by the patriarchs and as written in the patriarchical *Periodical of the Modern Language Association*. And when we went forth to teach the word, we appeared to be part of the old boy network. Carolyn Heilbrun terms the inability of successful women to conceive of other successful women, fictional or real, a "failure of the imagination" (1979, p. 72), and in our acceptance of and adjustments to the structures of male authority—in canonical and curricular decisions, in standards of critical theory and style, as well as in appointments and salary—we seemed to deny our Mollups, to endorse our own distortions, and to falsify our own humanity. Certainly it was during these later years of schooling that Mollup, my muse, my evolving, expanding, and energizing imagination, was laid most low. I find myself like Lee Edwards, who, in reviewing her education, concludes:

Like most women, I have gone through my entire education—as both student and teacher—as a schizophrenic, and I do not use this term lightly, for madness is the bizarre but logical conclusion of our education. Imagining myself male, I attempted to create myself male. Although I knew the case was otherwise, it seemed I could do nothing to make this other critically real (1972, p. 226).

But Mollup did not fail me altogether. Having been nurtured by the littlest mermaid and Baba Yaga, having been humanized by Jim and Esther, Mollup discovered her particular identity with outcasts and with women. Her subversive existence meant that I might do something "to make this other critically real." I could become sanely schizophrenic. Sandra Gilbert's and Susan Gubar's madwoman in the attic indeed! Like those British women writers and like Emily Dickinson, whose lives and works Gilbert and Gubar review with such brilliant illumination (1979), I found expression in alternative language forms. In college I had started keeping a journal and writing stories. Here I could abandon critical theory and style; I could describe rather than evaluate, narrate rather than analyze, see metaphorically rather than abstractly. If the journal, like Dickinson's poems, was my private letter to the world, the stories, which struggled to comprehend my private life as a woman in relation to the lives of other women (a fact I didn't realize till now), were public letters. Their subject was not successful women in Heilbrun's sense, but women seeking to survive, to understand themselves, and occasionally succeeding in becoming fully conscious of their circumstances. There were stories of my friendship with Jim, my friendship with Barbara, my innocence abroad; a middle-aged woman's friendship with a young woman, a middle-aged woman's attempt to create a community, my aunt's sad, proud isolation; an old woman's trial during floods, an old woman's determination to build her house on mastodon bones, my grandmother's senile dignity.

Having embarked in graduate school on the study of American literature, however, I discovered that the primary American myth focuses on a young man's penetration of the wilderness. This myth excluded women as the canon of American literature excluded women writers. Humanity, even for Hester Prynne and Isabel Archer, was measured in philosophical rather than social terms; gender was not an issue. Mollup waited in the wings with my feminine consciousness. Not until political and social circumstances shook the structures of imperialism, racism, and sexism in the sixties did Mollup assert herself openly; not until then did I become whole. Not until then, in the cracks that appeared in these structures, did the Mollups in many of us find public voice and begin to restructure.

My first reaction during this cataclysmic time was to America's oppressive and insidious institutionalized racism. Perhaps my protective and persistent schizophrenia made it possible for me to postpone reacting to America's oppressive and insidious institutionalized sexism; perhaps I still felt I could be one of the boys. Teaching Afro-American literature, I knew I wasn't black although I was frequently up against the blackboard. And forced to identify against my race if not against myself. However, as imagination had moved me to identify against my gender and to rage with the misogynistic King Lear, so I became a black man on the run, a black boy sneaking into the circus, a black girl swooning before a pear tree, a black slave refusing to be beaten ever again. And so Mollup became conscious of paradox: even as my experiences as a human being and an American were extended through Afro-American literature, I was reminded I was not a black American.

Historically, literary critics have changed in their response to black American experience as reflected in Afro-American literature. They focused first on the damaging effects of racism and slavery upon people from complex African cultures; second, on the triumph of survival—the vigorous reaction against slavery and racism, often militant, often ingenious and ironical; and third and recently, on the creation of a new culture—the transformation and fusion of African and American cultures into a distinctly Afro-American culture with a history, sociology, and style distinctly its own. As I came to write about Afro-American literature, I struggled to understand the damage of oppression and the triumph of survival and creation, but I knew my style could not be Afro-American; I could express neither with my body, nor my words, the vibrancy, the vitality, the soul of Afro-American culture; my language has been straight out of PMLA.

My growing consciousness of the integrity of Afro-American literature, however, directly precipitated my feminine consciousness. If I was excluded from the primary American myth and excluded from the Afro-American experience, I nevertheless recognized parallels between the phases in the history of Afro-American literary criticism and feminist literary criticism, especially as it applied to American literature. Elaine Showalter explicitly identifies three phases in the history of feminist literary criticism: first, a concentration "on exposing the misogyny of literary practice"; second, "the discovery that women writers had a literature of their own, whose historical and thematic coherence as well as artistic importance, had been obscured by the patriarchal values that dominate our culture"; third, an effort to "define the difference of women's writing as the expression of a female aesthetic" (1985, pp. 5–8). With a gasp, I saw the damage of persisting schizophrenia, the triumph of Mollup's survival, and the possibilities for her creative work within my community. With a gasp, I realized that Mollup, wild woman, was critically real and central to my sense of self. Freed to regard myself, my work, my life as female, I felt restored to an original wholeness and renewed.

With the encouragement and enlightenment of feminist writers—both critics and creative writers—and of feminist friends and with the autonomy of the classroom, Mollup, my muse and my imagination, came into her own. No longer did she have to exist secretly and subversively; no longer did I have to be schizophrenic. No longer did she have to exist reacting to stereotypes and conditions determined by a society and a profession dominated by male values. A mature Mollup guides my life and my work— my reading, writing, teaching—expressing the perspective of women, embracing paradox, synthesizing antithesis, delighting in difference and similarity.

With other feminists, I have thus become committed, as Gilbert suggests we are doing, to re-inventing, re-reading, re-writing, re-interpreting, reviewing, re-vising, re-storing, re-forming, re-newing the central texts of Western culture (1980). In terms of American literature, this has necessitated the re-examination of those male writers designated as shaping periods in American literary history and as satisfying the characteristics of the primary American myth. The writers whom I knew best stood newly revealed. I came to see that rather than Arthur Dimmesdale, whose suffering now seemed self-serving, correspondent with his societal ambitions, Hester Prynne, courageous and caring, was the true hero of *The Scarlet Letter*. I came to see that Ahab, whose searching now seemed to epitomize the desire for imperialistic conquest, represented conventional masculine values whereas Ishmael, committed to seeing all sides and to weaving them together, represented feminine values. Just as Simone Weil (1940) had long ago shown me that *The Iliad* must be read as a poem challenging the brutalizing nature of war, I realized that feminist critics—Nina Baym (1975, 1978), Judith Fetterley (1978), Annette Kolodny (1975, 1984), Adelaide Morris (1985), Carolyn Karcher (1980), Joyce Sparer Adler (1981)—threw the most penetrating of lights on the canon and myth of American literature. Women writers such as Emily Dickinson, Harriet Beecher Stowe, and Edith Wharton stood revealed as revolutionary writers, and women writers such as Rebecca Harding Davis, Elizabeth Stoddard, Charlotte Perkins Gilman, Mary Wilkins Freeman, Kate Chopin, Meridel LeSueur, Edith Summer Kelly, and Zora Neale Hurston simply and strongly stood; relegated previously to obscurity, they are now revealed in their common concerns as women and in their wonderful diversity as writers. Genres of literature in which women had excelled—letters, journals, diaries, autobiographies— whose value had been underestimated by the patriarchal publishing industry and the academy sprang into light and life. The challenge in my classrooms remains to transcend tokenism, on the one hand, by introducing selected texts by women and Afro-American writers into the curriculum, and ghettoization, on the other hand, by generating separate courses committed to women or ethnic writers. The challenge is, as Gilbert writes, "to decode and demystify all the disguised questions and answers that have always shadowed the connections between textuality and sexuality, genre and gender, pyschosexual identity and cultural authority" (1980, p. 36). The challenge for me as a teacher is to encourage all the Mollups crouched in my students to come forth.

So we renew ourselves through literature and re-tell our own stories. Knowing herself at last, Mollup can express herself in her own particular voice as female, American, and human, as self and member of society. It's been several years since I've written a story, in part, I sadly realize because the academy forces me to specialize, and in part, I gladly realize, because I'm being guided by my muse to experiment with a new voice. Now able to write myself into my writing as I can't do in writing about Afro-American literature, with some astonishment, I see myself writing, not by prescribed formula, but by Mollup's bright light, a feminist aesthetic. The result resembles Lee Gershung's description of feminist inquiry:

In discarding masculine maps that polarize female and male into hierarchies, feminist writers have attempted to blend reason and feeling into a unified sensibility. As a result, forms of feminist inquiry merge poetry and philosophy, history and myth, psychology and the personal and the political (1984, p. 192).

I have resumed my journal. The entries often comment on the state of my garden: the tenacity of weeds, the infestations of aphids, the surprise of larkspur, the luxuriance of lilac. The light is golden. I walk out the door into the garden to greet my eighty-nine-year-old neighbor who comes across the yard to give me a bouquet of pink and white sweet peas. She tells me what her grandmother had told her, "If you don't share your garden, it won't prosper." Mollup climbs down from the tree and agrees.

Notes

1. Perhaps especially noteworthy among feminist literary works written from an autobiographical impulse are two anthologies (Ascher, DeSalva, and Ruddick, 1984; Ruddick and Daniels, 1977) and three works of criticism (Brownstein, 1982; Heilbrun, 1979; Olsen, 1978).

2. See Brownstein (1982), Heilbrun (1979), and Ostriker (1986).

References

Adler, J. S. (1981). *War in Melville's imagination*. New York: New York University Press.

Ascher, C., DeSalva, L., and Ruddick, S. (Eds.) (1984). *Between women: Biographers, novelists, critics, teachers and artists write about their work on women*. Boston: Beacon Press.

Baym, N. (1975). *The shape of Hawthorne's career*. Ithaca, N.Y.: Cornell University Press.

————. (1978). *Women's fiction: A guide to novels by and about women in America*. Ithaca, N.Y.: Cornell University Press.

Brownstein, R. (1982). *Becoming a heroine: Reading about women in novels*. New York: Viking Press.

Edwards, L. (1972). Women, energy, and *Middlemarch*. *Massachusetts Review 13*, 223–238.

Fetterley, J. (1978). *The resisting reader: A feminist approach to American fiction*. Bloomington: Indiana University Press.

Gershung, L. (1984). The linguistic transformation of womanhood. In R. Rohrlich and E. H. Baruch (Eds.), *Women in search of utopia* (pp. 189–199). New York: Schocken Books.

Gilbert, S. M. (1980). What do feminist critics want? Or a postcard from the volcano. In E. Showalter (Ed.), *Feminist criticism: Essays on women, literature and theory* (pp. 29–45). New York: Pantheon Books.

Gilbert, S. M. and Gubar, S. (1979). *The madwoman in the attic: The woman writer and the nineteenth-century literary imagination*. New Haven: Yale University Press.

Heilbrun, C. G. (1973). *Toward a recognition of androgyny*. New York: Harper and Row.

―――. (1979). *Reinventing womanhood*. New York: W. W. Norton.

Karcher, C. L. (1980). *Shadow over the promised land: Slavery, race, and violence in Melville's America*. Baton Rouge: Louisiana State University Press.

Kolodny, A. (1975). *The lay of the land: Mataphor as experience and history in American life and letters*. Chapel Hill: University of North Carolina Press.

―――. (1984). *The land before her: Fantasy and experience of the American frontiers, 1630–1960*. Chapel Hill: University of North Carolina Press.

Miller, C. A. (1981). *A sociology of knowledge of feminist scholarship: A conceptual approach*. Paper presented at the annual meeting of the Midwest Sociological Society, Minneapolis.

Morris, A. (1985). Dick, Jane, and American literature: Fighting with canons. *College English, 47*, 467–481.

Olsen, T. (1978). *Silences*. New York: Dell.

Ostriker, A. (9 March 1986). American poetry now shaped by women. *New York Times Book Review*, pp. 1, 28, 30–31.

Ruddick, S. and Daniels, P. (Eds.) (1977). *Working it out: 23 women writers, artists, scientists, and scholars talk about their lives and work*. New York: Pantheon Books.

Showalter, E. (1985). Introduction. In E. Showalter (Ed.), *Feminist criticism: Essays on women, literature and theory* (pp. 3–17). New York: Pantheon Books.

Weil, S. (1940). *The Iliad or the poem of force*. Wallingford, Pa.: Pendle Hill Press.

Other Ways of Seeing: The Female Vision

16

ANN WEICK

For all of us fortunate to have eyesight, the act of seeing appears to be among the most commonplace of human activities. Moment by moment we trust our ability to turn the blurs of light striking our retinas into intelligible shapes and meaningful patterns. We believe that the world "out there" corresponds to our mental images of it and we count on its predictable familiarity. We find comfort in this familiarity and develop innumerable ways to maintain this sense of certainty and stability. All of this speaks to a taken-for-granted quality in our everyday lives that is difficult to see. But underlying the layers of automatic acquiescence is a deeper terrain worthy of our investigation. It is there we can discover the radical potential of a new way of seeing and, in that seeing, find a bridge between the personal and social dimensions of our lives.

In making this journey, we will pass through an intellectual terrain that can help us understand the social ramifications of our taken-for-granted lives and the emancipatory potential (Sampson, 1983) of learning to see differently. At stake in this journey is the development of a perspective that allows us to see both ourselves and the world in a new light and that gives credence to our ability to create new meanings in place of the old. Learning to see in this way is a radical act because it shows us, to paraphrase Thoreau, that looking is not seeing. The sensory data accumulated from using our eyes are not the same as the meaning derived from them. It is we who have the power to construct and reconstruct the meaning of what we see, and the expression of that power is, for each of us, a very personal gift.

The metaphor of seeing through women's eyes highlights the parallel processes of change that can occur for women and for society at large when unexamined aspects of life are brought to light. The outcome of such assessment can lead to a new synthesis of the personal and the social aspects of our lives.

Learning to See

The most critical aspect in learning to see differently is a recognition that it is possible to do so. This statement may seem disarmingly simple and yet behind it lies the resistive forces of every human society. Under the guise of authority and in the interests of self-preserving stability, social institutions create the illusion that things are the way they are because it is in their nature to be so. The rules of social conduct constantly reinforce a view of human relationships that seems to be immutable and, more importantly, true. From our earliest moments, we learn to shape the welter of impressions bombarding us into culturally acceptable forms and, with the acceptance of a particular way of seeing, we forfeit the possibility of alternative views. The process of socialization is a process of image-making. We learn to see through the particularistic eyes of our culture, the content packaged in a way that compels both belief and compliance.

Given the persuasive force of these social processes, it is worth examining how inroads are made in this perception monopoly. In an interesting way, the social and the personal routes bear some striking resemblances. In each case, the critique begins with impertinent, powerful questions: What if things are not as they appear or as we have been led to think they should appear? What if the definers of reality, whether pope, president, or potentate, are purveyors of a desiccated version of what human society is and can be? What if the power to define comes not from what a thing "really" is but what we believe it to be? At the heart of the social and personal critiques is the question of the role of the definer. As we shall see, it is the shift in attention from what something "really" is to who is defining it that represents the first dramatic step in learning to see differently. Discovering that we each have the power to define our own reality begins to loosen the ties that bind us to socially prescribed definitions of who we are and what we should be.

There are always small fissures in any set of cultural rules and beliefs. A few individuals see the cracks of inconsistency and in sometimes prophetic tones try to signal the need for change. But these voices are often swallowed up in the rush of history. It is when the few voices are joined by many that the more serious forms of critique begin to emerge. In recent decades, there has been a growing critique of the assumptions underlying the prevailing social definitions of the way things are. In fields as diverse as feminist scholarship (Gilligan, 1982; Ruether, 1983), quantum physics (Capra, 1982; Pagels, 1982; Zukav, 1979), and holistic health (Dossey, 1982; Weil, 1983), writers and researchers are contending with the old worldview and struggling to develop radically new ways of seeing. Although the language of the critiques varies, they center on a common insight: that the dominant Western paradigm is based on an incomplete and therefore erroneous definition of the nature of reality. In its place is a growing recognition that what was thought to be the objective, verifiable foundation of the natural and human worlds is instead a fluid pastiche of belief, intention, and socially negotiated meaning.

An early crack in the existing consensus was begun when Berger and Luckmann (1966) published *The Social Construction of Reality*. In contrast to the prevailing wisdom about the objective character of perception, they gathered evidence to show that reality is not of a piece, and that what we perceive has more to do with social agreement than with some purportedly intrinsic character of the object seen. Whether it was in a carefully controlled laboratory setting or a scene from everyday life, it was recognized that people brought themselves into the act of seeing and in doing so, projected onto the objects unpredictable and idiosyncratic qualities. To borrow from Gertrude Stein (1971), they brought into the realm of academic scrutiny the question of whether there is any there there. The upshot of their scholarly discourse was to show the complexities imbedded in that question and to demonstrate their case for understanding reality as a socially constructed phenomenon. Because the impetus of social sciences was moving in precisely the opposite direction—that is, toward greater reliance on measurement and objectification—Berger and Luckmann's apposite and intuitively pleasing interpretation of the vagaries of people's perceptions seemed compelling.

During this same period, Thomas Kuhn (1962) presented a similar but more far-reaching thesis in *The Structure of Scientific Revolutions*. Perhaps because he focused his analysis on the scientific enterprise, the reverberations caused by his arguments are still heard today. For of all the definers of social reality, Cartesian science has been preeminent. The Newtonian revolution was far more than a method of investigating nature's workings. It set in place a set of assumptions that made scientific inquiry the supreme arbiter of truth. The realm of legitimate human knowledge was narrowed to embrace only those facts that could meet the test of the scientific experiment. And it was the belief in objectivity that made this truth-standard possible. As Bernstein (1985) reminds us, "At the heart of the objectivist's vision, and what makes sense of his or her passion, is the belief that there are or must be some fixed, permanent constraints to which we can appeal and which are secure and stable" (pp. 161–166). Kuhn drove a fatal wedge in this belief structure by showing that the idea of science as a mechanism for discovering this fixed and secure foundation was an illusion. The choice of new theories or paradigms was not "a matter of proof or appeal to evidence" but a matter of historical and human processes. From the Kuhnian perspective even science, thought to be the best and, for some, the only route to achieving truth, could be viewed as a process of social construction.

Women as Other: Feminist Perspective

The process of seeing in a different way is a mysterious one. When Kuhn described a scientific revolution as a change in worldview, he was emphasizing the fact that a new paradigm dramatically changes what is seen. After a major paradigm switch, the world is, in important respects, a new place for its viewers. What was recognized in the old light is seen in an entirely different way. In Watzlawick's (Watzlawick, Weakland, and Fisch, 1974) terms, a second order change has occurred. Rather than struggling to solve the problem in the same old ways, the problem itself is reframed and in doing so, a startling new solution can be found.

Talking precisely about how this switch occurs is difficult to do. There seem to be a number of factors associated with its occurence: the presence of crisis (what Pirsig [1979] might call "getting stuck"); readiness to entertain different views; a creative, intuitive, playful, intellectual style; and a weak allegiance to the status quo. There is also, I believe, another factor that can be added to this list. It is related to the issue of allegiance but goes beyond it. And it is the factor most often shared by women and by minorities. That factor is an awareness of being the "other." Indeed, it is this awareness of "otherness" that has been a prime source of fuel for the contemporary feminist movement. Seeing oneself as "other" can be a matter of profound human estrangement but if that estrangement is understood in larger terms, it can become a powerful force for radical change.

The experience of "otherness" is a universal aspect of women's lives. In a culture that reveres maleness, women are necessarily viewed as the "second sex," Simone de Beauvoir's (1953) term for the socially ascribed, inferior status of women. It is not possible for women to live in a sexist society and not be aware of this negative appraisal. From their earliest memories, they have a sense of being "other," of not fitting the model of male attributes that is universally preferred. There is, then, a pervasive self-consciousness about being somehow alien and less desirable than male counterparts.

The negative message is repeated in myriad ways, sometimes starkly, sometimes coated with a sugar that hides its bitterness. To be told that one is not as deserving or as capable as a boy when experience suggests the contrary requires a young girl to ignore what she knows in favor of what is to be believed. To have the difference of gender then interpreted not as a loss but as a gain requires yet another level of deception. So with the experience of otherness comes the lesson that one's feelings and judgments are not to be trusted. One is estranged from oneself and one's most reliable source of knowledge about one's life.

These lessons are ingrained in ways that make dispute difficult. But the sense of otherness the larger society seeks to maintain can become the mechanism through which a challenge is raised. When any group of people is systematically prevented from recognizing and acting upon their full repertoire of human possibilities, the seeds are sown for collective reaction and action. There are always individuals who will question their socially assigned place and dispute society's definition of who they are. Such individuals can be ignored or forcibly squelched. But when numbers of individuals begin to question society's definitions, then the possibility exists for a serious challenge to the predominant view of the way things are. It is the very fact of women's "otherness" that enables them to become the eloquent critics of the existing view and the visionaries for a different future.

This recognition of otherness and the rejection of it must certainly have been a critical stimulus for both the old and new women's movements. In the spheres of collective political action and scholarship, women have been developing a powerful critique of the social forces that aim at keeping us a second class. On the action front, barriers are being challenged in the workplace, in the family, and at the ballot box. Attempts to win equal pay for work of equal worth, to protect women's reproductive choice, to gain equal access to positions of leadership, and to constitutionally outlaw discrimination based on gender have all demonstrated a growing collective commitment to overturning the old, patriarchal order. On the scholarship front, feminist authors are producing a growing body of literature that documents the existence and consequences of a sexist way of seeing. Whether it comes from anthropological and historical reassessment of women's contributions to society, from research on gender and role, or from critical appraisals of religious, political, and social theory, the central finding is the same: the fact that women have been cast into the role of other is a matter of social construction. There are no qualities inherent in women that account for their inferior social, economic, and political status. Rather, their inferior status is a useful distortion that serves to maintain a particular male class in a privileged position.

As important as are the findings that come from such analyses, they are not always the most important element of this critical process. The aspect that needs equal attention is the act of creating a vantage point from which to recognize that the way things are is not immutable. It is not so much the realization that things can be viewed from a new angle as the equally strong realization that things can be viewed from many different angles. Thus, in taking the step involved in a critique of the way things are, we also can take an epistemological leap. Instead of substituting one orthodoxy for another, we can come to understand that the ground under our feet is constantly changing. Whatever it is in one moment of time depends largely on how we, as perceivers, see it to be. We learn that we have the ability to put on different lenses and see the world from many different vantage points. And it is we who can choose the vantage points.

The issue of choice is a central one. If an existing social order does not constitute an incontrovertible reality that exists outside our awareness of it, then we have the choice to construct a new vision of what it could be.

Rather than making traditional scientific inquiry the arbiter of truth, we must find other grounds for our choices. These decisions ultimately hinge not on facts but on beliefs. For those challenging a sexist social order, it is the belief in women's inherent equality with men that provides the base for revisioning a world beyond gender-based divisions.

The Personal Experience in Seeing Differently

Discovering this arena of choice typically signals a personal insight of revolutionary dimensions. In my own life, this discovery began on an intellectual plane: the message imbedded in Kuhn's scholarly critique shook me to my roots. It caused the sort of initial reverberation that many of us instantly recognize. A quiet voice inside says, "But if this is true, everything changes." And in contrast to all the earlier times when such voices nudged me, I felt myself being propelled into the giddy and frightening state of acquiescence. Somehow, I knew that what I was thinking was true—not because it was verified by external authority but because it fit instantly and precisely with my own deepest wisdom and experience. It was a period of conversion because old beliefs, thought to be and taught as true, evaporated in the face of this new and truer view.

As with all such experiences of radical insight, there then ensues an exhilarating but exhausting period where the insight goes underground to work itself out. It is as though the first moments of seeing differently occur on a different plane of existence—where intuitive processes provide a clarity that cannot be sustained. But unlike the dream state, where one understands something with startling acuity and then cannot recapture it once the alarm rings, the critical insight that allows us a new way of seeing can be recognized and reworked. One learns quickly that the flash of insight gives way to a good deal of work.

The process of bringing this view fully into one's life is a matter of unlearning and relearning. Whether the insight is stored by a critical view of patriarchy or of science, there are common dynamics involved. Central to these dynamics seems to be a recentering of oneself in relation to the world. In a way that reverses the import of the Copernican revolution, one finds oneself not an obscure planet circling round the sun but as a new star at the center of the universe. It is not an egocentric place because being central in this way is not a glorification of one individual at the expense of the others. Rather, our centrality allows us to acknowledge, perhaps for the first time, that each of us is uniquely important in the universe and that our individual power does not deserve to take second place to anyone's, especially those authorities who have hidden our power from us.

The question of authority is crucial to this unlearning-relearning process. People are able to be subjugated as long as they accept others as the only ones to legitimately define reality. As long as men have defined women's reality, churches lay people's reality, governments their citizens' reality, and science nature's reality, the collusive relationship of oppression is in force. Freeing ourselves from this relationship is as simple and as difficult as declaring ourselves active participants in defining our own reality. The simplicity rests with the fact that such declarations occur first in the privacy of our own heads. We tell ourselves that we no longer accept anyone else's authority as automatically more legitimate than our own. In doing this we accomplish two things. First, we validate our own knowledge and experience as sources of authority and power. Our views of reality deserve to be heard and reacted to as much as anyone else's. Second, we no longer see tradition and force as legitimate grounds for authority. It is no longer sufficient in our eyes for others to exercise power because it has always been done this way or because they have the force to silence us. Authority, and the power from which it derives, become appropriate targets of critique. The task of overturning long-standing social definitions is naturally fraught with risks and difficulties. Those who act as social definers have no interest in relinquishing their privileged positions and any attempts to challenge their monopoly will meet with vigorous resistance. This resistance comes from the sure knowledge that power of this kind is maintained by holding firmly to the definitional reins. People must never know that things are not or need not be as they seem.

The force behind this definitional oligarchy is both direct and indirect. In its direct forms, we see the elite speaking out and squelching those who try to propose their own explanations and definitions. History is replete with examples of such tactics of silencing: excommunication, burning at the stake, the Inquisition, public shaming. Contemporary examples add to the list: Mary Ann Sorrentino, director of Planned Parenthood of Rhode Island, who, the Diocese of Providence ruled, excommunicated herself from the Roman Catholic Church by acting as an "accomplice" in abortions (*New York Times Index*, 1986); Sister Agnes Mary Mansour, the Catholic nun who was directed by her archbishop to leave her post as director of the State Department of Social Services in Michigan because she refused to oppose state payments for abortion (*New York Times Index*, 1983); Sonia Johnson, who was excommunicated from the Mormon Church for her public support of the proposed equal rights amendment (*New York Times Index*, 1980). These provide evidence of the direct consequences of oligarchic single-mindedness.

In its indirect form, the process of social definition is much more subtle and, because of that, even more powerful. The subtlety arises from the fact that the overt message is delivered on two levels. There is the content level of the message, which delivers the active punchline: women are inferior to men, blacks are less intelligent than whites, elderly are senile and helpless. The hook in this message is that believing the overt message means not only accepting its content as true, but accepting the authority of those who are defining it. Thus, one comes to believe both the message and one's own inability to question it.

This is precisely the point at which the simple and complex levels join. The simple part is coming to the startling realization that the sphere of creating social definitions does not need to be left in the hands of the elite. One can "simply" choose to see oneself as having the power to define one's own reality. The difficulty in maintaining this realization, even once achieved, speaks to the underlying complexity. We have all learned long lessons about our inability to assert our own definitions of self and world. The force of these lessons makes us shy and uneasy in taking a more active posture in our thinking and in the way we live our lives.

Thus, seeing in a new way is a process, not a one-time moment of insight. Because what we are engaged in challenges the definers in such a fundamental way, we can expect to meet active resistance. At the very least, we can anticipate times when our ideas and actions will be discredited. Attempts will be made to show that we do not have the authority or knowledge to create new definitions. Depending upon the arena where such challenges occur, there may also be active efforts to silence or ostracize us.

At the same time, we must be vigilant on another front—where the Greek chorus in our head chants: but you're wrong, you're foolish. This chorus is the result of years of imbedded messages about our own inadequacies. The roots of these messages are lodged deeply in our psyches, creating a core of vulnerability that often undermines our own wisdom about our life as we experience it. The interaction between external and internal discrediting sources presents a tangled web from which we must continually work to extricate ourselves.

Disentanglement is not a simple process. Seeing one's world in a new way is a significant beginning but it unfolds into an ongoing process of change. To have the insight that women's reality is not inscribed by social assumptions of inequality is a necessary first step. If this awareness is sufficiently strong, that is, if it evokes a deep wisdom about our own experiences, then this new view of reality immediately supercedes the old. In biblical terms, the scales fall from our eyes. The world is, at least for an instant, a truly different place. But this insight is only a beginning. From this point onward, a new path appears—a path that will engage us in a lifelong process of transformation.

One of the first things we will discover is that the old view reappears in many guises. The social beliefs and practices that support sexism continue to deluge us, sometimes appearing even more vigorous in the face of our new resolve. The world has not changed; only our view of it has. Because we still carry the old view within us, we find that it expresses itself in many surprising ways. We may find ourselves judging our behavior or the behavior of others according to criteria that are incompatible with our new view. For example, we may find ourselves being critical of other women who have not had the insights we've had or who live their lives in ways that seem, from our perspective, destructive and bleak. Such attitudes about ourselves and others are continuing reminders that insight does not easily displace old habits of mind. Out of this, we learn a new kind of tolerance for our own frailties, a tolerance that also helps us become gentler judges of others.

We may begin to more actively search out other women who share our perspective and experience with them the support that comes from a mutually shared view of the world. This group cohesiveness has a different base than the traditional women-gathering carried out over the ages. In contrast to the reactive quality of many traditional women's groups (coffee klatches, sewing circles, Ladies Aid Societies), where women retreated into a safe atmosphere to share stories of their lot in life, women who are actively challenging these beliefs form groups to move out into the world. The support gained in this way leads not to retreat but to change on both personal and social levels.

Seeing the World through Women's Eyes

Understanding the connection between personal and social change presents a sticky problem. With the heritage of Western dichotomies, we tend to isolate spheres of life along polar dimensions. In the case of change, we see individuals and social structures as separate elements, representing "inner" and "outer" aspects of human life. We pose problems for ourselves about whether to focus on individual or social change in order to bring about desired results. The phrase, "the personal is political," cuts through that separation by recognizing the intimate relationship between both spheres. Every personal experience is shaped by larger social forces; society, writ small or large, is affected by the changes of individuals. The personal revolution women experience when they come to see the effects of patriarchy in their lives reverberates within their social sphere, changing relationships and behaviors. The problem is that we discount this ripple effect because it does not produce what we think of as radical change. One woman's, or even many women's, experience of seeing in this new way has not toppled patriarchy. But individual change is the necessary foundation upon which such far-reaching change depends.

Women's collective vision of a world where each person can express and contribute her talents and abilities without any artificial barriers and restrictions presents a goal for humankind. In the long track of species development, and in the short track of human development, we have come to that auspicious place where increasing numbers of women are seeing possibilities for a new society, governed by a new consciousness. This vision is joined by others who see the possibility of a world without war and without hunger. From an optimistic viewpoint, the rising tide of this new awareness may be the precipitator for a quantum leap to a new stage of human evolution. Or the "deathy ways" (Barth, 1972) of the modern age may bring another end. What is important to recognize is the capacity of the human spirit to see beyond where it is and to use that sight to imaginatively create a new and more humane world. From this vantage point, women's way of seeing presents a visionary potential to be reckoned with.

References

Barth, J. (1972). *Chimera*. Greenwich, Conn.: Fawcett.

Berger, P. and Luckmann, T. (1966). *The social construction of reality*. Garden City, N.Y.: Doubleday.

Bernstein, R. (1985). *Beyond objectivism and relativism: Science, hermeneutics, and praxis*. Philadelphia: University of Pennsylvania Press.

Capra, F. (1982). *The turning point*. New York: Simon and Schuster.

de Beauvoir, S. (1953). *The second sex*. New York: Alfred A. Knopf.

Dossey, L. (1982). *Space, time and medicine*. Boulder, Colo.: Shambhala.

Gilligan, C. (1982). *In a different voice*. Cambridge, Mass.: Harvard University Press.

Kuhn, T. (1962). *The structure of scientific revolutions*. Chicago: University of Chicago Press.

New York Times Index. (1980). Volume 68.

————. (1983). Volume 71.

————. (1986). Volume 74.

Pagels, H. (1982). *The cosmic code*. New York: Simon and Schuster.

Pirsig, R. (1979). *Zen and the art of motorcycle maintenance*. New York: Morrow.

Ruether, R. (1983). *Sexism and God-talk*. Boston: Beacon Press.

Sampson, E. (1983). *Justice and the critique of pure psychology*. New York: Plenum.

Stein, G. (1971). *Everybody's autobiography*. New York: Cooper Square.

Watzlawick, P., Weakland, J., and Fisch, R. (1974). *Change: Principles of problem formation and problem resolution*. New York: Norton.

Weil, A. (1983). *Health and healing*. Boston: Houghton Mifflin.

Zukav, G. (1979). *The dancing wu li masters*. New York: William Morrow.

Different Visions, Same World: The Transmission of Feminism

17

SANDRA L. ALBRECHT

This article is based on my experiences as a teacher. Specifically, I want to focus my comments on what I have learned from teaching a course on the sociology of sex roles. I developed this course out of an interest in creating greater awareness of what I see as critical issues that, on a very practical level, affect our everyday lives. Since the very beginning, I have introduced this course by explaining that I was teaching it because I am a feminist. I know that such an identification does not go over well. Very few of my students, female or male, identify themselves as feminists. Invariably, students will comment that feminism is a sex-biased word, will use feminism as an example of a negative stereotype, or will in some way or another convey their disapproval of the label feminist. Their sentiments reflect not only the climate on college campuses today, but a more general, more pervasive societal attitude. As Bolotin (1982) found in her interviews, young women are often sympathetic to issues of equal opportunity, cognizant of their own experiences with inequality, and yet vocally rejecting of the concept of feminism. For some, it is not only a rejection of the label, but a conviction that feminists are bitter, shrill, unhappy, tortured women. Both this depiction of feminists as "icy monsters" and the perception that women are free to select individual routes toward success work against identification with feminists as well as with a collective movement. As one young woman said to Bolotin, "Sure, there's discrimination out there, but you just can't sit there feeling sorry for yourself. It's the individual woman's responsibility to prove her worth. Then she can demand equal pay" (p. 31).

The attitudes of these young women are repeated throughout our society. Although public opinion polls report majority support for feminist goals, there is only minority identification with feminism (Ferree and Hess, 1985). Introducing my course with an explicit statement of my feminism makes overt opinions that are covertly held. The distancing that I initially cause by this explicit statement is easier to deal with than what I now see as a form of subtle distancing that occurs in the absence of such a statement.

The Dynamics of Interaction

For a long time, I was more aware of the differential perceptions between my female and male students than I was of this subtle distancing between myself and my class. By and large, my students are involved in the course. They actively participate in the discussions, are attentive within reason during the lectures, and are creative in their written assignments which are based on observations of their everyday lives.

Gender Differences

They seem remarkably willing to say what is on their minds, often aware that it is going to create disagreement in the class. Usually, we get through such disagreement and on to a more collective sense of how people's experiences differ as a function of gender. For example, in a workshop designed to focus on the advantages and disadvantages of the opposite sex, one women's group reported that the absence of everyday forms of harassment was a male advantage. This contention did not go over well with some of the males in the class, who felt the women were both exaggerating and overly sensitive. Their complaint was fair in the sense that substance needed to be added to document the women's allegation, so I asked the women in the class to provide some examples, using the last week only, to support their contention. About one-third of my female students came up with concrete instances of harassment, ranging from being whistled at and followed while running to being called "girl" by a younger, less senior, male office employee. Once the male students could see the reality of harassment in the lives of the females in the class, they were much more accepting of the women's general perspective that males have an advantage in this area.

There are many other examples of gender differences in the beliefs and perceptions of students in my class. Male students typically see divorce as a financial advantage to females, contrary to the evidence of women's sharp decline in financial resources after divorce (Weitzman, 1985) and despite the available data on the feminization of poverty and its link to female-maintained households. Female students are more sensitive to female poverty; some have even argued that for women to live longer than men is a disadvantage because of the high incidence of poverty among elderly women. These are just some examples of how students perceive the effects of gender, and how gender affects their perceptions. Despite sometimes heated disagreement, rarely do we end in stalemate. (There are, however, some comments that are difficult to process. After years of trying, I have yet to be able to formulate an answer to the rhetorical question, "If girls aren't willing to take the name of the guy, then why are they getting married?")

Personal Changes

Since the main emphasis has been on communication between my female and male students, I was less conscious of the interaction between myself and my students. A few years ago, however, I was lecturing, presenting a fairly structured lecture that elicited a good deal of student note-taking. Looking for intermittent eye contact as I spoke, I got a real sense that the students were attentive but not really absorbing what I was saying. This feeling is not unfamiliar to anyone who has taught, but I was more aware of this sense of distance in this class because it seemed to contradict what I perceived as the whole purpose of the course.

I had designed the course to increase their gender awareness, not my own. But the experience of their distance made me begin thinking about the process of how my gender awareness had developed. I recognized that over the time that I had taught the course, my own issues relating to gender had changed. These changes were partly a reflection of what I viewed as changes within the feminist movement and were influenced by both my personal experiences and readings of feminist scholarship. The second wave of the feminist movement, born out of the participatory movements of the late 1960s and early 1970s as well as in response to the rising demand for female labor in an expanding service economy, combined both national organizing and grass-roots activities (Evans, 1979; Richardson, 1981). This movement highlighted concerns for women's relative position in the labor force and political representation, as well as other issues such as childbearing, childrearing, and health care.

My initial involvement in feminism revolved around my own central concern of the time. I had just graduated from college and was most interested in being able to obtain a decent job. I couldn't. Although I had worked in college at low pay, sometimes under what I saw as despotic supervision, I didn't want to make a career of it. I wanted the same opportunities afforded to men; and I became convinced that I could secure equal opportunity only by going to graduate school. Such a pattern of educational interruption and resumption is fairly typical among women seeking graduate degrees.

My personal encounters with the occupational segregation of the labor force may have influenced my decision in graduate school to study the sociology of work. Both my experiences and research have influenced my teaching. Until very recently, the sociology of work has been the sociology of male work, with female labor standing on the periphery. Not one semester of teaching the sociology of work goes by without some student opposition to my attempts to discuss both female and male experiences in the labor force. So permeated are we with the perception that the work world is male, so separated by gender are the majority of experiences of workers, that it is still difficult to convey the legitimacy of examining the entire labor force, including unpaid as well as paid labor.

In teaching about sex roles, I have not always been able to avoid the biased perception that the world of work is best defined by a male standard and the female role is one of adaptation. This perception has numerous ramifications and bars one from really questioning assumptions about how work is organized. For example, I have always placed heavy emphasis on the need for the desegregation of the labor force, with a primary focus on getting women into the more highly paid, higher positions in our society, i.e., traditionally male-dominated occupations. When the issue of comparable worth was first introduced, I was skeptical and imparted that skepticism to my students. I believed that a system to insure comparable pay for comparable work would be cumbersome, impossible to implement, and would draw attention away from the problem of occupational segregation. I have since changed my belief and now see the fundamental importance of the concept of comparable worth. This concept attacks the basic assumption that work can only be valuable if it is done by males. Moreover, by enhancing the value of traditionally female occupations, it expands the possibilities for occupational desegregation.

Breaking up the assumption that the male is the norm for the work world extends the discussion from work structures to stylistic elements that sustain those structures. In John Molloy's 1977 book, *The Woman's Dress for Success*, the female was clothed essentially in the classic blue suit, with skirts exchanged for pants. And, the message was obvious. Not only our clothes, but our femaleness was to be left outside the office door. Women's acceptance of themselves, and of their female colleagues, was tenuous and ambivalent. Like the society around us, we devalued emotional-expressive qualities and concerns for connectedness. We too split the genders into the competent one and the expressive one. Integration of these two attributes into our understanding of a human, gender-free nature has been difficult and slow, but increasingly this split is being healed, as the division between private and public spheres is breaking down, as women's voices are being heard. There have been other changes as well. I have become more attuned to the use of language and the impact of images in the media. I understand the complex issues of violence against women and pornography better than I did before; growing older, I am more sensitive to and more concerned about the hardships facing women as they age. In each of these, and other, areas, I have had to struggle against long-held assumptions, and as I change, my own evolvement becomes incorporated in my teaching and my interactions with students.

Class Interchange

The exploration of gender differences by my students, in research and scholarship and in my own personal thoughts and concerns, leads to an understanding that gender role change both requires awareness and is an ongoing process. Sometimes students become frustrated by their growing awareness and argue that focusing on such issues as media stereotypes, language biases, and gender stratification only exacerbates the problem. Their assumption is that it is better not to be attuned to these matters because awareness only creates conflict where there was none before. I certainly agree that it creates conflict. For women, the first stages of awareness are often followed by anger and a sense of powerlessness. For men, awareness of misogyny and gender inequality erodes their invested belief that society is basically equal, and sometimes makes them feel personally defensive. Blaming individuals is not the intent of my course. I have found that both the feelings of victimization by women and of defensiveness by men can be best dealt with by emphasizing the fact that the course itself did not create the problem, but that it can possibly contribute to a solution.

The transition in my own views, from the well-formed to the unformed and sometimes uninformed, increases students' frustration. The educational process has led students to expect only the former of these perspectives, what I see as the presentation of the message without the medium. In part, I share students' expectations about the role of teacher, and there is always a conflict for me about how much disorder there can be amid order. But disorder, showing all the various twists and turns involved in how I think through an issue, breaks down the perception that ideas are formed without process, without change, and without grappling with the complexity of issues. Hopefully, the outcome of this kind of disorder is empowerment: the deeply rooted belief that individuals can understand their world and have the ability to make informed decisions about how that world is to be organized. Empowerment works against the assumption that others are more capable of determining the decisions that affect our lives. Empowerment also breaks down the barrier that students have erected between themselves and teachers and can decrease their distancing from the learning process.

But commonly held expectations of the classroom situation are not the only origins of distancing. The attention without absorption that I became aware of in my course creates distance as well. When I first recognized this response, my tendency was to engage in my own form of blaming, concluding that my students didn't understand the significance of the issues to their lives. With reflection, however, I began to question my initial conclusion. I realized that I had been able to moderate disagreement between the women and men in my course and incorporate my own changes into my approach to the class. But, in fact, I knew very little about how relevant the gender-related issues I regarded as vital were to them at this stage in their lives. I felt this particularly with my female students. Although I had begun my own feminization at their age, the historical period in which I had come of age was radically different from today. My female students had grown up along with the second wave of feminism and were coming of age in a period of noted gains in equality as well as an equally strong backlash. The subtle distance that can occur between them and me may reflect their sense that the issues I raise represent the historical biography of a movement rather than vital concerns that pertain directly to their lives. I remain invested in the centrality of the issues we cover, but I also understand the need to fit these concerns into their reality. This awareness has prompted me to begin to study the ways my students, especially my female students, construct their own reality and cope with the world as they perceive it to be.

Current Realities, Current Views

For most students, the college years are a period of transition and anticipatory socialization. They are gradually separating from their family of origin and beginning the process of establishing new family networks. In addition, they are preparing to enter the labor force. Similar to men, women expect to be involved in paid labor. But, unlike men, their perceptions of that involvement are much more likely to be connected to their perceptions of their role in family life. Two patterns emerge in discussions and assignments focusing on the relationship between family and work.

By far the most common pattern envisioned by young women is a period of employment, exiting the labor force for childbearing and early childrearing, and then, reentry into the labor force. They expect that husbands will initially share equally in household tasks, with the assumption that when they become full-time housewives, they will take over primary responsibility for the household. Typically, they do not address how tasks will be divided after they reenter the labor force.

Caution needs to be applied anytime one is looking at future visions; such visions are composed of wish fulfillment tempered by a sense of the possible. To the extent that young women make their decisions in terms of this particular vision, however, their central life chances may be altered. For example, if women believe that their first employment in the labor force will be only temporary, this may have ramifications throughout their labor force participation. Such a belief may decrease their perceived need for education in order to secure desirable employment; they can assume that the real decisions about education and career will be made later when they can anticipate stable employment. Assuming that employment is only temporary can also increase the willingness of these young women to take employment that offers low financial and job rewards. In effect, such a vision may postpone job-related decisions during a critical period that significantly affects women's employment and personal well-being throughout their lives.

Moreover, this vision does not conform to reality. Over 60 percent of women with children under the age of eighteen are now in the labor force. Since 1970, the most rapid rate of increase in labor force participation has been among women with children under the age of three. By 1985, 51 percent of these women were in the labor force, compared to 26 percent in 1970 (National Commission on Working Women, 1986). For those who have left the labor force, the period of disengagement has progressively shortened. What is assumed to be temporary employment may, in fact, become permanent.

There may be ripple effects as well. A woman's chances of making a salary comparable to her husband's may diminish with the acceptance of the concept of a temporary job. In turn, decision-making power in the family unit is affected by economics, with more power accorded to the highest earner; the greater the disparity in income, the more pronounced is the power ratio (Gillespie, 1971). With differential marital power, the desire to establish an equal division of household tasks may be undermined. In an interesting national study conducted by a leading woman's magazine (Heffner, 1983), 90 percent of the respondents believed that men were doing more in the household than in the past; but, almost an equal number, 89 percent, reported that in actuality they were performing over half or all of the domestic and child care duties.

What Blau and Ferber (1986) refer to as the "housework gap" between women and men has been slow to change. In the 1970s, the gap did narrow, stemming from the reduction in the time spent by women in household tasks rather than from an increase in male contribution. In the 1980s, male participation in the household, particularly among younger men, has further narrowed the gap, but women's responsibility remains predominant. Women's perceptions that their own paid labor is temporary may not only reduce their expectations for their labor market position but increase their expectations for their own role in the household, thus adversely affecting the equality of the household division of labor.

It may be unrealistic to propose that young women should prepare for the eventuality of being unmarried if that is not their desire. However, in 1983, 43 percent of all women over the age of eighteen were single, separated, divorced, or widowed (Current Population Reports, 1984). From 1972 to 1982, families maintained by women grew at a rate dramatically faster than that of other families, undergoing a 57 percent increase compared to a 10 percent increase for the others (U.S. Department of Labor, 1983). By 1985, one out of four mothers in the labor force was maintaining the family (National Commission on Working Women, 1985). The rising proportion of women who will be the sole support of themselves and children, with a greater risk of falling below the poverty line, increases the concern over early decisions that may not reflect the reality of the current situation.

The second pattern, mentioned by only a minority of my female students, may solve some of the problems above, but raises other issues. This pattern is one in which women plan to be involved in the labor force without interruption. They know that they want careers and are likely to have organized their educational activities around getting professional degrees, either at the undergraduate level or during anticipated graduate training. Their solution to the difficulty of combining work and family is often a decision not to have children. This decision may change over time, as it has for other women, and may reflect a general trend to delay childbearing. On the other hand, the decision may be carried out; our society is experiencing a declining birthrate and an increase in married couples choosing not to have children.

The decision to have or not have a child is intensely personal, but it also is influenced by the social conflict women experience in the relationship between work and family. In the first vision described by my students, women ordered their work lives around their concerns for family; in the second, women ordered their family decisions around their work lives. Both visions share the underlying assumption that it is not possible to have both a satisfying family life and satisfying work. If you make one a priority, then the other has to conform.

Discussion

These two visions of the future suggest a real awareness on the part of young women of the difficulties of combining work and family. This theme is more noteworthy for its persistence than its novelty. Diary entries of women throughout history have echoed the conflict between work and family, work and love (Moffat and Painter, 1974). Today, the popular media often raise the question, "Can women have it all?" referring to these conflicts for women. Rarely, and then typically only in a financial context, have I heard this phrase used for men. If the world is not much changed, then women who differ in age share common concerns. Where, then, does the distance between women occur? Specifically, how do I account for the distance between myself and my female students?

In the same way that my students are reluctant to see themselves as feminists, they seem to have a general reluctance to identify with my generation. There could be a number of explanations for this. First, they are in the process of establishing their own identity, and much of this involves their separation from their mothers. We may offer role models to them, but ones that infringe upon their own autonomy and independence.

Second, many young women see the search for a mate as an important part of their current goals. For them, to identify with feminism may appear to hamper their ability to connect with men; as Ferree and Hess (1985) suggest, fear of male disapproval may militate against considering oneself a feminist. The concern for establishing a permanent relationship may also decrease young women's sense of solidarity with other women of their own age, both in terms of their focus of attention as well as the potential for competition. For example, in my class, females and males consistently argue that male friendships are better than female friendships. This perception is not shared by males and females in my age cohort; perhaps competition among women diminishes over time as they form families and work at fairly similar jobs. For men, competition increases as they enter the work-force and begin to compete on their way up the ladder. Thus, periods of competition may differ for females and males, having a corresponding effect on their ability to form same-sex friendships.

Third, although many of the views of the feminist movement have popular support (e.g., ERA, pro-choice, equal pay for equal work, etc.), as a movement it has received more than its share of aggressive hostility. In a period of general conservatism, bolstered by the Reagan administration's policies of retrenchment in the areas of gender, family, and social programs, students who express feminism do not have the backing and support that my cohort had for such views. I always wonder what kind of student *I* would have been in the 1980s.

Fourth, this cohort of young women has watched and personally experienced the struggles of my generation of women, as we watched the generation before us. Acknowledging our heritage and similarity can be overshadowed by a desire to avoid the conflicts and problems encountered by those who went directly before us.

And, finally, no one escapes the misogyny of our society. Stereotypes that persist in the socialization of children are reinforced by the media, influence our behavior, and create distance not just between students and teachers, but among us all.

Previous analyses of why young women are reluctant to identify with the feminist movement proposed that these young women had come to expect what we have fought for as their "birthright" and grew up with the belief that they had a right to both work and family fulfillment (Cocks, 1982). The future patterns envisioned by my female students and the interviews collected by Bolotin (1982) suggest, however, the persistence of perceived conflict rather than the assurance of its resolution.

Thus, I would argue that young women do not see the world in a way that differs from the way it is seen by older, more avowedly feminist women, but that young women seek individual solutions to social problems. In the climate of the 1980s, the sense of collective action has been submerged, and individual solutions appear as the only viable route available. Even if they expect a temporary exit from the world of work, young women are fully aware that they will be part of the workforce for the majority of their lives; they know that the traditional concept of a single earner in a household of two adults is no longer financially feasible. Young women also are aware that in all likelihood the primary responsibility for child care will rest with them, not with their husbands. Confronted with these simultaneous demands, young women create personal solutions: intermittent labor force participation or not having children. In effect, they take personal responsibility for solving a dilemma not of their making; they do not seriously consider the possibility of collective action to change the structure of the demands placed upon them.

Over time, inherent difficulties in these personal solutions may create greater receptivity to the possibilities of solidarity. The perception that intermittent labor force participation is an option increasingly does not fit the reality. For those women whose early decision not to have children evolves into a decision to have children later in life, the conflict may be delayed but not resolved. Both "solutions" may, then, bring women to the same, continuing conflict. It may be at this point that identity with the feminist movement may take on greater significance, and the similarity in women's struggles may take precedence over the differences that sometimes keep us apart.

References

Blau, F. D. and Ferber, M. A. (1986). *The economics of women, men and work*. Englewood Cliffs, N.J.: Prentice-Hall.

Bolotin, S. (1982, October 17). Voices from the post-feminist generation. *New York Times Magazine*.

Cocks, J. (1982, July 12). How long till equality. *Time Magazine*.

Current Population Reports. (1984). Money income and poverty status of families and persons in the U.S.: 1983. Series P-60, No. 145. Washington, D.C.: U.S. Government Printing Office.

Evans, S. (1979). *Personal politics: The roots of the women's movement in civil rights and the New Left*. New York: Vintage Press.

Ferree, M. M. and Hess, B. B. (1985). *Controversy and Coalition: The new feminist movement*. Boston: Twayne Publishers.

Gillespie, D. L. (1971). Who has the power? The marital struggle. *Journal of Marriage and the Family*, *33*, 445–458.

Heffner, E. (1983, May). Motherhood. *Redbook*.

Moffat, M. J. and Painter, C. (Eds.) (1974). *Revelations: Diaries of women*. New York: Random House.

Molloy, J. (1977). *The woman's dress for success*. Chicago: Follet Publishers.

National Commission on Working Women. (1985). Child care fact sheet: Affordability, quality and wages: The link. Washington, D.C.

———. (1986). An overview of women in the work force. Washington, D.C.

Richardson, L. W. (1981). *The dynamics of sex and gender.* Boston: Houghton Mifflin Company.

U.S. Department of Labor. (1983, April). *Women at work: A chartbook.* Bureau of Labor Statistics, Bulletin 2168.

Weitzman, L. J. (1985). *The divorce revolution.* New York: The Free Press.

Index

About the Contributors

SANDRA L. ALBRECHT is Associate Professor of Sociology at the University of Kansas. Her research and teaching interests are in the sociology of work and sex roles. In the area of women and work, she has published such articles as, "Men, Women and Informal Organization in Manufacturing"; "Industrial Home Work in the United States: Historical Dimensions and Contemporary Perspectives"; and "Informal Interaction Patterns of Professional Women."

MIRIAM BERKMAN received her B.S. from the University of New Mexico in 1984. She currently is enrolled in the doctoral training program in clinical psychology in the Department of Psychology at the University of Missouri-Columbia where she is working on her Master's thesis on women, dependency, and depression.

DOROTHY BOWLES is Associate Professor in the School of Journalism at the University of Tennessee. She has had more than ten years of professional media experience, most of it with daily newspapers. She earned her Ph.D. at the University of Wisconsin-Madison. Her primary research interest is in communications law, and she is the author of the *Kansas Media Law Guide*.

SHARON S. BREHM is Professor of Psychology, Director of the College Honors Program, and Associate Dean of the College of Liberal Arts and Sciences at the University of Kansas. She has published numerous articles, chapters, and books in social and clinical psychology. Her most recent book is *Intimate Relationships* (1985).

KARLYN KOHRS CAMPBELL is Professor of Speech-Communication at the University of Minnesota and author of *The Rhetorical Act* (1982) and *Interplay of Influence: Mass Media and Their Publics in News, Advertising, Politics* (1983). She is writing a rhetorical history of the U.S. woman's rights/ woman suffrage movement.

CAROL E. FORD is Assistant Professor of Psychology at the University of Missouri-Columbia. She has published journal articles related to depression and to stress and coping, and co-edited a recent volume on clinical and social psychological perspectives on negative life events.

FRANCES DEGEN HOROWITZ is Professor of Human Development and Family Life and of Psychology; Senior Scientist in the Bureau of Child Research; Dean of the Graduate School; and Vice Chancellor for Research, Graduate Studies, and Public Service—all at the University of Kansas. She is well known for her extensive work in the areas of infant and child development and is the author of the forthcoming book, *Exploring Theories of Development: Toward a Structural/Behavioral Model of Development*.

ALETHA C. HUSTON is Professor of Human Development and Family Life and of Psychology at the University of Kansas. She has authored numerous articles and chapters on sex role development, including the chapter "Sex Typing" in the *Handbook of Child Psychology* edited by P. Mussen and M. Hetherington.

E. CLAIRE JERRY is Assistant Professor of Speech Communication at the University of Denver. She is the author of "Rhetoric as Epistemic: Implications of a Theoretical Position" in *Visions of Rhetoric: History, Theory and Criticism*, Proceedings of the 1986 Rhetoric Society of America Conference.

LEONIE A. MARX is Associate Professor of Germanic Languages and Literatures at the University of Kansas. She has published articles on modern Danish and German literature, and on German-Danish literary relations. Her books include a critical study of the works of the Danish author Benny Andersen, an edition of selected stories by Andersen in English translation, and a book on the German short story.

DIANE MCDERMOTT is Associate Professor of Counseling Psychology at the University of Kansas. She was Director of the University of Kansas Women's Study Program from 1979–1983. As a scholar and as a practicing counselor, she has addressed such issues as counseling with special populations (e.g., minorities, homosexuals), professional burnout, and substance abuse.

SALLY ALLEN MCNALL teaches writing in the English Department at the University of Kansas. Since the summer of 1984, during which she portrayed Willa Cather in an original script for the Chautauqua Society, much of her scholarly work and several of her poems have concerned Cather.

REGINA MORANTZ-SANCHEZ is Professor of History at the University of Kansas. She is the author of numerous books and articles on the history of women physicians and health reformers, including *In Her Own Words: Oral Histories of Women Physicians* (1983) and *Sympathy and Science: Women Physicians in American Medicine* (1985).

DORTHY L. PENNINGTON is Associate Professor of African/African-American Studies and of Communication Studies at the University of Kansas. She has published in women's studies, intercultural communication, and public address. She has lectured and served as a curriculum evaluator for the Equal Opportunity Management Institute of the Department of Defense. She recently visited West Africa to observe the roles of women in the family and community.

ELIZABETH SCHULTZ is a Kansas University Endowment Association Professor in the Department of English at the University of Kansas. She has held Fulbright and N.E.H. Fellowships. Her published works include numerous short stories, personal essays, and critical essays on American literature, Afro-American literature, Japanese culture, women's friendships, and popular culture.

JOEY SPRAGUE is Assistant Professor of Sociology at the University of Kansas. She received her Ph.D. from the University of Wisconsin-Madison in 1986; her doctoral dissertation is entitled *Getting to the Bottom of the Gender Gap: Gender Differences in Political Understanding*.

MARLENE SPRINGER is Professor of English and Associate Vice Chancellor for Academic Affairs and Graduate Studies at the University of Missouri-Kansas City. She is the author of *Edith Wharton and Kate Chopin: A Reference Guide*, *Thomas Hardy's Use of Allusion*, and numerous articles. She is the editor of *What Manner of Women: Essays on English and American Life and Literature*, and *Plains Woman: The Diary of Martha Farnsworth*.

ANN WEICK is Associate Professor and Acting Dean of the School of Social Welfare at the University of Kansas. Her publications include the edited book *Women, Power and Change* (with S. Vandiver) and articles and chapters on holistic health, women's issues, and philosophical issues in social work.

SANDRA L. ZIMDARS-SWARTZ is Associate Professor of Religious Studies at the University of Kansas. She specializes in Christian theologies of history and devotion to and thinking about the Virgin Mary. Her publications include *Joachim of Fiori: A Study in Spiritual Perception and History* and several articles on modern Marian apparitions.